T0354360

Key Master

Key Master

Peter Anthony

3rd Edition

KEY MASTER

iUniverse books may be ordered through booksellers or by contacting:

iUniverse
1663 Liberty Drive
Bloomington, IN 47403
www.iuniverse.com
1-800-Authors (1-800-288-4677)

ISBN: 978-1-4401-3572-9 (sc)
ISBN: 978-1-4401-3571-2 (e)

Print information available on the last page.

iUniverse rev. date: 09/03/2015

Scripture quotations marked KJV are from the Holy Bible, King James Version (Authorized Version). First published in 1611. Quoted from the KJV Classic Reference Bible, Copyright © 1983 by The Zondervan Corporation.

Dedication

Brussels, your name hides from memory, however your profound words light my path. I hope I can honor your message?

Ethan Moss. You left us in 2000 of January leaving behind the gift of life. Our lives are guided by natural glorious moments, manifesting magical places, situations and amazing people. When the time is right our teachers appear on the horizon sharing their loving wisdom, allowing us to embrace our destiny. How blessed am I to have Wanda, Harry, Will and Linda as my Pied Piper's.

Acknowledgements

There are many amazing people to honor with the writing of this book. My most sincere thanks to Anna Skinner, my editor, whose words of encouragement guided me to continue this story when others said no. Fernanda's most treasured and invaluable opinion that took the time to read this inspirational tale in the beginning stages and said, "This *story* must be shared." It takes a special lady to recognize a beautiful flower before it blooms. Thank you Lynn Claxon for being the *Lady by the Bay*. My most sincere thanks to Ted Babcock for grasping the importance of this life-altering moment in time and putting this transformational story into a screenplay. There are those who cross your path and those who climb with you all the way to the top. Ted, you are my dear friend and confidant. Rick O' Berry made an innocent comment years ago at a spiritual conference in Los Angeles that transformed my life. His comment, "One person can make a difference on this planet." Rick, you changed the lives of thousands because of your passion for the safety of *Dolphin* and inspired a troop of enlightened beings to understand the importance of these innocent creatures. I will try my best to follow in your footsteps.

Through out the many years of my entertainment career, I have been fortunate to encounter numerous women from every sphere of media. Your stories of failed relationships, personal obstacles and triumphs provided me the insight to go forward with this inspirational story so that other people could witness the courage it takes to be spiritually open in a world that demands logical explanations for the unexplainable. Especially in this land called *Hollywood.* You are truly the teachers of this planet. Your lessons must be shared so that others that venture into *The City of Angels* have candlelight to show them the way.

My dear friends of Alcoholics Anonymous who welcomed me with open arms and did not care that I was not an alcoholic, but rather a person who showed up with one of their own to listen to his story of resurrection. Little did I realize that this statement, *"Do the footwork and let God do the rest"* would ignite a fire within my soul? Perhaps if our world leaders would practice a twelve-step program there would be more accountability.

And I must acknowledge Nancy Pelosi, Hillary Clinton, Marianne Williamson and Oprah Winfrey for being the front-runners of womanhood for generations to come. You are the *Female Collective Consciousness* that was foretold to me by a nameless man I shall refer to as *Brussels.* God Bless you for making a difference.

Table of Contents

The Landing
Part I

Chapter 1 St. Thomas...3

Chapter 2 Brussels...15

Chapter 3 Black Beard's Castle 35

Chapter 4 Pied Piper 61

Chapter 5 Stalker...73

Chapter 6 Fire and Ice 87

Chapter 7 Brussels' Return 109

Chapter 8 Message 141

Resurrection
Part II

Chapter 9 Flat line 173

Chapter 10 Key Master 217

Chapter 11 Guardians 257

Ten Years Later - Easter Weekend 273

Introduction

This story is inspired by true events. Various people, places and situations have been changed to respect the privacy of the many in our television and film industry. There is an unspoken law we come to honor and obey in our "Biz." The term "Behind The Scenes" is embossed upon our tongues once we step foot into this insidious world we call Entertainment.

"The golden moments in the stream of life rush past us and we see nothing but sand; the angels come to visit us, and we only know them when they are gone."

—George Eliot

The Landing

Part I

St. Thomas

Chapter 1

I can hear his footsteps behind me. He's close, and I imagine I can hear his breath in my ear and feel its heat on my shoulder. I'm too afraid to turn around, so I focus instead on getting away. I hear his pace match mine. The only thoughts rioting through my brain are that I'm human prey, and that the end of the chase is almost finished. I'm in despair. I begin thinking of ways in which I can cause him physical pain. My breath comes in short bursts. How can I hurt him? I'm a foot shorter and a hundred pounds lighter than he is. "Kick him in the shins!" my mind shouts. Absolute panic sets in and I ignore the growing pain in my side as oxygen-deprived muscles protest every step. I'm running as fast as I can, but this is not fast enough. I don't know where to go. All I know is that he's keeping up with me. He's gaining on me.

I spot a group of trees at the end of the long, sandy beach where I think I might be able to lose him. I figure I can at least outmaneuver him. However, as my speed increases, so does his.

"Stop!" he shouts—

"Ladies and gentlemen, please return to your seats. The captain has turned on the fasten your seat belt sign. All trays should be their upright position."

Overwhelmed by exhaustion, I wake up, twisting and turning in my seat. Perfume clings heavily in the cabin, as the flight attendant quickly walks by checking every seat back and tray. A small red pillow falls from behind my neck as I reach for my duffle bag. My dream was just that— a dream.

The plane descends into San Juan as I gaze out the window, tense and apprehensive. Heat from the sun fills my seat, but the window feels cold. I'm a young man searching for change. Anxiety weighs inside of me and doesn't ease up despite my constant deep breathing. That I am in a large metal object, suspended thousands of feet in the air, is almost too much to contemplate. I'm torn between awe and fear.

As I watch the clouds wrap around the wings of the plane, the earth zooms in. A searing abdominal spasm disrupts my quiet composure. The ache is familiar; still, it frightens me. Doctors haven't been able to diagnose the cause of my agonizing pain. The Tagamet, an anti-ulcer medication, and antibiotics they provide offer relief at times. Damn, this isn't one of them. Sighing, I look at my best friend, JB, who is passed out in the seat next to me.

I stand up and stretch my legs to relieve the tension that has crawled up the back of my legs and spine. Ignoring the seat belt sign, I work my way to the rest room in the back of the plane, I try to ignore the pain in my stomach. The reflection in the mirror belongs to a young man in his early twenties. He's thin with dark, curly hair and pale, smooth skin. Burden hides behind the dark eyes and in the boyish face, but innocence dominates my expression. As I wash my face and brush my teeth, a tingling within my body captures my attention. "I wonder if plane water is safe to drink."

The captain informs us that we'll be arriving shortly and to prepare for final approach. Returning to my seat, I see that JB has begun to stir. He pulls in his first deep breaths of Caribbean air, filtered through the plane's stale ventilation system, and arches his back as his jaw gears open. Then, like an orchestra holding a final note for the grand finale, JB exalts his yawn. We chat as the plane descends.

JB idly talks of his life as a hairstylist, and his excitement about this vacation. His enthusiasm keeps my thoughts from my own dilemmas. This is a first vacation for both of us, and we share the same sense of adventure. He notices my nervousness, though, as we near the ground and grabs my hand to comfort me as we begin to land.

The San Juan airport bustles with the liveliness of people on vacation. Everyone scurries to different destinations. At an arrival/departure monitor, we notice that our next flight departs from the other side of the building. With only minutes to spare, we run through the airport. As we approach the gate, the crowd thins and a few people mill about. The plane we are to board isn't a commercial airplane. It's a hideous contraption covered in vomit-colored shades of orange and yellow. I immediately begin sweating and run scripts in my head of crashing into the ocean. Once again, JB notices the concern in my face and promptly does his best to assure me that all is well and that we'll make it to St. Thomas.

Before we board the plane, I instantly note the vast differences between this one and the commercial airliner we just left. Nausea grips me and I drop into my seat like a rock. As the plane starts to lift into the air and the wind cradles its underside, the sick feelings dissipate and I begin to relax. I notice that JB is engrossed in his paperback. He's oblivious to the world, so I leave him alone and envelop myself in the painful feelings that devoured me earlier in the day.

I used to think ignorance was bliss. I now believe it's the scariest thing on the planet. I've left behind heartbreak in Dallas and the bleak, lingering feeling that being pure of heart isn't enough anymore. Has my innocence ended? Will life ever seem as exciting as it does when an affair first begins? This trip to St. Thomas couldn't have come at a better time. People are more open to listening and learning when the ladder has been knocked out from underneath them.

***

We land in St. Thomas and the first thing I notice is the storybook-quality of the islands and how they are randomly scattered about as if God just tossed them to the wind and let them land how they may. The foliage covers the land like a blanket, with many different shades of green. The mountains push through the jungle just enough to make their presence known. The blue water brushes the islands' shores as if worshiping their beauty.

As the plane lands and starts to taxi to our destination, JB wakes up and notices the strange look on my face. I feel horribly dizzy.

"Are you okay?" he asks.

"I think I'm sick."

"Relax! As soon as we're off this plane, you'll get some fresh air."

The airport resembles a flea market. We make our way in to retrieve our luggage alongside the chickens, goats, and other creatures moving about in the baggage area. People whose faces tell stories flood the airport and hustle the animals through the crowd. Some of the travelers are very tan with blonde hair and dark eyes; others have pale skin and European features. I feel overwhelmed by the surge of dialects and the abundant animal odors filling my still dizzy head. We finally escape into the ocean air with our luggage. The cool breeze is a relief and calms my senses.

JB's friend, Rick Tourney, waits for us outside with a calm smile. After writing JB about Carnival in St. Thomas, JB invited me, knowing that I had just ended a relationship and feeling that a trip would be the best thing for me. He and Rick are ready for a party and frolicking through the streets. I, on the other hand, am completely prepared for a quiet evening with a good book. I introduce myself to Rick and know right away that he's a sincere and generous soul. He stands tall and has kind eyes that always focus on whomever he speaks with.

We throw our luggage into the back of his Volkswagen jeep. Surely it has seen combat, tattered and torn with green-and-brown camouflage that can't hide the tackiness of the metal contraption. Climbing into the jeep, I notice gardeners in the distance chopping down a patch of sentry-like birds of paradise. We make our way through town and down the dirt roads. The green, wet smell of morning foliage and the hypnotic beauty of palm and sea grape trees growing along the sides of the road take my breath away. I look down at the jeans, loafers, and dress shirt I have on and wonder if I'm overdressed.

We cross the top of the hill and find the town of Charlotte Amalie spread out beneath us. We near the bay at the bottom, and the water is filled with monstrous cruise ships and sailboats. The land extends outward through a maze of old wooden piers. Passengers from all walks of life flow onto the island from the ships standing by. One of the ships looks familiar.

"Hey, Rick, is that the Love Boat?" I ask, as a joke.

"Actually it is," he replies. "They're filming here today."

The narrow streets are cluttered with wood signs, taverns, and antique stores. Alleyways creep between buildings into other alleys into a cobblestone labyrinth. The breeze comes off the ocean, reaching down and picking up any bit of salty odor it can and sweeps through the city streets. Music seems to flow from every direction, as people negotiate the bumpy roads, involved in their daily routines. An old sign above the entrance of a tavern catches my attention as it swings back in forth in the wind. Its banana-leaf green-and-turquoise lettering seems typical of the island's color scheme.

I ask Rick where people live who can't afford the city. He tells me they live in the mountains, where we're headed.

The road twists up into the hills, which are well fortified with two towers, Bluebeard's Castle and Blackbeard's Castle. Thirty-four cannons from pirate days face the harbor. We wind our way up and around the mountain until we finally pull in front of the flat, home for the next few days.

All the windows in the flat are open and the long, sheer white drapes fill the room as the wind lifts them up in slow motion. A green leather sofa sits next to a couple of straw chairs that are bound with green fabric. The stone floor has a rug placed in the center of the rustic-colored room. Shelves and shelves of books are everywhere. I pick up a tattered and worn hardbound and open it. The inside page speaks of a student of God who mystified the world by his writings. I can almost relate to the skeptic apostle Thomas. I can't go on blind faith. I am agnostic.

JB suggests I lie down and rest. Rick leads me to a bedroom with two full-size beds, surrounded by three windows that overlook the island. I lie down on the frilly white-lace bedspreads and pass out almost instantly. A nap that seems only minutes long turns out to be several hours, as I find out when JB wakes me.

"Get up. We're going to a party."

Groggy but excited, I throw on my Calvin Klein jeans, a fitted white shirt, and a pair of tennis shoes. We jump in the jeep and make our way back down the mountain. The sky has drastically changed to a burnt shade of orange. The anticipation is building. What I am here to experience is not far away.

When we reach the village, Rick explains that we're going to a small party first and then we'll carry on to Carnival, a wilder version of New Orleans' Mardi Gras but with a lot more nudity and drugs.

After we find a place to park, we walk through the streets to an old stone building. Two weather-beaten, wood doors at least twice my size with weighty, tarnished brass handles stand before us. Rick bangs the oversized knocker, and an elderly Creole woman with graying hair invites us inside. We walk down a few steps to a large room with an Old Spanish feel, filled with burning white candles on antique candelabras. People speaking in a language I can't understand and dressed in white, festive robes surround Rick, JB, and I.

Rick greets a man in baggy bell-bottoms, Jorge, whose hair is braided and has silver beads adorning the ends. The front door bangs shut and everyone turns to look in its direction. A tall woman enters the room with an older man who seems to tower over everyone. He scans the room and stops, his eyes lighting on mine. Staring at me, he makes his way through the crowd and heads in my direction. I immediately feel uncomfortable and turn to Rick to ask who the creepy old guy is.

"He's my guest. I have invited him," says Jorge in a heavy Trinidad accent.

I turn around and discover that I'm now face to face with the white-haired giant. His probing blue eyes shoot right through me. I immediately look away.

Long hair surrounds his tan face like white wings. I excuse myself and work my way back up the stairs, knowing he's still watching me. This man seems to exude power, which is not a good combination with my heightened insecurities right now.

I'm more than eager to flee the room and get back in the jeep. When JB finds me and says we're going to Carnival, I feel relieved. On the drive, Rick mentions that we're going to meet with Jorge and his tall friend.

The square is crowded with dancing and laughing people. The air hangs heavy with body odor, along with salty sea air. Rick leads us to the spot where we are to meet later in the evening. JB and I wander off to the nearby vendor stands watching Rick fade into the decadent partying crowd. The crescent moon dangles from the evening sky. Suddenly, a hand is placed on my shoulder. It's the man from the party.

"You enjoy the moon," he says knowingly. "This will become a sacred ritual in your life in future days to come."

Oh my god, what a freak. I try to excuse myself, but he stops me.

"It would be nice to talk to you in detail." His grip on my arm is firm.

"Um, well, I am busy," I respond, "I, I must go find my friends."

I turn and race through the crowd with my heart pounding. When I find JB, he immediately sees that I'm upset and asks me why. When I try to tell him what happened, he says it sounds like a silly conversation and not to worry about it.

We continue to walk, admiring the fireworks overhead and joking about the dreadful food the vendors peddle. The tall man in the distance glides toward us with cat-like movements. I quickly look down and move behind Jorge, JB, and Rick, hoping to avoid him. The others chat about plans for the weekend, and JB commits both of us to join them. I keep quiet.

We decide to meet Saturday for breakfast and then spend the day on a beach called Morning Star. JB and Rick walk ahead, leaving me lagging behind. A hand taps my shoulder.

"We'll speak tomorrow, young man."

I turn and it is the tall man. He fades into the crowd. I hurry back to the jeep.

***

When I wake up the next morning, I find two of Rick's roommates reading in the living room. Marsha and Diane are both from New York and decided to come down to what they refer to as "the end of days."

"I'm an actress," says Diana. "I just booked a *Love Boat* episode yesterday."

"That's really cool," I tell her.

"So what do you do?"

"Oh, enough to keep me interested," I reply. It's embarrassing when your life isn't what you want it to be.

After a while, JB and Rick wake up and join us in conversation while Marsha decides to make scrambled eggs. We agree to break our plans with Jorge and to simply enjoy a relaxing moment at the flat with one another. Instantly I feel much better since I won't have to be subjected to more nonsense about soul energy and the moon. In the shower I realize that the pain in my abdomen has briefly subsided and surrendered to the painkillers.

We make our way down the mountain and find a portrait sandy beach, which seems to stretch around the island like a yellow-and-white ribbon. The air is more humid than usual, someone says. Villagers are completing their morning routines and finding their way to the beach. Norwegian cruise ships can be seen coming in from the horizon. The turquoise water shimmers in the sun, its color changing due to high and low sandbars. We all lay out our towels on the sand. I find a spot that suits me behind everyone, preferring to observe rather than participate. I always feel that other people have more to contribute to a conversation than I do. A small radio next to the girl's, spits out early 1960's songs from *The Mama's and Papa's*. Bits of their conversation about bathing suits drifts in and over Rick telling JB how New York makes him feel burned out. The problem is, once you've been to New York, the rest of the world just seems to move in slow motion.

Marsha decides she wants to go in the water and the others join her. I, of course, want some time to lie down and feel sorry for myself. As I'm looking for my suntan lotion, I glance to my right and see a giant foot next to me. I notice a toe ring and look up to find the white-haired tall man staring at me. I look away to avoid eye contact.

"We spoke briefly last night," he says. "Do you mind if I join you?"

I toss my hand toward the beach, keeping my eyes focused on the sand. He sits down next to me.

"So, are you enjoying your stay in St. Thomas?"

"Yes," I mumble.

"What have you done so far?"

"We went to a party last night, then to Carnival, and now to the beach."

I sound like a robot, but I can't help myself.

"I see," he says, gazing at the water. Then he turns back to me.

"I'm from Scotland, but live in Brussels, Belgium. Where are you from?"

I look for the others, hoping to join them, but there's no one to be found. Maybe if I'm rude to him he'll get the message and leave me alone.

"How old are you?" I say, smirking. "You must be at least 100 years old."

"Why do you ask?" he says, smiling gently.

Pointing to an elderly couple down the beach, I say, "It seems like you should be talking with someone your own age."

"I am talking with you. I am trying to befriend you," he calmly answers.

"Well you need to go befriend someone else! I'm not interested in making any friends right now."

"You do not want new friends. That implies you are putting limits on the possibilities of a new beginning. You never know who you are going to meet."

I don't how to respond to this. He continues questioning my animosity and remarks how I'm always behind my friends or avoiding interaction. He's been watching me with his piercing gaze. I know it!

"Are you bored with your friends and their conversations?"

Suddenly, this gets my attention. "My friends talk of frivolous things that really don't matter." I avoid eye contact.

"At your age," he continues, "everyone feels that no one understands them. You must learn that you have something to contribute in a conversation and don't be afraid to speak up. And most of all stop wrestling with that silly inner-dialogue inside your head, because you will never win that battle. Perhaps you should surround yourself with those who are making a difference on the planet?"

My mouth gapes open. Brussels doesn't look like the odd man I first thought him to be. He stands up and brushes the sand off his pants.

"You need to come to peace with yourself. You may find you have more to say than you think."

Nodding his head, the man from Brussels turns and walks away, never losing his steady eye on me. A few moments later, JB and Rick stroll up and invite me down to the water. I pick up my things and hurry along with them. As we slowly walk through the sand, I look behind me and notice that the old man has stopped and is watching me. I turn around and decide to forget about him and get on with my day. I find a joint inside my short's pocket and light it up. "Who brought drugs?"

Brussels

Chapter 2

The day begins to wind down, and we all return to the flat. Marsha grabs a book. Rick and JB finish their conversation. I fall onto a sofa and take a deep breath, still trying to absorb this unfamiliar world. I look at the bookshelves, reading all the different titles, and notice Marsha is reading a book about Nostradamus' predictions.

"Have you read all these books?" I ask.

"Oh, I love to read," she says, putting her book face down in her lap. "They're not just my books but Rick's as well."

She goes back to her reading.

"Why did you come here?" I say, sitting in the chair opposite her.

A serious expression falls across her face. "St. Thomas is the last of paradise and I want to enjoy as much of it as possible before, well, you know, the end days."

"What do you mean the last of paradise and the end days?"

She looks at Rick, and they exchange glances.

"Oh, never mind."

Having no idea what she's talking about and feeling excluded from whatever it is that I'm supposed to eventually understand, I excuse myself and turn in for the night.

The next morning while everyone sleeps; I wake up early and decide to go to the other side of the island to a place called Magens Bay. Rick had shown us the bay on our way home from the beach the day before. I fix myself breakfast—bananas, mangos, and peanut butter—and leave a note for everyone to meet me there later in the day.

The cab makes its way to the north end of the island, along a bumpy road that's absent of traffic. On the heart-shaped, empty beach, I stand alone in awe again of the postcard-picture bay. The shimmering, cobalt blue water meets the white sand, which radiates the morning light and ends into tree-covered mountains that surround the bay. Legend has it that Sir Francis Drake sat in a large stone chair at the top of the hill, watching as British fleets sailed into the island. I settle for something much less regal and find an agreeable spot on the beach where the bay is spread out before me. Laying out my towel, books, and marijuana, I feel the rising sun take the edge off the cool morning air.

A local with dreadlocks dives for seashells down the way. He sets the rhythm for the beach, diving into the ocean and returning with a treasure of shells that he places on the sand. He dives back into the ocean then heads for the sand, over and over, at a steady pace. Everything is still and tranquil, except for a Native American Indian man jogging on the beach.

My eyelids grow heavy, but when I sense myself falling into sleep, I awake with a startle and sit up. The local is gone. So is the Native American man. I notice a moving shadow in the corner of my eye and glance over my left shoulder. Brussels is walking toward me. My heart begins to pound violently in my chest. I try to pretend I don't see him, hoping that he might not recognize me. As he puts his left hand on my back, I struggle to get up, but he gently settles me back down on the sand. Darting my head up and down the beach, I think he must know how panicked I feel. The morning is early, and I'm too far north on the island for a rescue.

"How odd it is to see you here, young man. How is your morning?"

"I'm fine," I blurt out.

"Do you mind if I join you?"

"Uh, I'm just getting ready to meet my friends who should be here shortly," I say to him, as I begin to collect my belongings and bag of marijuana. "If you don't mind, I'm going to go ahead and leave."

"Well, then I will walk with you."

"No, no, that's okay. I should really go now," I say, never making eye contact with him. "Well, have yourself a nice morning," I add.

I start walking to my pretend meeting point, nervously dropping my sunglasses along the way. I don't stop to pick them up. Instead I pick up my pace and am alarmed when he does the same. I risk a quick look behind me and see him. His face is a mask of determination, and I feel the hair on the back of my neck rise. I drop all pretensions, and break into a run. If I can just run faster, maybe I can get away. I can hear his footsteps pounding behind me. He's gaining on me. I run faster and faster. His steady pace is unbelievable. An excruciating abdominal pain strikes my left side. Panic sets in as I realize my nightmare on the plane has become a reality.

"Stop!" he shouts.

"This man is fucking insane," I think to myself.

***

"What do you want? Leave me alone! Why do you keep following me?" I yell between gasping breaths.

I watch him stride purposefully through the palm trees. He is within arms reach of me. If he wants to harm me, I am finished. I run faster. He runs even faster. I twist along the beach, looking behind me. Another jolt to my abdomen forces me to falter. I hit a large stump and fall to the sand like a girl, gasping for air. My heart is pounding so hard I think it might jump out of my chest. That would scare him away for sure. He's looking at me, as if he's waiting for me to catch my breath. My breaths are pounding in sync with my heart. His breaths are composed. I freeze when he finally reaches me and places his heavy, large hand on my shoulder again.

"Ethan, you have been running all your life!" he shouts.

He stands facing me with his hands on his hips, dangling my sunglasses between his thumb and index finger, as if this moment is ridiculous to him.

"Stop feeling guilty about the relationships you have ended. Why do you continue blaming yourself?" he says, as he shakes his head.

"What do you mean? What are you talking about?"

"You know what I speak of, young man?"

I look at him with such confusion. I know what he's talking about. What I don't know is how he knows not only about my failed relationship but the guilt I carry with me. Is it that obvious? Do I have that much insecurity expressed on my face?

"Ethan, your decision to end the relationship was a wise choice. As much pain and sorrow as it causes you now, it was the right thing for you to do."

"How do you know my name?"

"Dear boy, we were introduced Friday night."

"We were?" I don't remember this man's name, nor do I care to know it at this point in time. I keep looking over my shoulder for anyone on the beach. I just want to end this conversation quickly. I reach for my glasses.

"Please do not be afraid. I am not going to harm you."

"How do you know about my relationship?" I ask.

He just smiles as if it is a silly question.

"Ethan, you keep allowing your negative thoughts to sabotage your day?"

I look down to where I've dug a hole in the sand with my heel.

"I still don't understand why you're asking me these questions? What do you want?"

"I want you to become aware of all the thoughts about yourself that randomly fill your head. Stop doubting yourself. All thoughts should be positive thoughts? Your thoughts are not allowing the beauty of your soul to come through?"

"What?" I continue to look down at my feet, not really understanding what's going on. Though what he says makes sense, I don't know how to respond.

"You ran after me to call me down on my thoughts? That's freaky! You don't know me," I say, finally looking at him. "You don't know me at all."

"Ethan, I do know you. I know you very well. Your drug addictions are destroying your life."

"I don't know you. I don't know anything about you. Who told you I was doing drugs?" Clouds begin to fade away. Sound vanishes completely.

How *can* he know anything about my life? Maybe I do carry a lot of pain with me? So what if I surround myself with people who are equally riddled with their own pain. My friends are speed junkies, cocaine users and alcoholics. That's how we play the game of self-esteem, and I'm just along for the ride because these people accept me. It's a lot easier to avoid taking a hard look at yourself in the mirror. My thoughts are plagued with self-doubt, confusion, and loneliness. As hard as this is to deal with, that's just how it is. I have no idea what time it is nor do I know if Rick and JB are coming. I don't even know where my watch is. Hell, at this point I don't even know if I own a watch.

"Let me ask you," says Brussels, continuing his bizarre inquisition. "Does your drug addiction limit you, or does it empower you?"

I sneer, feeling irritated by this approach. "What? Where is all this leading?"

"Ethan, I'm not asking you to answer these questions now," he says, sighing patiently. "But what I am asking you to do is to consider that maybe it is time for you to change your life. Create a life that you never want to give up. Wouldn't you agree? Do you have any dreams or aspirations?"

"Yes, I do."

"Do you wish to share them with me?"

With absolutely no confidence in my voice I say, "I'm trying to pursue the entertainment industry as a special effects make up artist."

He places his hand under my chin, raises my head to face him, looks in my eyes, and says something that I will never forget.

"Allow others to look into your eyes. There is a beautiful spirit inside of you, Ethan. Does this make sense?" Everything around me spins in slow motion.

I look back down at the sand, embarrassed. All I've heard lately is how much of a failure I am, courtesy of my ex.

"There is something incredible inside of you, young man. Before you leave St. Thomas, you will discover a new pathway for you to embark upon."

"I don't understand? I will discover a new pathway? What does that mean?"

"I want you to think about what I am sharing with you today," he says, gathering himself up as if to leave. "Please think about it. We will speak at another time."

Before Brussels leaves, he reaches out with both hands to shake my hand. As I look into his piercing blue eyes, I notice a golden halo surrounding his entire being.

"Will we talk again?" I am mesmerized by the golden light.

"Indeed, we will. Soon," he replies.

"Where are you staying? What's your phone number? How will I find you?"

"I will find you," he says, absolutely.

As I watch Brussels walk away, I feel as if a weight has been released off my shoulders. I see JB and Rick in the jeep, waving at me. I look down the beach and the local with dreadlocks diving for seashells has reappeared. The Native American man passes by. All sound returns. Clouds return. The beach restores itself to normal speed. My marijuana is spread about in a perfect circle, along with a puddle of blood.

***

That night, my flat mates and I make our way to a disco called the Monster. We walk through the club's restaurant, a quiet room with white-linen tablecloths and gold flickering candles. To the left is a rustic bar made of polished wood. A wall of assorted international liquors waits behind it. A bartender minds his own business, polishing glasses in the corner. We pass through a connecting corridor into a dark staircase that leads to the dance floor. A spinning disco ball fills the room with colored lights, and eighties disco songs bounce off the walls. It's still early in the evening. The club is empty.

As the evening rolls on, the crowd begins to thicken, as do expectations for something better. The tiny dance floor becomes overwhelmed with people shaking their half naked bodies. Small groups are crammed around the little tables that are scattered throughout the room. Some of the crowd sniffs cocaine, others do poppers. My group decides to join the masses on the floor, and I follow along as usual. We all join in, sniffing cocaine, doing poppers, downing tequila shots and dancing. I'm already thinking, "Here I go again, following everyone else."

Closing the lid on the poppers and handing it off to Rick, I'm feeling okay until the speaker's start blasting a song I hate. Oh well, my buzz will kick in and it won't matter. Then Brussels walks in as I stare at him with my frozen high. The disco is filled with people more than half his age as he towers above everyone. People begin snickering and pointing at his conservative attire. Dressed in a white, pressed button-down shirt and beige khakis with brown sandals, he makes his way to the edge of the dance floor and sits down at a table, all the while staring at me. I'm too buzzed off my poppers to truly grasp the oddity of the situation. I turn around pretending not to see him but can see his reflection on the mirrors around the room. I turn back to my friends on the dance floor hoping they have not noticed him. Rude laughter and people pointing at his run of the mill clothing make me feel embarrassed for him. I walk up to him and sit at his table.

"Hey."

He turns to look at me.

"Please, do not feel the need to sit with me. Join your friends and continue dancing," he says in a commanding but kind voice.

"Why are you here?" I yell over the music.

"I've come to have a conversation with you. But first, go to your friends and dance. Do your drugs."

"No," I say, feeling emboldened by the drugs. "If we need to talk, let's talk."

I stand up and motion to the back of the disco.

He stops and says, "Come with me. There is a café upstairs."

I stumble over to JB, Rick, and the girls to let them know that I'm going upstairs to the restaurant, but I don't tell them why. They'll think I'm bored as usual, and shove cocaine up my nose. "I'll be back shortly," I say. Something tells me I need to hear what Brussels has to say.

We walk up the dark stairs to the restaurant near the entrance. It's still empty, except for the bartender. Brussels leads me to a table in the back. I can tell by looking at the menu that this is going to be a pricey meal. I feel hesitant. Our waiter circles the table, but seems to be pre-occupied with another table of disruptive customers. He quickly stares at my white tank top and Levi's and then turns his glare back to the rowdy table of four young men wearing tank tops and jeans. He avoids any eye contact with me and asks Brussels what he would like to drink.

"Why don't you give us a second?" Brussels kindness melts the waiter.

"I'll have glass of water with lemon and four ice-cubes. Squeeze the lemon slightly into the water, but don't leave it in the glass."

The waiter rolls his eyes, "Would you like me to go outside and cut the lemon off the tree so that it's nice and fresh?"

"Excuse me?" I feel my anger rising.

"Why don't you give us a few minutes," says Brussels. The waiter walks off.

"Are you uncomfortable?" asks Brussels.

"As a matter of fact I am," I say, sarcastically.

Brussels English is proper, and he speaks articulately and thoughtfully. I, on the other hand, can barely complete my sentences due to my drugs and alcohol.

"Ethan, this man is responding to your negative energy."

"What do you mean by that?" I can feel my high surging.

He repeats himself. "Your behavior, is allowing a negative reaction."

To me, energy powers television and cities. I don't have any energy that I'm aware of, unless I have a battery in my pocket.

Brussels smiles and removes the folded white napkin and lays it in his lap.

"You might call it personality or charisma. Or lack of. When we walk into a room, people intuitively feel someone's energy."

"How can that be?" I ask.

"Energy is all around us and inside of us," he says. "Anyone who has a pulse has the ability to feel strangely attracted to someone they just met. This can have the opposite effect as well."

What the hell is he talking about? The waiter stares at me obnoxiously as he makes his way over to the table. He slowly leans forward to whisper in my ear.

"What are you doing with this old man? Is he your sugar daddy?"

I can only imagine that it looks like I'm hanging out with Brussels so I can milk him for his fortune. I stare coldly at the waiter as he hands me my water. I purposely miss the hand off, dropping the glass of water.

"Oh dear, look what I have done? I am so sorry." I look over to an empty table. "Hand me that napkin over there so I can clean up my mess. Please hurry."

The waiter slowly turns, grabs the napkin from the table, tosses it into my lap, and storms away.

"Ethan, why did you do that? Creating a problem because you think there's a problem only creates more problems?" Brussels says calmly.

I tell him what the waiter said, thinking he'll agree with me. Instead, Brussels replies, "Do not judge his action or his reaction will create further actions."

"What? Action and reaction doesn't make sense? What do you mean? He was rude to me. He can't treat me that way!"

"Ego to ego only creates more conflict. There is no need to be nasty to our waiter. You do not know what kind of day he has had thus far. Or do you? Perhaps you should be more understanding and maybe our waiter will be more understanding."

"You mean, if I stop being rude," I say, slowly, "He won't be rude?"

"Indeed," he says, as if we're finally speaking the same language. "Diminish the lesser side of yourself and let the greater side of your true self shine through. Ethan, the key to living a more productive life begins with kindness and understanding."

This makes a little sense. The lower side of myself, is my low self-esteem? Or is it my ego?

"Ego tends to contribute to the greatest amount of conflict in one's life," he continues, speaking in a low and soothing voice. "Ego is a mask for insecurity. You are too wrapped up in reacting to other people's actions. Do not become a slave to your ego. Instead, raise your thoughts to a higher way of thinking. This can be a very complicated thing to explain, Ethan. It begins with learning to pray for peace on a daily basis."

"Praying? What are you saying?" I ask him sarcastically. Once again, I start to think that maybe he *is* crazy after all. "I don't believe in prayer."

"Perhaps you don't understand prayer? Most people pray to God to acquire more things," he says, drawing out the last word. "We should pray for wisdom, understanding, authentic purpose, and peace. We bargain with God and call it prayer. Wallowing in self pity is often times caused by one's addiction. Drugs, cigarettes, sexual promiscuity, poor choices and other bad habits pollute your body and destroy your body's energy field, distorting your perception and judgment. Challenge yourself to a different way of thinking. Begin your day with peace. Say a little prayer." Brussels grins with delight.

"That's your answer? You think the key to life is peace?"

"Indeed, I do! Start by doing simple things. Compliment people in your life and mean it. Make them feel good. People always enjoy being appreciated. Say hello to people and really listen to them when they talk. Make people feel special. It will have a very positive effect on you. Embrace life, experience failure alongside success, and cherish the struggle as well as the happiness. Believe in yourself and know that you have absolute power over your destiny. That can only happen when you are at peace."

Utterly overwhelmed, I sit back in my chair and look around the room. The bartender chats with the bitchy waiter. Occasionally they glance in our direction. If they only knew what was being said at this dimly lit table above a thumping disco. What would they think? I'm not sure even I know what to think about it.

"Ethan, treat the body as a temple. It is God's gift to you. Stop taking drugs! Substances damage the body in such a way that a person's perception is greatly affected. Your spirituality is at risk. I suspect you know this? It has been a gradual, way of thinking for you for such a long time, that you have allowed it to become your way of life. Perhaps it's time to bring spirituality back into your life."

"Doesn't all this talk about spiritual energy contradict God?"

"Spirituality comes from the Latin root *Spiritus*, which means breath. It refers to the breath of life. Whether you choose to believe in God or not, there is an underlying order to our universe that did not happen by chance."

His words are beginning to make sense, but it's still a lot to take in. I feel like I could use a drink, then immediately feel guilty for having the thought. I'm still trying to get comfortable with the world as it is. Trying to understand everything he says is difficult to say the least. The waiter brings us our water, eyes Brussels, and shuffles off to the bartender again.

"Ethan, what was the initial attraction in your last relationship?"

"Beauty," I say, smiling and immediately feel shallow for being so flip. Well, may as well go for broke. "Also, it was great sex!"

He looks at me and wraps his large hand around my wrist.

"Ethan, perhaps you went into this relationship with the wrong values. Did this ever cross your mind?"

"I guess. It's a possibility."

"When did you notice a change in the relationship?" he asks, letting go of my wrist and folding his hands together on the table. "When did things become strained? When did the mistrust and anger begin to surface?"

I am shocked and confused how he knows so much about my relationship.

"Ethan, do not be embarrassed. Answer the question—if not to me then to yourself."

"You want to know when everything went south."

"Yes," he replies.

"Three months. It went sour in three months."

"You noticed mood swings, drug addiction, and anger in a three-month cycle. Is that correct?"

"Yes? How did you know that?"

"If you had noticed these things the first night, would you have slept with this person?"

"Oh, probably not," I answer. "I don't know."

"When did you realize that it wasn't a *positive* relationship?"

"It was exactly three months."

"Why did you stay, Ethan?"

"Honestly, I thought I could make a difference."

"So, did you?"

"No, I didn't." I furrow my brow, recounting in my mind ugly scenes. "In fact, it got worse every day. I wanted to leave but I felt guilty. I thought that leaving would cause more harm and grief. I felt guilty all the time."

"Perhaps by staying, you lost yourself," he says.

We are silent for a moment as he lets me consider this.

"I would suggest from now on that you build all your relationships on a solid foundation," he says, gently. "Be mindful of your intimate relationships."

The waiter comes back again to take our order. With one hand on his hip, he acts as if he has many people to wait on, even though the room is empty. Just as he begins reciting the day's specials, Brussels interrupts him and orders for both of us.

"Take your time," he adds gently and with a hint of charm. The waiter rolls his eyes and walks away cursing. I can't understand how Brussels can tolerate his behavior.

"What a jerk!"

"Didn't you behave the same way toward me the other day on the beach?"

He's right. Looking down while playing with my napkin, my voice very low, I mumble an apology. He reaches over and lifts my chin to make eye contact with him.

"Never be ashamed to apologize for a wrongdoing."

"I'm sorry about the comments I made to you and the remarks about your age."

"I understand, Ethan. You were reacting because of anger. Do you understand how energy and your ego work with or against people?"

"Yeah, well, sort of?"

"When the waiter returns, notice his body language. His is upset about something we know nothing about."

"Yeah, he is impatient and hostile."

"Ethan, our waiter is upset about something that happened before he arrived to work. When you are happy and the energy within your brain is higher, it creates a higher frequency, regardless of previous circumstances. In turn, higher energy attracts other forms of high energy. Low energy tends to attract low energy. Is this making sense?"

He says this so confidently, as if anyone with half a brain knows this stuff. I look at his white hair and alert eyes and wonder how he learned these things. Who taught him?

"You must remember that the entertainment industry is a business filled with layers of ego," he says smiling and lightening his tone. "Learn to walk into a casting room with a smile on your face; emit positive energy. Those people in the room will recognize this. However, Ethan, it does not guarantee that they will employ you. Your lesson is to maintain your self-worth whether they employ you for a job or not.

Brussels moves in closer, whispering a passage that seems rather odd.

"Be aware of those who praise themselves as devout subjects of God. Sometimes these vexatious angels wear *glued-on-wings* so they can tear down the freedom of human rights. Often, the person with the most financial sway in the room is the one creating the rainstorm. Perhaps it is best to seek inner guidance from above, rather than subject to their dominion to control the thunder. And Ethan, not everyone that holds political title holds honor. *This will make sense in decades to come.*"

"Huh?" Confusion sets in again.

Our waiter approaches us and slams our food and drinks on the table. Pasta is halfway off the plate. Without an apology, he walks away. I am so angry I want to cuss him out. I guess if I do that I apparently will be lowering my energy and giving into my ego because of his ego and giving into bad energy and…whatever! I want to knock this guy across the room. Then it dawns on me that Brussels is right. Can I change my behavior just like flipping a switch? It's going to take some time.

"Excuse me sir. I believe we got off to a bad start. I want to apologize for my rude behavior. I am so sorry." The waiter stares at me. Suddenly, his coldness dissipates and a warm smile takes over his face.

31

"Ethan, what a wonderful gesture you demonstrated. What a glorious meal we have to feast upon! And what glorious company I have before me. Thank you for coming up here under such short notice and listening to me," says Brussels. "I am grateful."

This is such a surreal night. I'm speechless. Brussels' is so courteous, and it's quickly becoming clear to me that I need to start changing my behavior.

"Ethan, I want you to know that these viewpoints are not that difficult to apply, especially once you learn to lead your life with an open heart."

"Uh, okay?"

"Living a life with an *open heart* attracts *abundance*." He points to my stomach. "This is known as the *intuitive zone*, where compassion, love, integrity, and kindness reside. This is no more than a giant electrical circuit. Different emotions vibrate at different frequencies. Some of these frequencies are emitted at different points within the body. When this circuit is disrupted, due to many things we spoke about earlier this evening, you feel it within your stomach. Your wrong choices have resulted in the decline of your health. This is why you have so many problems with your stomach."

"How do you know about my stomach?" I say surprised by this new revelation about me that he has mysteriously acquired. He nods his finger as if to dismiss my question.

"The medications you are on are not helping you. They are only creating more toxins within your system. You must find other ways of healing the body."

"How do I do that? What about—"

"Start by going home and clearing out the skeletons in your mental closet," he interrupts. "Come to terms with your addictions and decide how to change them. Find peace within your soul and come to a better understanding of God; however you perceive God to be. Trust the *Universe* enough to know that you, like everyone else, are here for a reason. It is the opinions and judgments of humankind that have damaged the higher teachings of God through out the centuries. God is merciful and forgiving! Not condemning. Ethan, strive to have faith in you and come to the table with the purest of intentions. Keep your heart unadulterated. It is not success that measures you. You know that? It is your courage, integrity, and belief in a *Higher Purpose* that tie together your destiny."

As Brussels and I finish our conversation, the waiter picks up our plates, places our check on the table. Brussels reaches for the bill and pulls out his wallet. I excuse myself to go to the rest room. When I return Brussels is gone, and a note sits on the bill for the waiter. It reads, "Thank you for such wonderful service, God Bless." I sit and wait, but he never returns. JB and Rick walk in and ask where I've been.

"I just had dinner with an acquaintance."

"You did? Who was it?" Rick asks.

"Some man from Brussels," I answer. "I can't remember his name. He's originally from Scotland."

"We were beginning to worry. You've been gone for over three hours," JB tells me.

"I was?" I try explaining what Brussels and I talked about, but I can't do our conversation justice. JB and Rick look very confused.

"This all sounds very strange, Ethan," says JB. "You know how you tend to attract weird people. Just be careful. Let's get out of here. I'm hungry and I'm tired."

As we leave, I look back to the empty table and wonder where my dinner guest has gone. The waiter comes over and says, "I want to apologize to you. I had a fight with my room mate over money. There was no need for me to take it out on you tonight. Okay?"

"I understand. I really do."

Black Beard's Castle

Chapter 3

The following morning JB wakes me to go sailing. It's 5:30 and in my dreamy state I wonder if what took place the night before really happened. The girls decide to stay home because they're hung-over. The guys and I shuffle through the flat trying to get ready.

Upon reaching the marina, I can see the sailboat and other people getting on board. In the Caribbean, locals take two-or three-day cruises on smaller sailboats or yachts. I wonder about our other passengers.

The sky is still luminous with a shimmer of stars like glitter tossed up to the sky. The dark-blue night sky is slowly fading to an early morning's paler shade. The light from over the horizon slowly creeps along the edges of the island. As we make our way onto the craft, I look up in awe at the massive sails that dance above us. Still drunk with exhaustion, I ask one of the crewmembers for a quiet place to continue my slumber.

An unwelcome flash from JB's camera awakens me. I stumble to the deck to find the sun above the sail boat with no land in sight. Making my way to the end of the boat, I find a quiet spot, away from everyone else, and sit down to get my bearings. The roaring blue ocean seems to break into waves and slosh around in slow motion, as if to show off for us.

I hear footsteps and turn to see a stout, older man with brown hair and a kind face coming toward me. Quickly, I turn away and pretend not to see him. I want this selfish moment of peace and tranquility. The man taps me on the head and I turn around to greet him.

"Hi, my name is Mr. Jerry Goldberg," he says.

"I'm Ethan."

I assume he's the owner of this yacht because he has an air of wealth about him. The large diamond ring on his hand is a big clue, as is his movie-star smile filled with perfect, porcelain veneers.

"Do you mind if I join you?" he says.

I nod my head toward the empty seat next to me.

"Why aren't you with everyone else?" he asks. "They say you're the quiet type."

Great, more questions. I am not ready for an interview about my quiet behavior.

"They always say that about me."

"Well, I believe the quiet ones usually have more to say than they let on and what they have to say is often very intriguing."

I nod my head in agreement.

"Why are you here?" he asks me, as he applies a French suntan lotion.

"You mean here on this sailboat?"

"No, I mean here on the island. Usually people come to St. Thomas to find themselves."

"Well, I came here with my best friend," I say, pointing at JB who has a crowd around him laughing at his jokes, "to escape a few things I guess you can say. Why are you here?"

He tells me that he owns his own law firm and that he loves to escape to St. Thomas every year. He begins to talk about the jewelry store he owns on the island, when JB excitedly interrupts with news of a whale shark swimming alongside the boat. Mr. Goldberg starts to stroll to the front of the boat, and then stops.

"Don't you want to come and see the whale?"

"No, I'll see it when it passes me."

"No," he insists. "Come with me."

I stare at this brown clump of a fish swimming through the water and think to myself, "Yep. Uh-huh. Okay, back to the back of the boat." Before I can walk away, Mr. Goldberg introduces me to a young man, David, who looks to be in his late teens and has a very strong southern accent. We say hello, and David explains that he's here on spring break and that his father is Jerry Goldberg's brother. As Mr. Goldberg and I walk around the boat, he explains, "Oh, like you, David is trying to escape a few things."

"What do you mean?" I ask, intrigued that someone so young is on a self-imposed journey.

"His father wants him to be a lawyer, but David wants to be a musician."

"You mean David is going to be a lawyer so he can please his father? He is feeling guilty because his dad's opinion matters more than his own?" I know I'm repeating what I heard Brussels relate the night before, but it feels like a smart thing to say. "You would think he'd speak up about something he's so passionate about."

"Ah, you seem like a wise person. It looks like I was right. The quiet ones do have something to say."

Since I now feel like I'm ready to have an adult conversation with this man I decide to introduce a more intellectual topic.

"Do you believe in God?" I ask him.

"Well of course I do. Don't you?"

"No, not really. I had a conversation with an older man last night that got me thinking about a few things. I guess I don't really know yet."

"You should know that there is an unexplainable order to our universe," he says. "I happen to believe in past lives. In one lifetime, we may be poor and in another, rich. We get the chance to experience different avenues of life, and with every lifetime we evolve. Every person here is evolving together, to find their authentic purpose?"

"Really," I add, pretending that what he has to say is old news.

"At the end of our journey," he continues, "We come to understand the equality of life."

"I have no idea why I'm here," I murmur.

He laughs. "Well, maybe you're here on a life-changing mission? Perhaps you're a *Doubting Thomas*, trying to find truth as you come to understand it?"

Our vessel pulls into a small cove, JB, Rick, and some of the other people on board dive into the cobalt blue water. Mr. Goldberg walks David back, sits him down next to me, and starts to turn away.

"Mr. Goldberg!" I shout. "Maybe you should stay here."

"No. You two boys get to know each other. And Ethan, you can call me Jerry."

This is an odd Kodak moment. David and I stare at our flip-flops in complete silence. Irony at its finest! I now understood what everyone else must see in me.

I turn to David and ask, "What do you like to do?"

He shrugs his shoulders. "Uh, I don't know."

"Do you like music?"

Oh, there it is. The expression on his face changes, and I know I've said the magic words. He just needed someone to listen. Now I can't get him to stop talking. One of the crewmembers puts on a song by Christopher Cross, called, *Sailing,* and cranks the volume up. *"Well, it's not far down to paradise; at least it's not for me. And if the wind is right, you can sail away and find tranquility."* David's face lights up as he lip synchs the words.

The crew decides to light up a few joints and bask in the sun as everyone splashes around in the water. David, Jerry, and I decide to continue our conversation at the back of the boat. It's one of the first times I've decided not to participate and give in to my addiction. It feels pretty damn good. For the first time in my life, I have met a younger boy and an older gentleman who are on the same page as me.

"Before you leave the island," says Jerry, "you should come have dinner at my house in the mountains."

"I'd love to."

"What about tomorrow evening? I'll throw a small party, invite a few of the people from the island, and make you the guest of honor."

"Oh, please don't do that. Make David the guest of honor."

"Don't worry. It will be a great party and you, my friend, will be the guest of honor. Why don't we invite your two friends along as well? But let's keep it at you and your two friends." He stands up and walks over to JB and Rick.

"You must have made an impression on him. He doesn't invite people to his house, especially since he's still remodeling," says David. "My father and Jerry are so opposite of one another. To tell you the truth, I feel closer to Jerry than to my own dad. Uncle Jerry is the only one who encourages me to be a musician. My dad wants me to be an attorney. Just like him."

David stares into the foamy, white trail the ship leaves behind. I look at his face and recognize the pain. I guess we all have our pockets of hurt that we carry inside us.

***

We sail back into port a couple of days later. Jerry Goldberg comes up and gives me a bear hug. "We sailed from Heaven's Gate, all the way to the Holy Cross. Now let's hope that Calypsos folklore comes to pass."

"What do you mean by Heaven's Gate and Holy Cross?"

"They are known, as Magens Bay and St. Croix. They are considered to be sacred waters, according to Calypsos folklore. Locals believe that every Easter Sunday, angels come ashore to St. Thomas and discover a scribe. I have been taking writing classes for years. I am finally ready for this celestial encounter."

"You believe that?"

"I certainly do!" I've given Rick directions to my house, so I'll expect to see you tomorrow night," he says, nodding his head.

"Okay, sounds great."

As we load our things back into Rick's jeep, he and JB stop and stare at me.

"What?"

"Ethan, do you know who that is?" Rick asks.

"Yep, his name is Jerry Goldberg."

"Yeah, but do you know who he is?"

"No, I guess not?"

"Ethan, there are two castles on this island. Mr. Goldberg owns Black beard's Castle, and he's throwing an Easter party for you there tomorrow night!"

"So? I'm more interested in his friendship than his house," I blurt out.

I notice David and Jerry climbing into their car and wave them down.

"Jerry, since you're throwing this party for me tomorrow night," I tell Jerry, "the least I can do is cook."

"Ethan, I have someone that will do that."

"I feel like I should do something. Let me at least cook. Have you ever had chicken-fried steak, mashed potatoes, and corn bread?"

"That sounds absolutely, splendid," he giggles. "You have yourself a deal."

I get into the jeep and tell Rick and JB about my dinner offer. I can see by their facial reactions that they sense a change in my personality.

Later that night, I give JB a hug and thank him for the trip to St. Thomas.

"Ethan, are you okay? There is something different about you?"

"Yes, I am. I'm actually happy for the first time in a long time."

***

The next night the jeep pulls up to the castle, sliding a few inches in the gravel. We climb out with our jaws dragging, taking in this fantastic fortress. We walk across a bridge that crosses a moat filled with rocks and saltwater fish. In front of us is a large wooden door with a portal window. No sooner do we knock than a cocoa-colored man wearing denim red pants, a bandana, a colorful green shirt, and matching bright-red socks greets us. Could he possibly be the butler? JB, Rick, and I step inside, admiring a spiral stone staircase that leads to a tower. Colorful stained glass windows line the ascending wall.

"Damn, Ethan, good score." Rick is flabbergasted by the entranceway.

In the center of the room, a very long wood table with two large throne-like chairs, at each end and eight other chairs dominates the cathedral ceilings. Paintings of galleons with sails aloft and old maps of the island fill the walls while antique candle-bearing sconces dimly light each corner of the room. Gold-rimmed china is laid out on the table. An overflowing basket of tropical fruit is the centerpiece.

The newly remodeled kitchen is adjacent to the dining room. A giant, antique-iron stove grounds one wall, and next to it a bay window gives a majestic view of Magens Bay. I shake Jerry's hand and tell him how wonderful his home is. He walks us around, showing us his antique tapestries, bronze statues, and 18ᵗʰ-century English portrait paintings.

After the tour, Jerry and I are in the kitchen preparing dinner, enjoying an easy conversation. "Try this local tonic water." I take the glass from Jerry's hand.

"Oh by the way, Ethan, I forgot to mention that I invited a man I met at my store. For the life of me I can't remember his name. I've always been dreadful with names. Anyway, I remember he said he's from Brussels."

"Are you kidding? Did he say anything unusual?"

"Yes, he did. I couldn't help offering an invitation to him. He was so mesmerizing. A funny thing happened while we were talking. It seemed as though time stood still? All sound seemed to vanish?"

I cough up my tonic water all over the kitchen counter as Jerry continues. "I'm so sorry. Where's your bathroom? I need to wash up." Jerry points to a hallway just past the iron stove. I venture down a long corridor beyond the main entrance of the castle.

Guests begin to arrive. My eyes stop on a bohemian collection of men and women, as they begin introducing themselves to me one at a time. I politely try to excuse myself but it falls on deaf ears. One tall woman, Sulivia, works at a metaphysical bookstore in the village called, *The Octopus*. A white, lace dress is wrapped around her ageless body. An amethyst necklace, though striking, pales compared to her piercing blue-green eyes that lock onto anyone that looks into her eyes. Another woman, Shari, is dressed in a black gown. She constantly digs for filter less cigarettes in her handbag. The rich and elite, continuing to gather at the entryway, greeted by the coco-colored man, whose name I learn, is Anthony.

David nervously strolls in. He looks at all the guest gathered in the parlor and immediately rushes over to me, offering to help me in the kitchen anyway possible. A pounding on the front door halts the flow of conversation. Instantly, the room becomes still. Brussels walks in, magnificent and imposing. All eyes are focused on him as he enters. He shakes the hands of every person in the room, and then walks towards the kitchen.

"Come with me David, now." I grab David's arm and rush him into the kitchen.

"I'm so glad you took the time to share this evening with us," says Jerry, walking over to clap Brussels on the back.

"I wouldn't have missed this for the world."

"Have you met our guest of honor, Ethan? And this is my nephew, David."

"What a pleasure it is to meet two fine young men." Brussels smiles intently.

***

Conversation is light and mainly dominated by Anthony, the coco-colored skin artist, hired by Jerry, to paint his bell tower. Brussels sits quietly, smiling, and listening attentively to everyone.

After dinner, Jerry and I gather the dishes and carry them to the kitchen, eager to finish cleaning up so that we can continue enjoying the conversation. I'm anxious to see if the table talk will lead to something other than Anthony's wealthy clients.

Jerry attends to his guests as I finish washing dishes. Brussels comes into the kitchen, and without looking up I know he's there.

"You left the restaurant in a hurry?"

"I sensed your friends were looking for you."

"I wish you could have stayed and met them."

Jerry drifts in and out of the kitchen, offering desserts and coffee. Some of the guests stroll into the kitchen, picking up towels to dry and stacking pots and pans in their rightful places. Jerry points me in the direction of the back door, which leads to a lush yard, and tells me to take a break. I eagerly agree.

Brussels and I go outside, walk to a cliff that shows an incredible view of the bay.

"You're not being your profound self tonight?" I say, sarcastically.

"Oh, now you're eager to hear what I have to say?" He chuckles. We chat about the island for a while when Jerry walks out and asks if we want dessert. I turn around and notice everyone is staring at Brussels from the kitchen bay window.

"We'll take whatever your feel is best," I say.

Jerry nods and goes back inside. Brussels turns to me with serious eyes.

"Ethan, why did you come to St. Thomas?"

"I needed to get away. I, I, have been lost for quite some time."

We all lose our way, make poor decisions, and we think that by wanting more *things* we will find happiness," he says, his voice quickly becoming more somber.

"I guess I've never really thought about it that way."

"Most people don't," he says.

We move to a stone bench and sit down. The sky is littered with stars and the air smells sweet, like the honey scent of gardenias.

"All that matters is the car, the home, the sex, the money, the career, social status, the need for a relationship, and where to vacation each year.

"Yep, that's me." I say, nodding my head.

"The insatiable *need-want-have-to-have-more* things are contagious. It is easier to allow yourself to become seduced by the trappings of wanting more, rather than contribute to causes that really matter. Most people focus on making more money on a daily basis, rather than *being of service* to the planet. Meanwhile Mother Earth is slowly slipping into a point of no return. Learn to start thinking about something other than money, Ethan. Make a difference within yourself first. Ask God to be of service. That is cosmic maturity."

"Okay? But the other day I heard Rick talking about Nostradamus' predictions. What about all the end-of-the-world prophecies? If all this bad stuff is going to happen, why should it matter anyway? I might as well take what I can get before it's too late."

"Prophecies are mere warnings signs. Look at them as road signs that advise us when to pull off the freeway. We all have the ability to stop things from occurring. But first, you must discover your authentic purpose. Ethan, purpose leads to inner happiness, which allows a shift in consciousness. Imagine every man and every woman connected to their true calling? Prophecies wouldn't be necessary if you knew you were on the right road?"

Jessica and Shari come outside with their drinks, exclaiming how beautiful the weather is and what a gorgeous night to be sitting outside. Sulivia makes her way towards Brussels and whispers something in his ear. He nods his head, smiles, and excuses himself. I am mesmerized by Sulivia's beauty. Her eyes are catlike, almond shape; almost beyond this world? A long, white dress compliments her perfect choice of opaque sandals, almost camouflaging a silver toe-ring on her left foot. Her regal presence seduces the starlight.

"Please come with me, Ethan." I feel light, almost invisible, as I follow Sulivia inside this magnificent castle. "Come, Ethan."

We make our way towards the main entrance of the castle. Sulivia points to a winding tower of stone steps that goes upstairs. "He waits for us in the tower."

Our footsteps slap against the stone floor, and the temperature seems to feel cooler the higher we climb. Our voices resonate and echo off the stone walls. Reaching the top, I can see a scaffold where Anthony has been working. The painted tower is filled with images of saints and angels with majestic wings looming up the circular walls. The moon creeps into the room, and a cool breeze off the ocean pushes through the trees and makes its way up to the loggia where we stand. I look at a portal window and turn to ask Sulivia why we are meeting Brussels in the tower. She is gone? Where did she go?

Brussels stands beside me, his hands clasped behind him and white hair shining in the dark. He turns to me. "Ethan Michaels, I ask for you hand as a scribe."

"What?" I look at Brussels with confusion.

"Carefully listen to what I am about to say." Golden light blazes through out the tower, highlighting a large bell that resides at the top of the dome ceiling.

"Ethan, the awakening of feminine consciousness is near. Women's kindheartedness has prevented the demise of this planet for decades."

He slowly paces back and forth, working out his thoughts with each step. I'm intrigued, yet skeptical. Why am I listening to this stranger? Is he crazy? Or am I?

"The rise of women holding political title will send a message that the time has come. Men's continual need to desolate the Earth will cause planetary catastrophe, if women do not come forth in numbers."

"I don't understand what you are talking about?"

"Corrupt, greedy, men have controlled churches and government institutions through out the centuries. Conquering lands, murdering innocent men, women and children, in the name of God has undermined the truth. Women have watched the dismantling of morality for centuries. The time has come. Ethan, what do you know of Joan of Arc?"

"She was burned at the stake, wasn't she?"

"Why?"

"Because she was a heretic," I say, guessing.

"According to the church!" exclaims Brussels. "She was captured by the Burundians; Charles VII offered no ransom and sold her to England for 10,000 pounds. When she declared that she answered only to God and not the church, she was tried as a witch and a heretic. Ethan, corrupt men destroyed one of the strongest female energies on this planet. Men's compulsive addiction to war, power and self-indulgence left its footprints on womanhood for ages.

Brussels' blue eyes seem to glow brighter with every word he utters. The night sky ushers in a tropical breeze. On the tower walls, the painted images seem to silently whisper approval of his words.

"The hand of power shall continue to plague the earth. In the year 1997, the Rose of Europe will be diminished, but the flame shall live. This event will trigger the collective female consciousness to rise. When Mars pierces the sky as a neighbor to Earth and the oceans storms from the East, the rise of female energy will come to fruition within the American government. Despite the increase of men's hunger for authority, it is the river of womanhood that will shatter the glass ceiling."

I can hear the rise and fall of laughter, as everyone moves into the grand living room. But my thoughts are quickly brought back to where I am now. Flooded with apprehension, I wonder how I will remember all that Brussels has shared with me.

"Discord began when men chose to control the church with absolute authority, forgetting the true essence of the Christ teachings."

He stops and looks at me. A warm smile flashes across his face.

"I realize that you are hearing many things for the first time."

"I am not one to believe in Jesus or the church. You can't expect me to understand any of this, nor do I want to," I say.

"You did once before? And you will again. In time my dear boy."

"I chose to leave the Catholic Church for personal reasons. I don't plan on going back. Besides, I won't remember any of this once I leave St. Thomas?"

"The mind is brilliant! Recall will prove favor at the right moment, Ethan," Brussels says, assuredly. "*Two* women will come into your life.

The first woman will come to you in the *midst of the day* playing like a *Pied Piper*. *Fire and Ice* will give clues to the second woman's arrival. Her lesson to you is love. Both women are your life teachers."

Looking out over the island, I can't help but feel unsure. My mind feels more inundated than when I first arrived, yet something tells me to trust this old man. I will listen until it becomes too outlandish. "Two women are coming into my life?"

"Yes!"

Brussels turns to me and takes hold of my hands.

"Do you believe that Adam and Eve were actual people and that it was the rectitude of a few to decide the world's fate for centuries? Or do you believe that maybe they were an analogy, a parable?"

"I don't know. I never really thought about it. I guess I thought they were two actual people, because that's what I was raised to believe."

"Exactly," he says, excitedly.

My view from the tower is picturesque. We move to sit in the stairwell, which is painted to resemble the Sistine Chapel. The hand of God reaches down to give Adam life. I glance out the window to catch the twinkling lights that blanket the village. Brussels nudges my foot to recapture my attention.

"How could Adam and Eve be an analogy?" I ask.

"Much of the Bible can be interpreted as poetic passages laced with symbolism. Language interpretations, analogies texted in Hebrew, if altered or edited in the slightest way can take on an entirely different meaning. Editing the Bible with their *hypothesis* about how God would approve or not approve, can weave a web of *intolerance* for all mankind.

Unfortunately, men of title edited dogma throughout the centuries and costumed *fear* with a *cloak and dagger*. What was the truth became the lie, which became the truth. Women continue to learn lesson after lesson, in every lifetime, despite the obstacles thrown their way. Men's misuse of power will continue until women take the reigns of government. Perhaps men could learn a lesson from women, rather than allow *greed* to dominate their every move?"

Brussels' eyes fill with sadness as he hesitates for a moment.

"Women have borne the stain of first sin for many lifetimes. Yet it is she that bears the womb's fruit and gives hope. Perhaps Adam, having reached eagerly for the forbidden fruit, should have carried the responsibility?"

I realize Brussels isn't preaching to me, but rather sharing diverse points of view. "This is something I really need to think about," I say under my breath.

"The women I predict will come into your life will significantly change you," he says, slowly. "Listen to their words."

"Okay, I say half believing.

Humankind has the opportunity to shift this planet into a new consciousness in 1987, 1992, 1994, 1997, 1998, and 1999. If this *shift* is ill-treated, the year 2001 will take a detour. Pray that this shift will empower truth and fairness. Remember this, while masculine energy continues to wage war for avaricious outcomes, it will be female consciousness that saves us from ourselves."

Suddenly, my name is called out. "Damn it, I want to hear more."

"Meet me next Friday at four o'clock at *The Octopus Book Store*. There we will have our last conversation. Ethan, this doesn't have to make sense now. What you choose to remember will come forth at the appropriate time."

I can hear JB calling me. Footsteps echo up the stairwell.

"I have to go."

He stops me and puts his hand on my shoulder.

"Study the conspiracies of the world's greatest leaders. You will open Pandora's Box. Those who stand to profit become your clues."

"Huh? Do you mean Abraham Lincoln or John F. Kennedy? Martin Luther King? Or, do you mean Caesar?"

"All their stories are the same."

He is silent for a moment, and then whispers as we wind down the tower.

"The queen of hearts will rule for eight days and shall preside over the scandal. Earth will pause for one moment and honor the *House of Kings*. Feminine Consciousness will stir in the hearts of those souls who are kind," Brussels squeezes my hand.

"*November the 11nth* will come into your life like a winter storm. Do not lose faith. *I will be there when you reach for the light*. I ask that you become a scribe, Ethan. Research, read, and learn to become what it is you are meant to be. You will know when you are ready to share this story. Until then, you must study."

JB approaches the top of the stairs. Brussels excuses himself politely and walks back down the stone steps. Blue orbs descend down the stairwell, as though they guide Brussels to the main foyer. JB looks at me with puzzle.

"Are you okay, Ethan?" JB asks me. "You've been gone for over an hour?"

"What? Are you sure? I guess I lost track of time?"

"Are you high?" he asks me.

"No. Not anywhere close to that" I look away.

"Well, you look like you're fucked up on something."

"I'm so overwhelmed by this castle. You're buzzed, aren't you?" I ask him.

He has a silly smile on his face. "Of course I am! Want a little snort?"

"No thanks." I walk down the winding stairwell and leave JB behind.

***

I call Jerry the following Friday. On his suggestion, I go to his jewelry store in the village to pick up what he calls 'an appreciation gift.'

"David has decided to speak to his father," he tells me. "He has decided to follow his passion and pursue music. Thank you for encouraging him, Ethan."

"Well, I, uh…I didn't do—"

"Ethan, just say you're welcome. What are your plans for the rest of the day?"

I explain that Brussels has invited me to The Octopus Book Store.

"The Octopus is an amazing metaphysical book store. That is where the Mamas and the Papas wrote '*Monday, Monday* and '*California Dreaming*,'" Jerry tells me.

We exchange numbers, and I thank him for the wonderful dinner party.

"Ethan, you have brought David and me so much pleasure. Your thoughtful chicken-fried steak dinner will always be a treasured memory. I will hold it dear."

He extends a warm embrace and hands me a blue rosary. "I know what you are thinking? Why would a Jewish man give me a rosary?"

"Well, yeah?" I look at the rosary and feel a cool sensation in my hands.

"This will bring you luck at the right time." Jerry hugs me. "Good-bye."

I wander through the cobblestone streets peering into various antique shops. I nod to strangers and say "good day," and I'm surprised to find that most of them smile and answer back. I keep mulling over the information I've learned. I've definitely felt a change in my thinking. I'm beginning to like myself. It's liberating.

As I turn the corner, I see Brussels waiting at the entrance of the Octopus. He stands tall and proud with a smile on his face. He's dressed in his usual pressed white shirt with pressed khakis and sandals.

"Ethan, thank you. It's nice to see you today."

"Thank you," I answer, confidently.

We walk inside and I notice Sulivia sitting on a cement floor in the back of the store. She's wearing a white dress embroidered with silver thread, and a large turquoise necklace. Extending her hand, she says, "Come. I have been expecting you."

Brussels taps me on the shoulder and motions for me to sit down. Sulivia tells me to remove my shoes. She then takes my left foot into her hands and begins to examine it. She glances at Brussels and smiles.

"*Il est une âme très ancienne*," she says to him. "He is indeed an old soul."

"*Très bien*," he answers back. "*Quel âge a-t-il.*"

"*Il est très ancienne.* Au revoir."

Brussels kisses Sulivia gently on the cheek, excuses himself and walks out into the bustling streets. Sulivia looks into my eyes and says, "Go to the Charlotte Amalie Pier after our session and conclude your conversation."

"Yeah, okay. What do you mean old soul? And why did Brussels leave?" I ask.

"This is my gift to you. I asked for our time to be private. Do you understand reincarnation?"

"We've talked about it some," I tell her.

"Do you know why you have met Brussels?"

"No. Not really."

"He is a *Courier* of words. Try to retain as much information as possible. Do not disregard his message. Use your common sense and newfound enlightenment. Decide for yourself what is truth."

Sulivia shuffles a deck of tarot cards and spreads them on the cement floor. She closes her eyes and asks that I turn over three cards. I can't take my eyes off her toe ring. "Let me know when you have chosen your cards."

"Okay." I grab three cards and flip them over quickly. "What's the significance of your toe ring?"

"Only a few are solicited to wear them," she explains. "The legend of the Celtic toe ring has been passed down for centuries and speaks of men and women known as, *Key Masters*. Once the toe ring is placed upon the left toe, a sacred initiation opens the *Akashic Records*. The request of the toe ring is simple: Begin your day with *gratitude* and the doors to heaven will grant true abundance."

Sulivia touches my three cards with care. "The 16/7 card represent the *Falling Tower*. Loss will come to your doorsill on a winter's night. Do not fear. You will rise from the ashes with purpose."

Sulivia holds the *Messenger Card* to her chest. "You will become the *Messenger of Truth*. Stand in your truth, despite those who criticize you." She looks intently at my last card and speaks.

"The *Master Card* represents the teacher and the student. You are asked to become the *apprentice* before you become the *messenger*. Once you become a great student, you will be asked to share your word."

"None of this makes sense?" I look at Sulivia at a complete loss.

"You will be fine, Ethan," she announces. "You will find ways to come to terms with the information I have shared with you."

Sulivia removes a silver ring from a small wooden box. She motions for my bare left foot and places it gently on my second toe.

"Ethan, every time you look at your toe ring, remind yourself that St. Thomas is your vantage point. Each time your foot hits the ground, remind yourself that destiny calls!"

Clasping my hand, Sulivia smiles and speaks softly. "I'm glad we had a chance to meet during the Easter holiday. I must attend to my next client. Farewell."

"Oh, okay? Thanks. I really appreciate the reading and toe ring."

Sulivia stands up, smiles at me warmly, and retreats to rows and rows of books. I notice that cash lies inside her small wooden box. How could I be so rude and not pay her? I jump up and scurry off to catch up with her. As I run through the store trying to find Sulivia, I notice black and white photos of *The Mama's and Papa's* proudly displayed behind a lacquered wooden bar that serves as a register. An old lady closes her register.

"Excuse me. Did you see a very pretty, tall lady wearing a white dress? I forgot to pay her for my tarot reading." I am out of breath as I look around the store.

"A tall lady did a reading for you?" The old lady is somewhat troubled.

"Yes, her name is, oh dear, I can't remember her name? You can't miss her? She's at least 5'11 or taller?" Her eyes are, well, they are incredible."

"Sir, no one has done tarot readings since the 1960's, when *Mama Cass Elliot* was visiting our store. See?" She points to an old photograph of Mama Cass standing next to Brussels.

"Oh, my god, that's, never mind. How do I get to the main pier?" I toss the cash down on the lacquer bar and wait for the lady to write down directions. "I have to go."

***

Scores of sightseers crowd the pier. Cameras flash snapshots of newlyweds, children and old couples walking down the wooden planks. Cruise ships dock on the waterfront walls, allowing tourist to assemble off the yachts, anxious, no doubt, to meet their sight seeing guides. I see Brussels in the distance, surrounded by children feeding seagulls.

"Hey, Brussels," I shout out.

"Over here," Brussels yells back.

I run down the pier, moving through the crowds, not paying attention to anything other than Brussels. "Excuse me, I am so sorry," I hear my words of apology, but I don't mean one word of what I am saying. I need answers and I need them now! This meeting is not a coincidence? I reach Brussels panting with confusion.

"Okay!! You and your lady friend are way out there! She, well, she fucking disappeared! And I saw an old photo of you and Mama Cass. You have not aged since that photo was taken. I need answers. Who are you? What do you want?" I pace up and down the pier, ignoring the children that reach inside Brussels pants pockets for coins.

"You have an art deco beveled mirror. Do you not?"

"Yes? I, how do you know about my art deco mirror?" I blurt out.

"You have an art deco mirror surrounded by Chinese-red walls? This mirror will fall to the ground and break into a thousand pieces. All around this mirror, I see *fire* and *ice*. Footprints will go in a thousand directions. Whatever happens, do not lose your faith. *Find strength within the rubble.*"

"What do you mean? How did you know about my red walls?"

Ignoring my startled response, Brussels continues.

"You will fall three times. Each time will feel like death. Rise above the circumstances and find your courage."

Brussels strolls toward the town square as I stumble behind him, confused yet again, and more than a little freaked out. He stares at the cruise ships locked neatly to the large wooden piers. He speaks without looking at me, and I listen.

"October 15 will play a majestic role in your life. Never forget that. Look back to St. Thomas as your beginning. Hold steadfast to your *open heart*. This will be your greatest asset. Follow the road of gratitude, Ethan, and not the road of greed. And never forget that you are a *Speaker of Truth*. I choose you, to be my scribe."

The traffic of pedestrians crowds the streets. A flock of seagulls soars directly above us. A faint cry of church bells resonates through the town, chiming six times. A cool breeze rolls in off the water as the sun sheds its layers, glowing orange and then red.

"I must go now, Ethan."

He turns around to meet my sad brown eyes. Children walk down the pier, encouraging Brussels to follow.

"I don't know how to write anything," I say to him, trying to be persuasive.

"You will know exactly what to pen when the time comes."

"No! You need to go find Jerry. He's been waiting years for this chance."

"I choose you, Ethan. Brussels smiles and turns to walk down the pier.

I give him Jerry's number, trying to be subtle, but it doesn't seem to matter.

"Good-bye, my dear Ethan. Thank you," he says one last time as he turns and fades into the cityscape. Children surround Brussels, laughing, joyous to be near him.

"Come back here old man!" I wave to him, but he doesn't see me. Will I ever see him again? I keep waiting for the credits to roll at any minute. They never do.

I turn toward the village and begin walking. My thoughts fill the air with confusion, yet there's something different within my soul. Brussels will never know how grateful I am to feel alive again. I turn around hoping for a last glimpse. But he's nowhere in sight. I find a deserted corridor of endless alleyways, and cry tears of gratitude. The next day, Rick drives JB and me to the airport. I feel as if I've been thrown out of a cave into the sunlight. What should I do next? Will I learn to write? What will I write about? I need to go home and rediscover everything I've put aside and start my journey with one foot in front of the other.

"Then the eyes of the blind shall be opened and the ears of the deaf unstopped... The people that walked in the darkness have seen the great light; they that dwelled in the land of images, upon them in the light has shone."

— *(Isaiah 35:5, 9:1)*

Pied Piper

Chapter 4

A gentle rain has been falling all morning, leaving a phantasmal mist slithering around the trees in the distance. Raindrops drip from the foliage, and I am caught in the dwindling sadness that rain can sometimes bring. Burnt-orange leaves cling to the ground as the onslaught of an early autumn nears. I glance over my shoulder at the clock and notice that it is ten minutes until two. It has been six months since my encounter with the one I call Brussels. Since returning from the island, I have changed salons and now spend my time making up the faces of the wealthy and the elite.

Mrs. Harris scrutinizes the final touches of her makeup. She peers into the mirror, analyzing every wrinkle and mole. Turning my attention back to the trees, where the low-hanging fog still clings to the feet of the forest, I yearn to rush her along, and yet I'm hesitant to annoy her. I have a go-see in ten minutes that could boost my special effects make up career. I tell her that my next client is waiting and so our time is limited. I don't want to seem uninterested in her concerns, especially if a tip is involved. She takes the hint and blesses me with a double-cheek kiss. The receptionist gives me a thumbs-up as I hurry out the door, letting me know that I scored a big tip. This helps overcome the melancholy mood that has saturated the air around me.

"I have a dental appointment, Mary. I'll be back in an hour."

No way am I going to tell her about the interview for the three-day booking on a low budget film. If I get the job, I will call in sick and worry about the repercussions later.

"Don't forget, Dr. Scalier has confirmed her appointment and said she needs you to spend some time with her," Mary calls out as the door closes behind me.

My dirty-white bomb of a Toyota is waiting for me alongside the building. I always try to park it in an unobtrusive place, but that's difficult when the lot is filled with Jaguars and Mercedes. My car coughs and gags every time I start it. A hubcap is missing from the driver's side and a dent in the passenger's door was a present left for me in a grocery store parking lot by a runaway shopping-cart. As the dew in the air settles across my face, I toss my bag into the back seat and turn out of the parking lot. The mist outside is thick enough to distort my view through the glass but just thin enough to cause the windshield wipers to drag and bounce across the window, creating an annoying racket. I cast a furtive glance to my passenger seat to make sure I have my portfolio and take a deep, nervous breath. Before long, the address I was given is finally in front of me, and a parking space away from the building's windows makes me feel like this is a positive sign.

"I will get this job. I will get this job."

With a confident, purposeful stride and my portfolio in hand, I enter the glass doors.

"Excuse me, can you tell me where the casting call is taking place?" I ask the receptionist.

She points down the hallway.

"You can go into the waiting area with the other makeup artists, and they will call for you when they are ready," the receptionist says, in a monotone voice.

Making my way down the hall, I find the waiting room and sign-in sheet. The room is painted hospital-white with modern black chairs and tables positioned around the room. Framed posters of movie posters hang on each wall. Magazines displaying the latest fashions of the eighties are staggered on the coffee table. One door in the room remains closed.

My plan is to meet the assistant director; even though I have been assured that the booking is mine. A vacant chair is positioned to capture a full view of the closed door and everyone else in the room. Eagerly, I take my seat and begin sizing up the other people who have come to play the game. A rather large woman dressed in black with long blonde hair and excessive purple eye shadow sits on the other side of the room. To my left is a thin man with long hair and spiked bangs. He wears an elaborate, asymmetrical jacket patched with hues of brilliant blues, greens, and yellows that covers his black slacks. Another man, to my right, sports red-and-yellow shoulder-length hair. Safety pins dangle from his ears to his collarbone, and hand painted slippers with curling, pointy toes decorate his feet. My lightweight brown slacks, argyle socks, and loafers scream Yuppie.

A young woman wearing a black pantsuit, with her brown hair pulled into a French bun, opens the closed door. She must be the assistant director's assistant. She looks at no one as she softly calls the large woman to enter the room and bring her book. The room behind her seems unusually dark with a barely discernible light in the distance. The door closes and opens in what seems like no time at all. The large woman quickly exits with a tearful face. Black mascara streaks down her cheeks. She lights a cigarette with trembling hands and makes her way out the door. The assistant nods and motions for the man with the multicolored jacket, to follow her. I find myself staring at the man on my right side, with safety pins in his ears, wondering about the scene we have just witnessed. Tension hangs in the air just long enough for anxiety to weigh in my chest. My colleague does not appear to be worried. His portfolio lies next to him, a large and worn leather satchel. He turns to me but I quickly turn my gaze to the ground.

A minute has passed. The door opens and releases the man with the multicolored jacket. His face is contorted into a deep frown. The assistant nods and motions to the man on my right, to step forward. He smiles as he approaches the assistant. I try to convince myself that everything is okay. The other makeup artists obviously aren't getting the job because Jason has promised me the booking. The door opens again and the man with the safety pins comes out muttering to himself. The assistant motions for me, and I grab my portfolio and make my way to the door.

"Hello, my name is Ethan."

"Hi Ethan, my name is Sheila," she says, and points to a table across the room.

There is unmistakable evidence of fear in her face. It is obvious that she does not want to be here.

The entire room is black except for one overhead light that illuminates a drawing table and a lone figure hunched over it. I walk toward the shrine as time suddenly seems to crawl. Over my shoulder, Sheila fades into the darkness. The shadows of the room lay completely still.

The endless silence hovers over the table while a feeling of blankness slips through my body. I see a woman with short, gray hair furiously scribbling on a stack of folders. Long, shedding ashes hang from the cigarette in her mouth. Her lips are wrinkled from many years of smoking. I stand patiently, staring into the darkness around me, and wait for her acknowledgement. Scribble. Scribble. Nothing! Scribble.

"Put your book on the table," says the woman.

"Put your book on the table please, Ethan," Sheila calls out in a timid voice from across the room.

I place my book on the table and still nothing. The nameless woman continues to write. She takes another drag off of her cigarette, playing odds on how long those ashes will last before they topple down in front of her work. The nervous tension begins to set in my stomach as I look back in Sheila's direction.

"Open your book, Ethan," Sheila calls out. "Please."

I step toward the table and open my book, pushing it in front of the stoic woman. Seconds pass then the woman finally breaks her silence.

"Next!"

The ash falls from her cigarette in what seems like slow motion and lands on my open portfolio page.

"But you haven't looked at it," I say.

"Your book is boring. Get out."

I am dumbfounded by her response and left speechless. Sheila's hand is on my right shoulder and gently urges me to move.

"It's time to go, Ethan."

"But she didn't look at my book."

Sheila nudges me again to leave. I walk back through the void then stop. Racing toward the table, I open my book again.

"Excuse me, but you haven't seen my book yet."

"I said your book is boring so leave now!"

"How do you know? You didn't look at it."

She grabs my book and opens it.

"Look at this photo. If this is the photo you are opening your book with, then it is obvious that the rest of your book is boring."

"What do you mean?" I can't comprehend what she is saying because this is definitely not what I have come to hear.

"If this is the strongest thing in your book," she said, "you are not a special effects makeup artist. So you must leave! Get out now!"

"Have you spoken to Jason?" I implore, in a desperate attempt to regain any control of my career.

"I will speak to Jason and tell him that he is not working with you. Now get out. I shouldn't have to tell you this more than once," she snaps.

I fetch my book and stomp toward the door filled with anger. I want to scream, but even in my angry state I know that telling this woman what I think of her won't salvage the situation. A sinking feeling comes over me, as if I am in a chair falling backward and struggling to regain control. I stumble on the threshold of the doorway as I leave the room.

The sky is black and a torrential thunderstorm is crashing against the buildings. That subtle air of melancholy that I felt earlier had now become a monster, namely my complete feelings of failure and lack of self-worth.

I thought this job was mine. It's funny how the rain can play two characters. It's either a holiday parade complete with the crashes of a bass drum and cymbals from a marching band, or it is the wrath of hell that makes you run home and hide under the covers.

The salon parking lot is brimming with BMWs. I can't remember driving back, but I know I have to suppress my anger before I go inside. I run into the salon and make my way to the back room so that I can dry myself off. There are still a few minutes to go before my next appointment, which provides me the time to desperately go through my address book. Maybe Jason can help me?

"Yes please, is Jason there?" I ask the voice on the phone.

"I'm sorry but he's out on a shoot. They should be back soon, since the rain is so bad."

"Can you tell him Ethan called and to call me at work?"

"I sure will."

During my next appointment, Mary calls out across the salon.

"Ethan, there's a Jason on line one."

I hurry through the salon, passing a row of women stationed under dryers. My stomach sinks. What has he been told? What am I going to say? I fumble for the phone.

"Hi Jason, this is Ethan."

"Hey, Ethan, I heard what happened."

"Your assistant was so rude. I was really quite shocked."

"Yes, I know. She can be tough. I'm sorry you had to go through that, Ethan. I'm also sorry because she picked another artist. I really like working with you, but it just didn't work out this time."

There is a long, uncomfortable silence on the phone. I'm eager to hear something positive from our phone call, but my brain tells me that won't happen.

"Tell you what," adds Jason. "There's a party tomorrow night for industry professionals. It's invitation-only. Photographers, models, and makeup artists all get together to network. It's a very exclusive party, and you'll be able to show your book and meet a few people. I'll leave your name at the door. That's the best I can do, Ethan."

"Well, of course, I would really like that. Thank you."

"And Ethan...."

"Yeah, I am listening."

"You might want to choose another print for the front of your book."

"Thanks, Jason."

"I'll see you later," he says and hangs up the phone.

A commotion in the back of the salon captures my attention. The rain has stopped, and everyone is focused on an unfamiliar woman. Scattered bits of high-pitched laughter come from the shampoo area, but my view is blocked by a crowd of customers.

The woman's blonde hair is pulled back and held by a pencil, which seems a little odd considering she is wearing Chanel. Her manicured hands wave around as she talks, as if she is directing a symphony and pausing to accentuate the laughter from her audience. Tired, I sink into my chair in no mood for frivolity. The brouhaha softens as I peer over my shoulder.

I see the salon owner point the woman over to my station. Gliding toward me, the female stranger takes off her fur-lined raincoat and adjusts her black cashmere sweater over her black slacks. I notice the other women staring at this duplicate image of Grace Kelly, hypnotized with admiration for her classic beauty. Her piercing green eyes lock onto mine as I leap out of my chair to meet her. A large diamond wedding ring sparkles on her French manicured fingers as she reaches for a Moore cigarette.

"What is your name, doll face?"

"I'm, Ethan Michaels."

"Well, my name is Nora. Damon says you are a wonderful makeup artist. You know, I am in the mood to spend some money. I don't know if it will be today, but perhaps next Thursday I should come in for an appointment. How does your schedule look for next week?"

"I'm happy to help you. Check with Mary at the front when you leave today, and she'll pencil you in for Thursday."

"So what can I buy today? Are these lip colors good? My face is shiny. Do you like Dior?"

Nora's words race together. I wonder if she will stop to take a breath.

"Maybe I need some hand lotion?"

I show her some powders and display them on the counter. Maybe she'll change her mind and stay for a makeup application?

"Oh, I don't know how to put these on correctly," she says, shyly.

"Why don't you sit down in my chair and I'll show you."

Nora puts out her cigarette and sits down, crossing her legs. She is gorgeous and has a powerful presence, yet I sense sadness. Perhaps it's just me projecting my horrible day onto the world.

"What can you do for an old lady like me?"

"Dear heavens," I respond smiling. "You are not old at all."

All the women in the salon are transfixed on Nora. Her every move is being studied and memorized for later. A small girl, no doubt a client's child, approaches us and tugs at Nora's cashmere pullover sweater. Her big brown eyes stare innocently at Nora.

"Lady, you are so beautiful," she says with a squeak.

Nora throws her head back and laughs while embracing the child, kissing her on the cheek.

"Oh, you are so sweet," says Nora, as she gently touches the girl's cheek. "Run along, Honey. Go find your mother."

Without hesitation the child disappears into the huddle of women. Nora turns back to me and grabs a loose powder.

"Do you like loose powder? How many powders do you think I should buy?"

"I think you only need one," I answer.

"I need one for my car, one for my purse, and one for my bathroom and…oh I'll need one for the summer."

"It's October the 15 nth. You don't need to be thinking about summer right now."

Nora pauses for a moment as I carry the translucent powders to the front register.

"Oh, why not buy them all," she exclaims, and gestures her hand to the side, knocking over the translucent powder and sending a golden cloud into the air. The powder explodes like fireworks on my shirt, my face, and my hair as the sound of laughter breaks my embarrassment. A captive audience of salon women breaks into a train of collective hilarity. Nora suddenly cries out in a burst of laughter, joining the roar of the other women in the salon. She twirls the remaining golden powder onto my face, and I begin to laugh helplessly. I grab the other loose powders and hurl them at Nora, showering her Chanel outfit in a golden rain. The two of us tag each other, and at that moment our connection begins.

I hear heavy breathing and look up to see my boss with his hands on his hips. He stares at the two of us.

"Damon, I am so sorry!" she says with a smirk. "I'll take care of everything."

"Ethan, clean this up now!"

His steely gaze locks onto my powdery face.

"Damon, please be a gentleman and show me to the powder room," Nora giggles. She locks arms with him and guides him toward the back of a salon.

Turning around, Nora blows me a wink and a farewell kiss.

"We'll catch up soon? Perhaps we can meet next Thursday, Ethan?"

An overwhelming feeling comes over me. I feel a connection, one that I have felt only one other time. Is this the woman Brussels spoke about?

Stalker

Chapter 5

The storm's serenade has concluded its final movement of the day. Only puddles remain. I drive home and pull into my parking space behind my decaying wood apartment building. As I close my car door and run for the rotting steps, a man wearing a gray, hooded sweat jacket races past me, striking my left shoulder. He looks like trouble. I ignore his disrespect and make my way up the broken concrete steps.

Douglas Place sits gloomily on a grassy knoll. The hallway is poorly lit, and every step noisily announces the presence of each tenant. The landlord is a grumpy, old Middle Eastern woman who passes her days watching television and screaming at tenants about missed rent. Most of us are surprised the city hasn't condemned this property. We don't complain because the rent is so cheap.

My two cats greet me at the door after a busy day of tangling with cockroaches, which scatter behind the walls in the kitchen when I turn on the light. Unreliable contractor's hands have duct-taped the wiring of this old scrap I call home. My pipes moan and groan every time I shower, sending a notice to all the tenants that my daily cleansing ritual has begun. My mattress sits on the bedroom floor with a small black-and-white television cradled in front of it on a sturdy plastic crate. Aluminum foil crowns the antennae, which channel nighttime soap operas into my dark room.

As I change clothes, I stop and gaze into my newly organized closet. I don't miss the cocaine, or the marijuana stash or my fancy roach clips. Vitamins and rigorous workouts have become my new addictions. Tennis shoes near my workout bag filled with sweats remind me to head for the gym. I scurry to my car and crank up the radio. Madonna sings of lucky stars as I watch out for stray cats that might be hiding in the alley. My rearview mirror catches a glimpse of the man in the gray, hooded sweat jacket as he fades into the onset of early evening. Perhaps a good workout will help me lose the feelings of stress and paranoia that dog me. The very thought of the social gathering awaiting me at the open house makes me nervous.

Later that evening, I find myself searching for parking on the street since the lot at the meet-and-greet is full. A parade of trendy eighties ensembles winds its way between the cars to a long line in front of the building. Men sporting perfect hair and polyester shirts, and women in asymmetric tops with matching haircuts all huddle in little groups waiting to get in. I glance down at my neatly pressed khakis, swallowing whatever pride I have left, and march through the sliding-glass doors. My insecurities fill my body all the way down to my argyle socks. You can do this, this is your night, I tell myself silently, over and over. Clutching my portfolio with sweaty fingers, I make my way through the entrance and follow the herd into a large studio filled with photographers, art directors, models, and makeup artists. An uninteresting assortment of houseplants is arranged carelessly in the windowsills. Long fold-out tables are labeled with sign-in sheets for photographers, casting directors and modeling agencies. I inconspicuously make my way to the bar, avoiding the center of the room. A waiter hands me a glass of white wine and disappears into the forest of egos. Dear God, make this feeling go away, I mutter.

"Excuse me, why are all those people standing in line?" I ask one of the female models.

"Oh, that's Jeff Monroe's line. He has to leave early, so we're all trying to show our books before he goes."

She stares me up and down with condescending eyes and stops on my khakis. I eventually shuffle to the front of the line, riddled with fear. Tear sheets from *Elle, Town and Country, Glamour,* and foreign magazines whose names I can't pronounce adorn Monroe's portfolio, whose pages he shuffles as he talks to people. Maybe he'll take pity on me and see my potential.

Jeff Monroe rushes through my book and quickly hands it back to me.

"Thank you. Who's next?"

"Excuse me, Mr. Monroe. I'm new to the industry."

He yawns and looks elsewhere.

"Well, I was wondering what I can do…and maybe—"

"You need to test," he says, interrupting me. "You have a really bad book."

He breaks his concentration and peers around me to find the smile of a gorgeous female model that is waiting in line behind me.

"Thank you for your time, Mr. Monroe."

I pick up my portfolio and nervously walk away. Where are the drinks? Should I leave? Are they talking about me? My inner conversations plague me helpless.

I find a chair in the corner of this unsympathetic room and watch everyone laughing and air kissing each other. After thirty minutes of this torture I leave. As I pass the new arrivals, I notice that no one is wearing khakis. If I ever come back to this hellish event, I'll have to leave the preppy look at the door. Maybe I should save for a trendy outfit?

I reach my car feeling nauseous and mad. According to Brussels, I'm supposed to find my purpose. This meet-and-greet certainly wasn't that. What does he know!

As I open the car door I notice a lit cigarette lodged against the driver's window. Who would do that? I drive back to my hellish tomb of an apartment with my leaky faucet, broken down television, creaky wooden floors, annoying landlady, and roach population. Home never sounded sweeter.

Thursday morning arrives like a lion in winter. The buzz of the day greets me as I walk through the salon's doors. Mary's snappy tone tells me it is going to be a busy day. I decide to quickly pass the reception desk in case she decides to turn her legendary temper on me.

"Good morning. Salon, please hold. Good morning. Salon, please hold. Good morning, hold please!"

Mary hands me three pink slips, covers the receiver end of the phone, and whispers to me.

"Some lady from CBS called. She said she'll call later to set up an interview."

"Did you say interview?" I ask, confused.

Mary never looks up and continues her repetitive game. A beautiful red-haired lady finds her way to my makeup chair and begins to finger the tools on my counter. She seems oblivious to my watching her, which annoys me even more. Plopping down into my chair with a heavy sigh, she sips the cup of black coffee that sits in front of her and immediately begins to apply her own makeup.

Mario, the plant man, sits patiently and waits for the woman to finish her private time so he can water the fichus tree that stands next to my station. Mario's politeness is beyond the call of duty as she fumbles around, ignoring him as if he exists to serve her. I make my way to the counter to stop this nonsense just as a hairdresser's assistant calls the woman to the dryer.

"Mario, next time anyone is rude to you, call me over."

My support is wasted on ears that barely understand English.

"Gracias, Mr. Ethan."

"I can help you move the fichus tree later this afternoon? Okay?"

"Gracias, Mr. Ethan."

"Call me, Ethan." I smile and give Mario a thumbs up gesture.

Glancing down at my messages, I notice that Nora called about making dinner plans for this evening. In Mary's cryptic handwriting, Nora's message says: "Can't come in today. Meet me at Café Noire at 6:30p.m. Dress nice, casual." My watch says 10:30, and by the look of my schedule I better stay on track. Clients bustle in, and the morning hours turn into the afternoon while a hectic atmosphere fills the salon. The rush of the day sings its finishing note as my most recent appointment bids farewell. My feet are numb, my back hurts, but I have to get my second wind. Dinner with Nora seems like the only bright spot in this pathetic week.

"Thank you, Ethan. I love my face," says my final client.

"You're welcome," I tell her, and then I dash to my car, aware that I have less than thirty minutes to go home, change my clothes, and get to the restaurant.

Approaching Café Noire's front door, I take note of the elegantly carved inlays dotted with blinko glass. The maître d' leads me to a table in the center of the room. White tablecloths are covered with enormous white-flower centerpieces in oversized vases. Crystal chandeliers hang throughout the room, illuminating the well-dressed men and women who huddle in conversation. I imagine they're speaking of golf games, vacations in Europe, business deals both dirty and clean. Lost in this reverie, I come to as the maître d' approaches, escorting Nora through the busy room to our table. Her muted-blue silk dress flows along the contours of her slim figure. Her jewelry is understated and highlights her green eyes, which seem to hypnotize every man in the room. Conversations come to a stop as she glides through the dining area.

"Hello, Darling. Have you been waiting long?" she says, as she extends her hands to meet mine. She smiles gently at the maître d'.

"No, I just got here."

"Thank you, young man," she says, bidding the hovering host good-bye. "How wonderful it is to see you, Ethan. Have you ordered drinks?"

"No, I thought I'd wait for you."

A waiter magically appears, as if he had been anticipating Nora's desires.

"Oh my," she exclaims, clasping his hand between hers. "What beautiful hands you have. You must be an artist."

"How did you know?" asks the waiter, with a shy smile on his face.

"What else could you be?" she says, releasing the waiter's hand. "We will have your best Australian merlot."

Nora winks and gestures for the waiter to hurry.

"Ethan, do you have a pen and pad?" she says, searching deep into her purse. "Oh, never mind, I found a pencil. Do me a favor and write your name and birthday on this paper. Don't forget the year you were born."

She instinctively turns her head just as our waiter is approaching us. He is carrying a tray with two large glasses of wine.

"What?" I say, baffled. "You want me to write my birthday…"

"The gentlemen at the bar have paid for your drinks."

The waiter's hand points to a large bar where an even larger mirror is hanging at an angle, ensuring ultimate people-watching for those who prefer to drink standing up.

I explore the crowded room and see two anxious-looking men with eager smiles.

How can this be? I think to myself. She just got here. Is she a regular?

Nora turns around to investigate the dining room and spots the men standing in the back.

"You both are absolute dolls," she whispers loudly across the room. "Thank you," she says, as she blows a kiss into the air.

I stare at Nora, wrinkling my brow and wondering if she knows I have no idea what is going on.

"Ethan, I am a Numerologist," says Nora.

She gazes past me, as if she sees something in the large window behind me. Confused, I turn around and follow her gaze. There's nothing there.

"I didn't know you were a doctor."

A bellow of laughter vibrates through Nora's body. Smiling, she reaches into her purse and places a small gold cigarette case box on the table.

"Numerology, think Astrology, but with numbers."

As she searches for her lighter, she lays out the contents of her purse: Tissues, gum, wallet, and notepads all decorate the tabletop. Seconds later, two masculine hands appear from nowhere, both with lighters. Nora turns to a gray-haired gentleman whose beaming youngish face fills with pride as she turns to him.

"The thoughtfulness of a gentleman is always appreciated, but I'm afraid the man on my left arrived sooner."

Nora turns to the man on her left, but the handsome gray-haired man on her right quickly ignites his lighter.

"Both of you are absolute dolls, however—" and before Nora can finish her sentence, each man jostles a lighter, simultaneously sending small flames onto her cigarette. Everyone in the room is in a trance, including me.

"Thank you," she politely tells them both. "I suspect your friends at the bar are anxious for your return?"

Nora bids both men good-bye with a single wink. She takes a drag on her cigarette and places her elbow on the table, extending her smoking hand away from me. She reaches for the pad and writes down my birthday, month, and year. A long silence descends on our table. Seconds turn to minutes as Nora determinedly calculates the numbers on the pad.

"I find this absolutely fascinating. Don't you, Ethan?"

"I'm not sure," I say, awkwardly. "I don't know what you're doing."

Another silence fills our table while Nora scratches figures with her pencil. A lock of her blonde hair falls and frames her cheekbone. Slowly she looks up and, sitting back in her chair, seems to be sizing me up.

"I see…" she says, and then stops to look at me again as if she is seeing me in a new light. "I see a shadowy figure with malice in his heart. Ethan, there could be danger around you. Perhaps you have a secret enemy?"

I roll my eyes, uncertain how to stop Nora from continuing.

"I've encountered a lot of mean spirited jerks at castings lately," I ruefully chuckle, thinking of the past week's various humiliations.

"I see?! This doesn't make sense. Someone's negative energy is all around you?"

She looks around the room as if she can find the source of her analysis.

"So, are you interested in anything outside of work?" she asks.

Why is she asking me these questions?

"I work out every night; run a couple of miles, but other than that—"

"I am sure you have other aspirations, Ethan? Working out and jogging is fine, but surely there is something that intrigues you?"

She leans forward as if I am about to say something very important. As I struggle to think of something interesting about myself, she interrupts my thoughts.

"My numerology findings tell me you should become a writer?"

"That's weird? Um, I, met, never mind. I'd like to become a special effects make up artist."

Nora's eyes gleam with curiosity.

"How wonderful, Ethan. Have you taken steps to make that happen?"

My head sinks. I was hoping my meeting with her would take me out of the funk I'm in. Nora takes note of my reaction and giggles. She turns her attention to the waiter, who has just come up behind her.

"Can we have two more glasses of this wonderful merlot, please?"

"Yes, of course, Madam."

The waiter has a puzzled expression on his face. He looks at me, but I just shrug. We're both wondering the same thing: How does she know when he is behind her? The waiter asks if we're ready to order, and Nora tells him to bring us something special, that she trusts his good taste.

"How do you do it, Nora?" I ask. "People are fascinated by you."

"Ethan, I am truly happy. People sense when we are in a great place. I believe my inner happiness helps me to attract good things into my life. It is the gift of manifestation," she says, and taps her pencil on the note pads with my birthday details. "Do you have the patience to pursue the film industry?" Nora asks, kindly.

"I haven't been given much of a chance. I keep doing the rounds but—"

"Ethan, all dreams are tough to achieve in the beginning. And they get even tougher as you become successful. A little luck and knowing the right people take precedence. Talent is just as important. But believing in you is the key."

"Knowing the right people is not my strong suit."

If only Nora knew the right people, I think for a moment, and then realize the egotism of my thought.

"Perhaps you are going through the wrong door, Ethan? Maybe you will have to enter through the back door rather than the front door. Both doors lead to success."

She laughs and reaches out for my hand. I slowly hand it to her. Her hand is warm, and as she squeezes mine.

"Ethan, learn to look at your life as a road map. Every morning, when you start your day, make sure that the road is going to take you somewhere. And rather than focusing on how long it's going to take, why not just enjoy the ride."

Nora's eyes fill with compassion as though her own journey was laid with many roadblocks.

"Ethan, once you learn to look at your journey as continuous stepping stones, then every day becomes a road of possibilities. Your life becomes a joyous ride."

Suddenly, I understand what Brussels meant. "Nora, you're the Pied Piper?"

"What did you say, Ethan?"

She nudges the cigarette to see if it's still burning. Sipping her wine, she seems to be enjoying the moment and takes a deep drag on her brown cigarette. Smoke fills the air and dissipates into the many conversations around us. I can see Nora contemplating her next move.

"Ethan, your secret to success is simple. Discover the heart of the client, and you discover their uniqueness."

"That's your secret?" I say, surprised.

I look around the noisy room, wondering if everyone else in this restaurant shares my sense that something important is about to happen. I dare not speak, and instead down my wine, anticipating our meal. The waiter places our food on the table ands silently retreats. Nora tastes her wine and pats her mouth.

"Ethan, treat every client like a celebrity. Treat each person with awe, respect, and learn to ask questions that relate to their lifestyle. How long have they been married? How many children do they have? When is their birthday? Let your heart lead the way when you ask questions. And always come from a place of authenticity. The doors will open at the right time, my friend. Am I making sense?"

"Yes," I say, struggling to keep up with her. Her advice seems so simple, yet there is something to this. I can't forget my conversations with Brussels.

"Nora, what you say makes sense."

I feel flattered that Nora has shared her opinion with me. We turn our attention to our food and eat in comfortable silence, each of us alone with our thoughts. When we finish, Nora turns yet again to our approaching waiter.

"If I did not know any better, I would think you called my best friend to ask about my favorite dish. Or maybe it's just that you have excellent taste."

The proud waiter smiles from ear to ear.

"Thank you Mrs. Berry."

Stacking the dishes in his right arm, he expertly sweeps the crumbs of the table with his left hand.

"Ethan, is there anything you need before this young man leaves?"

"I'm fine. My meal was delicious. Thank you, sir."

"Please enjoy your dinner and if you need me, I'll be over here."

The waiter points to the wait station. Nora motions for the young man to lean down. As he puts his head next to hers, she whispers, "Is a phone nearby?"

"Yes," he says, "over by the bar."

I notice Nora's face seems pale. She squints, as if she's having trouble focusing.

"Are you okay?" I ask.

"I feel very dizzy," she says, and slowly lays her head on the table.

"Are you okay? Are you okay? Nora, what's wrong?"

"Ethan," she whispers, "Call my husband now!"

I motion the waiter for cold water. The two men that had lit Nora's cigarette have come to the rescue. A small gathering forms around our table.

"Is she okay," I hear a stranger ask.

Nora whispers a telephone number, and I run to where the waiter directs me. When I return, she is sitting up, but her head hangs forward slightly. A sympathetic woman holds her hand as the two men try to comfort her.

"Nora, I spoke to your husband, Richard. He's on the way."

"Don't worry, honey. Your husband is coming," says the woman.

Within fifteen minutes, a large hand touches my shoulder.

"I'm Richard, Nora's husband," he looks at her.

He helps her stand up and puts his big arms around her. "Nora keeps having these dizzy spells? We need to go. Thank you." Richard looks at me with uncertainty.

The tone in his voice is enough to move you to tears. Nora slowly turns to me.

"Ethan, I am so embarrassed. Please excuse me. We will talk...."

Richard pats me on the back and assures me that all will be fine as soon as they get Nora home and that he will take her to see her doctor in the morning.

"I will call you tomorrow, Ethan," she says. "I promise."

Nora slips out the glass doors. The restaurant is silent as all eyes watch her leave the restaurant, then everyone returns to their private conversations.

"Excuse me, Sir, but she left this at the table."

Our waiter hands me Nora's note pad. I look at her doodling and become sick to my stomach.

Next to my birth date are these words: "*Fire and Ice / Stalker.*"

Fire and Ice

Chapter 6

Running out to my car with keys in hand, I feel the cold wind sending a dreaded message that winter, the poor man's least favorite season, is on its way. The Toyota's windows are clouded with a thin frosty film, obscuring my view of the car's dingy and cracked interior. I scan the semiprivate empty parking lot, looking for those who seem suspect. A thought of my interrupted dinner rendezvous with Nora finds me worrying about our future friendship. Café Noire will have to welcome Nora and I back for dinner another evening. The car starts without any hiccups, and I make my way back to Douglas Place. Seeing the old building fills me with relief. No shady people waiting to scream boo.

I bounce out of my car and race through the hall to get to my front door. The little one-room apartment feels cold, and the cats huddle on the bed. I eventually settle down for the evening and get lost in a travel magazine, savoring the idea of sun on my face, blue water in front of me, and warm sand under my feet. Then the phone rings. I ignore it. Only a wrong number would call this late. It rings again and again.

"Hello?"

"I am watching you," a muffled, deep voice says on the other end of the phone. This must be a joke. I quickly inventory my male friends who might think this was funny. But none of them would pull a prank like this.

"Excuse me?"

"Ethan. Ethan Michaels?"

"Who is this?"

The phone clicks, and I quickly hang up. My blood rushes from deep inside my body to my tingling fingers and scalp. Thoughts race inside my head and my heart begins to pound rapidly. My pores feel like tiny spigots as sweat covers my shaking upper lip. I immediately walk to my front door, almost stepping on one of my cats who have gotten up to investigate the change of emotion in the room. I check the locks and feel a little more secure. Still a little uneasy, I look around the room and move a solid-wood cabinet under the doorknob. I walk over to the bay window and shut the curtains. Then I move a fantail palm tree in front of the window, hoping it will block any light coming through from the moon. Will this flimsy plant block a creep's view, I ask myself? In my bedroom, I wrap the blankets around my nervous cold body and watch the heavy cabinet under the doorknob. My eyes feel heavy, and I struggle to keep my focus on the door. Eventually the warmth from my sleeping cats' bodies lulls me into sleep.

In the morning the apartment feels chilly. I glance at the front door and the plant in front of the window, and feel a little ridiculous.

Wrapping the blankets around me, much to the cats' displeasure, I phone Nora's house, but there's no answer. I replay her numerology notes over and over in my head, trying to erase the crash of riotous insecurities that greets me almost every morning. Jump-starting the workday will keep me focused and help to chase away my reservations. And today I'm faced with clients whose only concerns are looking good for the weekend's activities. Even superficiality has its place.

***

The day goes by in a whirl, faces and hair all blending together. I clean my station after my last client bids me a glossy, lacquered good-bye. Mary wishes me a good weekend, and I bid farewell to a work week that was less than stellar. She hands me my last phone message before closing out the register. "Julie Gautier called from CBS again. She wants to interview you. She will call back in two weeks from New York City." Sparkling thoughts play like Alka-Seltzer in a murky glass of water as my head dissolves with the finish of the day. Too drained to be excited about the bewildering message from CBS, I turn my attention to my throbbing feet and welcome the worn-out seats of my car. Frosty air splashes my face from a broken defrost fan, reminding me that winter clothes must be sorted and placed in the closet. Gray clouds dot the sky, matching the moodiness I feel. Even the smell of pinion seeping from someone's fireplace into my vent, fails to fill me with anticipation. I glare as I turn into the driveway and feel like a stranger entering the building. No sooner have I walked into the hallway than the landlady darts up to me.

"Mr. Michaels. Mr. Michaels. A man comes by your apartment today but I tell him you no here."

"What?"

"He said he had appointment with you."

"No, I don't have an appointment with anyone, Mrs. Habib. What did he look like?"

"He mean-looking man! He wears a dirty gray hooded jacket. He wants to know where you are, but I no tell him. I not trust him. I tell him leave his name and number and I give to you, but he no give me nothing."

A sick feeling trickles through my body, accompanied by a very hard pounding in my chest. My palms begin to sweat as I walk toward my door.

"Thank you. I'll take care of this. Please let me know if you see him again."

"Yeah, okay. No want weirdo's 'round my building," she grunts.

A game show blares through her front door as she waddles into her place. I don't bother greeting my cats and instead go straight for the drawer that holds batteries, coupons, to-go menus, and other odds and ends. Finding a hammer and a plastic baggie of nails, I head for the kitchen window and nail the window shut. In the bathroom I do the same. As I finish the last nail, the phone roars from across the apartment. I freeze. The ringing sends coldness down my spine, and I feel my heart rise in my throat.

"Hello?"

A dead silence. No voice, but I can hear nasal breathing.

"Hello? Hello?" I shout.

Stillness continues.

I hang up the phone and begin to pace. My stomach clenches. The phone rings again. Do I answer? Do I let it ring?

"Hello!"

"Hi, Ethan, it's Nora. Are you okay? You sound upset?"

"Nora, thank god it's you. Are you okay?" I ask, dismissing her question and feeling concern for my friend.

"Ethan...."

She hesitates for a moment.

"What is it, Nora? Is there something you want to tell me?"

Someone pounding on the front door interrupts our call. Outside there is a shuffling of feet.

"Nora, stay on the phone please," I plead.

"Ethan, there is something wrong!"

"Hold on and let me see who is at my door, Nora."

The pounding intensifies. Footsteps pace outside my door like sandpaper to a freshly textured wall. I hold the phone up so Nora can hear the commotion.

"Ethan, its Mrs. Habib. You come to door now."

"Nora, it's my landlady. There's no telling what—"

"Ethan, you come now," Mrs. Habib screams at my door.

"I'm so sorry, Nora. I can't talk this moment. Can I call you right back?"

Nora urges me to call her back, but Mrs. Habib's pounding makes it difficult to her.

"I'm coming. Hold on, Mrs. Habib," I shout. "Nora, I promise I will call you back as soon as I can. Is everything all right?"

She pauses again.

"Ethan, Richard and I are leaving town tonight. I'll call you when we return. Is everything all right?"

"Nora, the other night when you—"

My sentence is interrupted by loud conversations in the hallway.

"Never mind, please promise me you'll call when you get back?"

"I promise. Good-bye, Ethan."

"We'll speak soon, Nora. I promise."

When I hear her hang up, I rush to the front door. Shouting voices ricochet down the musky hallway as I jog to the back of the building. I'm struck with the thought of the dire circumstances that must have brought each tenant into finding such a place to live. Screaming TVs do battle with raised voices from each apartment. Mrs. Habib waits for me in the back parking lot wearing an expression of disgust.

"I told you no more," she demands. "That man! That man was here again. I told you no more."

"What? What are you talking about?"

"That man who was here the other day. I said no more and he was here again. I call police. I will raise your rent if he comes back."

"Wait a minute—I can't afford for you to raise my rent. I don't even know who this man is."

"I no care, Mr. Michaels. I raise your rent."

She mutters as she walks to some tenants near the back garage. A young married couple packs their van, ignoring the drama that's being played out. Clothes fill their Volkswagen while Tony, another tenant, and another man move boxes out the back door and stack them outside.

"Excuse me," I ask the wife. "Are you really leaving?"

"Yes we are. That damn Mrs. Habib raised our rent by a hundred dollars. This place isn't worth it. We couldn't get her to repair the plumbing in our bathroom. My husband has had his share with that crazy woman."

I look toward the back hallway and walk toward the broken cement steps as Tony and his friend maneuver a dresser through the doorway. I look back at Mrs. Habib, trying to second-guess her next move.

"What about Tony and his roommate?" I mumble.

"She raised their rent too," says the woman. "Everyone's moving out. What about you? Are you going to stay?"

I stammer for an answer, unsure of what to say. Shrugging my shoulders, I break eye contact with the woman, ashamed that my finances can't protect me from being screwed by the unstable Mrs. Habib.

"Excuse me, I'll be right back."

The back entrance is surrounded by cardboard boxes.

"Hey, Tony, can I speak with you for a second?"

Loading the last of their belongings into the trunk of the car, Tony acknowledges my waving hand gestures. His eyes dart away from me and land on the heated conversation that has just begun between the married couple and the landlady. The husband shakes his head emphatically and steps close to Mrs. Habib, who begins to shriek in Lebanese.

"You are insane if you think I am paying you any more money," the husband yells.

Mrs. Habib steps away from the couple and looks in our direction. When she spots me, she walks toward us.

"I suppose you going to move out too?"

"Well…I don't—"

"I raise your rent like everyone else. You don't like it, leave."

Ignoring Mrs. Habib, the two men place the last of their belongings into the truck.

"Leave now if you want. We'll help you move out of this shit hole today."

"I'm broke!" I shout, as one of them starts the engine of their truck.

Guess I'm stuck, I mumble under my breath. I watch Tony and his roommate race away into the coming winter night. The married couple quickly follows, and I shuffle back to my den of an apartment, find my car keys, and head to the gym. I'll work out the bits and pieces of my distress on the treadmill.

***

I drive into the back of the apartment complex, slurping on a protein drink and feeling slightly less tense. The parking lot is empty, and the building has no lights on. All my neighbors are gone? Walking up the back steps, into the entrance, forces me to come to a stand still. A light rain has just begun to dampen the cracked steps. Silence permeates the dark hallway. Reluctantly, I make my way toward my apartment, my feet heavy on the creaking wood floors. A crunching noise under my feet catches my interest. Squatting down, I reach for what I can't see. Why does this sound alarm me? I pull my hand back after touching something sharp. Could it be? Something is wrong. Leaping up, I race to my apartment, seeing darkness through my slightly open front door. My hand slides around the doorframe searching for the light switch. Flip. Nothing!? Flip. Flip. Flip. Nothing! My Siamese cat meows in the darkness.

"Baxter," I yell. I hear his cries near the closet. Slowly I creep into the blackness, listening to every deafening sound. I must remain calm. I must not panic. I must not let anxiety swell inside me. Remain call, Ethan. I repeat this over and over in my head.

I find my way to the nightstand hoping the lamp near the bed will destroy the shadows. My hands fumble to the top of the bedside light when I realize that the bulb is gone. A wave of nausea overtakes me. The crunching sounds beneath my feet continue. Instantly I realize that I am walking on broken glass. The missing light bulbs in the hallway, in my house…

Walking blindly through the darkness, I stumble into the kitchen. Searching frantically, I find the candles in the top drawer. Where the hell did I put those matches? Here they are. Shivering, I light the first match.

There's a pile of fragmented glass. A cold breeze hits my face, and I follow it to the kitchen window. Dear god. The window has been pried open.

My head rushes back to where I am. I tiptoe through the apartment, checking all the places where someone could hide. The faint sound of my cat moaning in the closet reminds me that I'm not alone.

The silence is suddenly disturbed by the sound of footsteps in the hallway. Broken glass gives the intruder away. I rush to the closet where Baxter is hiding. Where is my other cat, Honey?

"Hush, Baxter, I'm right here. Be quiet."

The footsteps get closer.

"Shhhh," I whisper to Baxter.

Crunch? Crunch! Crunch!! Honey suddenly races past the closet in the direction of the bed. Silence! My breathing stops. A long pause fills the air. My eyes begin to adjust to the dim light, catching a view of a man standing at the opening of my front door. Staring into darkness, the figure moves across the living room floor. Baxter meows. I draw a shallow breath. The lone figure moves toward the closet. I leap out and lunge at the invader.

"Get the fuck out of my apartment!"

"Ethan! Jesus Christ! It's Tony, your neighbor," he yells, confusion layering in his voice. "What the hell are you doing? Why are the lights off in the building? Why is your door open? Are you okay?"

"I think so," I say, my body flooding with relief that I am not alone.

"I came back to get the last couple of boxes and noticed the building's lights were out. I heard noises from your apartment and thought…well, never mind what I thought. Are you okay?"

Tony's eyes dart all over the room as he tries to calm me down. He wipes his brow and looks at the vacant expression on my face.

"Ethan, what is going on? Do you want to tell me? Hold on, you can tell me in a minute. I'll get a flash light and call the police."

"All right, Tony. Please hurry."

It sounds as if he's racing on gravel. His footsteps vibrate up the side stairwell onto the second floor. Vociferous drawer slamming above reassures me that he is close by. I squeak quietly to the nightstand and hear Baxter's screeching meow. Ignoring his plea, I reach for the phone and catch a glimpse through the bay window of a man standing outside. My thumping heart feels like it's beating through my T-shirt, and my mouth goes dry. My heart stops. The moonlit body turns toward my window. The man stops, lights a cigarette, tosses the smoky match to the icy ground, and moves toward the window. He inhales a long drag from his cigarette, as I fight to stay standing.

"Tony! Tony!"

My voice echoes through the empty building, bouncing off naked walls that were filled with life earlier today. Tony runs to the window and aims the flashlight at the shadowy figure. Both of us stand still as the mysterious man runs away.

"Did you call the police?"

"They're on the way."

Nervous anticipation keeps us frozen while both cats find refuge around my ankles. What lays ahead plays like a skipping record over and over in my head.

***

Morning light filters through the barren room, which has cardboard boxes lined up against the walls. I can hear Tony and John chatting about the best places to showcase their houseplants. The normalcy of their conversation is in stark contrast with the events of last night. I tiptoe to the bathroom, not ready to break this feeling of everyday life with discussions of what I should do. I relieve myself and splash my face with water. How nice that their water runs clear and strong, not like the mysterious tan trickle that comes out of my tap. A conversation in the living room catches my immediate attention.

"I'll be sure and tell Ethan, Mrs. Habib. Good-bye."

Tony speaks quietly through the bathroom door.

"Ethan, they arrested some creepy man last night across the street from our complex. I mean your complex," he says, chuckling at his little mistake.

"What? Are you kidding?"

"No. Apparently some lady called the police after she saw a man masturbating in her flower bed. She saw him in the parking lot looking in your bedroom window. I found out when I called Mrs. Habib and told her that you were staying with us."

"Great."

Mrs. Habib will have a fit when I get back home.

"Thanks, Tony."

I splash my face one more time and get ready to face the day. Dreading the return to my apartment, I brace myself for the brisk walk ahead of me. Tony throws an old sweatshirt my way to cut the vigorous wind that has transformed our neighborhood. I thank him and John for helping me and start the long walk home.

Approaching Douglas Place, I notice Mrs. Habib sweeping the remains of trash.

"They got that weirdo man."

Her words of anger don't penetrate me. My cats' cries coming from the hallway remind me that breakfast is past due. Baxter and Honey devour the Kitty Mix, easing the troubling thoughts from last night's drama. A red flashing light on my answer machine nudges me to my nightstand.

"Hey, Ethan, it's JB. I'm in town. Let's get together. Call me at the Garden Hotel and ask for room 111."

A spark in this depressing room, JB's message fills me with anticipation. I could stand to see a good friend right now. My mind flashes on Nora. What did she want to tell me? Where has she gone?

I carefully step around the glass on the floor, looking for the broom so that I can clean up the ruins of last night's episode. After the room looks somewhat normal, I sort my winter clothes and place them in the front of my closet, put my portfolio on the upper shelf, and remove the nails from the bathroom window. Then I call JB.

His tires squeal as we turn into the parking lot of the theater. Only true fans would stand in the freezing rain for the midnight showing of *The Rocky Horror Picture Show*. Well-versed fans decked out in black fishnets, wigs, and leather hint at the upcoming evening. The packed house makes my trouble disappear with each well-timed delivery to the screen. A standing ovation for the fans who rushed the stage to perform and the show is over. Everyone laughs and smiles as they leave the theater. JB and I walk to the car as it starts to snow. The ground is slippery and we hold on to each other's arms to keep from falling.

"That was great," says JB, laughing heartily.

"I know. Didn't you love it when the audience followed along with the movie?"

The car doors slam, and we both exhale. Little clouds appear before our faces.

"Oh my god, it's freezing!" JB reaches for his car keys.

"Hurry up, JB. Start the car."

"I am. I am, Ethan."

Laughing in unison, fingers frozen, and feet trying to beat numbness, we feel exhilarated by the cold.

"I need to piss," says JB.

"You can use my bathroom when you drop me off."

Covered with snow and ice, the Douglas Place parking lot is empty of cars except for my old Toyota. Pulling into the back of the compound, JB suddenly goes quiet.

"Boy this building is freaky looking, Ethan."

He looks at the dark building. Douglas Place is dressed in shades of gray and covered with snow. I spot a large box filled with old paint cans and paint remover sitting at the base of the trash dumpster. The residential trash bin is also full, of what looks like newspapers and old magazines. Instantly I start to feel the panic from last night filling my mind and body again. JB, not missing a beat, notices me staring at the overstuffed dumpster.

"Are you all right, Ethan?" JB wrestles in his cold seat.

"Yeah, I'm ok," I say unconvincingly.

"No need to worry. It's just a dumpster filled with trash. Deal with it tomorrow. I really need to piss."

We leave the car and walk to my apartment.

"That's weird."

"What is it?"

"All the lights are off in my building again."

"Again," asks JB. "What do you mean again?"

"Forget it. It's a long story."

"Well, maybe your landlady needs to be told a thing or two."

JB has no idea how right he is. We dash into my apartment, and he finds his way to the bathroom. While he is there, I quickly walk around the apartment and make sure that no bogeyman is hiding in a dark place. Reassured, I then check the safety latches on the windows. All is secure. Snow begins to fall heavily and with it comes the sound of heavily laden tree branches sweeping against each other. The windowpanes start to fog in front of my warm breath. JB enters the living room and notes my mood, which hangs heavy in the air.

"Ethan, are you okay?" He glances around the room before his eyes land on me.

"I'm okay."

My stomach is upside-down. I want so much to share the events of last night. Instead, I revert back to old behavior and keep my mouth closed.

"Don't worry, Ethan. Everything's going to be fine. Call me at the hotel if you need me, okay? I leave early tomorrow morning, but I'll see you next time I am in town. Okay?"

***

Flannel sheets and a thick bedspread comfort my doubting spirit. I descend into a state of exhaustion, worn out by the ups and downs of this emotional day. The space heater next to my bed chases away the harsh cold and comforts my cats. I place my bathrobe on the corner of the bed so they can enjoy a fuzzy warm robe if they decide that the floor is too cold. From the bed, I can see the glimmer of white snow in my Art Deco beveled mirror. I take one last look around the room and nuzzle deeper into my warm sheets. The sharp pain of anxiety lies heavy in my thoughts, yet somehow I manage to nod off into a bottomless sleep.

I dream of screams. A woman's crying can be heard. Lying still, half-asleep, half-awake, I slowly open my eyes. Her cries are still there. I jump out of my bed. The digital clock shines 1:11 a.m. The pungent smell of smoke fills my apartment. I call out for my cats as my eyes start to sting. Where are they?

"Help me! Someone please help me!" a weak voice cries out. "Somebody help!"

I run to the bay window.

"Somebody please help me."

Wiping the frost from the window, I see a body doubled-over on the driveway. Karen, my neighbor above me, is lying in the snow, huddle in a fetal position.

I pry open the window and yell out to the frozen ground.

"Karen, what are you doing on the ground? What happened? Are you hurt?"

"Please, Ethan, help me. I think I broke both my legs," she cries.

"What? What happened? Are you sure?" I think of my cats again, struggling to take in what she is saying.

Karen's face fills with panic.

"The building is on fire, Ethan! Call the fire department. Call the fire department now, and get out of there!"

"Oh my god, Karen, I'll call! Oh, shit! Don't worry. I'll call the fire department right now."

I dash to the front door, open it, and stare into a sea of flames approaching the south hallway. Bellowing smoke swirls past the married couple's old apartment. I quickly close the door. My heart pounds so hard, I can't focus. I shout to the telephone operator to call the fire department. I turn every light on in my room, wrap my bathrobe around my body, and make mental notes of what I must seize first. My apartment is full of smoke as I cry for my cats.

"Baxter! Honey!?" Where are you?

Frantic thoughts race inside my head. What do I do? Seconds turn to split seconds. Grab your winter clothes. Sweaters, jackets, sweat-pants and anything that will help me survive the cold weather that lies ahead.

"Baxter! Honey! Where are you?" I scream with desperation.

I grab the pile of clothes and race down the north hallway to the door of the building. The cold air hits me in the face as sirens shriek in the background. I throw my first pile of clothes against the northwest face of the complex. It's as if someone is telling me what to do. I'm not conscious of thinking or even moving my legs. I turn toward the front entrance and run back into a cloud of smoke. Flames the color of ginger circle the back entrance, inching along the old walls. Get your wallet, important papers. Don't forget your portfolio. I hear my voice. Inhaling smoke, I can barely see. My eyes hurt, and the smell of burning curtains and charred wood singes my nose and fills my lungs.

"Baxter! Honey! Where are you?"

I frantically shove my mattress to the side and scan the bed frame looking for my cats. I run to a box, grab all the papers, find my wallet, and rush to the closet for my portfolio, repeating the hellish challenge to the front exit. I drop my second pile in the falling snow. People are gathering outside as the fire trucks race up the building's driveway. Panicked faces gaze at the madness, while firemen unload the hoses and rush inside. Mrs. Habib scrambles into the ambulance that Karen has just been placed in. Her eyes show confusion as she looks at her burning investment. Adrenaline surges through me, and I leap past the icy steps and stumble back into the smoking hallway. Immediately my lungs ache as I choke on ash. I run past empty apartments. The orange flames molest the walls and devour the crumbling remains.

It's hot, and I realize I'm barefoot. I brace myself against the wall, coughing and wiping the soot from my eyes, finding my way back to the apartment.

"Baxter. Honey, please come." I croak.

A faint mew seems to be coming from the closet.

"Come out please," I beg, frantically.

Stretching my arm to the back of the closet I reach for a fury body. Black smoke cuts into my eyes, like tiny fragments of glass, causing a flood of tears. My eyes blur, and the heat pounds against me. Claws bear down on my thin bathrobe as I hug the trembling body to mine.

"You have to leave the building now, Sir," a voice calls out. The hazy air clears for a moment just as a large gloved hand grabs my shoulder.

"I am not leaving without my cats," I say to the fireman, barely managing to get sound out of my body.

"Sir, you have to leave. I'm taking you out of the building now. Where is your other cat?"

"I have no idea. I'm sure he's in the back of the closet. Please don't let my cat die in here. Please," I plead.

Rushed outside by a nameless stranger in a yellow suit, I gather my possessions around me, as paramedics rush for me. The frigid air fills my lungs. A crowd stands across the street from the burning building. A collective gasp fills the air as the shingled roof crumbles in a monstrous ball of flames falling in on Karen's apartment. Honey jolts from my grip, running toward the front entrance, back to the fiery hallway. Witnessing my loss of power, a firefighter lunges after my frightened cat and nabs her from the inferno.

I drop what few belongings I have and race to her.

"Thank you! Thank you," I yell with relief.

Honey bears down on my shoulder, eyes darting in every direction. The fireman makes another journey into the sweltering flames, meeting other firefighters, combing the vacant hallway searching for stragglers. His yellow suit vanishes from my view. My cat trembles in my arms as I watch the monstrous flames devour each unoccupied apartment. Caught in a second of defeat, I think I can hear the screams of my Siamese cat through the noise and disorder. I feel another rush of adrenaline explode within me.

"Watch my cat and don't let go of her," I shout out to an innocent woman who stares at me blankly.

I can hear Baxter's cries as I rush back to meet the flames. I see the steps, the firemen, the blackened, peeling halls. I focus on one thing—Baxter.

I hear the roof upstairs disintegrate under the hellish roar, devouring each moment of someone's past. Swimming through a river of smoke and flames, the helpless cry of Baxter's plea gets me to my front door. Excruciating pain cripples my lungs as they tighten from the onslaught of fumes. Twisting and meowing frantically, Baxter is paralyzed in my closet. I dive in, throwing clothes about in hopes of rescuing him from an enemy that I cannot defeat. The sweat from my face runs into my eyes, bringing soot with it.

Again, a man's hand grabs me, pulling me up from my closet floor and startling me.

"Get out of the building now. I will get your cat, but you must leave now," says a voice from behind a dirty mask. "Leave now!"

He shoves me through the scorched door, past red flames as the hum of destruction builds around us. Stumbling for the front door, completely void of strength, I fall against the seared walls. Firemen race to the back entryway of my complex. I stumble through a blanket of smoke. My stomach tightens and my heart stops as the faint cry of my Siamese cat goes unanswered. Baxter's cry for help renders me. I fall onto the ground, begging God to please save Baxter.

"Baxter, don't worry. Someone is coming to get you." Tears fall down my face.

The lady who holds Honey kneels beside me.

"Please don't cry," she says, embracing me. "They'll rescue your cat."

She hands my trembling cat back into my motionless arms. I turn to her with my heart in my throat and whisper, "I can't lose Baxter…I can't!" Her eyes flood with emotion, as she fades into the cold night, cupped in her husband's arms. She speaks to her husband, hoping I won't hear her words.

"I've never seen so much *fire and ice* in my life."

***

The inferno shows no mercy as the platoon of flames engulfs what remains of Douglas Place. Windows crack and glass bursts. Blue-red flames crawl up the giant oak tree, throwing orange ambers onto the secluded parking lot. The gross stench of burned furniture and carpet dominates the white night while the remains of people's possessions disappear into nothingness. The roller coaster finishes its second loop and then descends down the tracks. Hands in the air and stomachs churning as the speed increase, the winding curves take us down a wooden plank for a final excursion. The wintry sleet grazes my cheeks. My bare feet ache with numbness. Honey shivers, finding comfort in a tattered charred bathrobe that keeps us temporarily safe.

"Baxter!" I shout. "Baxter!" I fall to the icy ground and cry helplessly. "Why?"

"It is during our darkest moments that we must focus to see the light."

Aristotle Onasis

Brussels' Return

Chapter 7

Scattered snowflakes laced with bits of frozen ice gently touch down on the knoll. Adrenaline finally fades from my wrecked disposition as I fight back the fatigue. An old man wearing flannel pajamas inside a winter coat looks at the scene with dismay. Onlookers make their way past him, back to houses and apartments that offer heat. As he slowly makes his way through the snow toward the English Tudor that must be his home, he turns to me and nods his head in disbelief, acknowledging the landscape of anxiety that rests in my eyes. I look down at my bare feet and wonder how I have been able to withstand frostbite. My mind is racing. Flurries cover the pile of my personal belongings that did not survive the collapsed roof. Portfolio, wallet, and photos taken of my family the night before their fatal crash are all gone. My sister smiling from a silver frame fades with all other memories of a family I no longer have. Tonight is a night when your mother and father would take care of you and tell you that tomorrow does bring promise. That absent hug will rest in a portico I will always call Douglas Place.

Waves of despair march through me like enemy soldiers waiting for their final command. My right hand throbs with pain. I don't know how I injured the blue-black fingernail, but the ache is tremendous. The night sky blossoms with powdery flakes while orange blazes backdrop the complex I use to call home. Honey trembles in my arms, finding safety in a seared bathrobe that barely offers shelter. Within seconds, time comes to a shut down. Firemen who were racing to every corner of disaster seem to move at half-speed. Flickering ambulance lights seem to pause, while conversations between curious pedestrians are no longer audible. I look to the building's northwest corner. Is time standing still? Am I in shock? Tonight's disastrous marathon suddenly feels like an episode from *The Twilight Zone*, with every character of tonight's adventure suddenly paused to a freeze frame. Normalcy, if I can even recall what that means, has left this moment in time.

The frigid air is lighter. My heartbeat joins the listless pace, allowing me a split second of realism. Cat claws brace down on my shoulder as if to say, "You are not dreaming, Ethan. This is real." Silence and stillness take over. My eyes focus on white lights descending down from the cloudy sky, passing the silhouette of bare oak trees. I follow their brightness past the inflamed roof and stare into a glittery landscape night. Stars that resemble pincushions surround the mysterious sky and the moon fills the area with a ghostly light. A *whispering* voice calls to me: "*Find strength within the rubble.*"

***

A nudge on my shoulder breaks this isolated, suspended moment, while overwhelming thoughts of having escaped with my life start to fade. All movement speeds up to rapid, and distant conversations become comprehensible again. Somewhere between the sea of snowfall and ice, flashing lights flicker at normal speed, firemen return to being heroes, and the nightmarish roaring fire resumes its passage. Another shake on my shoulder startles me. I look to see a large hand dangling a pair of white tennis shoes and stare into the eyes of a familiar face. Reaching for the shoes with appreciative hands, I barely register that their extra large size will more than cover my feet.

"Come with me, Ethan."

Startled and confused my response slides off my tongue. "What are you doing here?"

"My brother does not speak English and says that you know each other." A beautiful girl with topaz eyes leans in for a closer assessment. "My name is Cecelia. I am Mario's sister."

"Mario," I utter again with exhaustion, "what are you doing here?"

He says something in Spanish that I don't understand, but his eyes are compassionate. He then bends down, grabs the shoes, and props me against his hefty frame. Lifting each of my feet from the icy ground, he places each one in a shoe, the way you would for a child.

"Come with me, Et'an. I take care of jew."

"Why don't you come with us, Ethan? We live several blocks away." Cecelia places her hand under my elbow and gently nudges me forward. Kindness in her eyes prompts me to follow as Mario copies her gesture, pointing me away from the scene.

Two strangers in the hours of darkness have become my allies as we toddle through snowfall mixed with sleet. Conversations dissolve into the quiet while my rescuers lead me to safety. A wooden door garnished with a holiday wreath welcomes my arrival. Honey nestles under my smoky robe as we make our way up the carpeted stairwell. Dim lights showcase family portraits along the walls. At the top, an arched doorway leads to the main living area where blue-and-gray furniture surrounds a gas-burning fireplace. I imagine intimate conversations taking place here. The sound of running water catches my attention. Mario smiles, nodding to his sister, and speaks a few words of Spanish. Cecelia has quietly disappeared and returned with fresh towels.

Conversations I cannot understand and gestures point me to the warm bathtub. A small pile of pajamas, robe, and fuzzy slippers sits atop a closed toilet. Steam from the bathtub relaxes my mind. I try to close the bathroom's heavy door, but apparently it's broken? I place Honey on the tile floor, and remove the robe from my body. The rush of water striking a filled tub seems more than appropriate in this moment. I slip into the balmy water, surrendering to a thousand thoughts that play like musical chairs. Tears join the bathwater. Honey jumps on the edge of the tub, meowing loudly. Is she crying for her lost companion too? I look into her frightened feline eyes and want to promise that I will never let anything happen to her. Maybe she knows better than to believe me.

I don't know how much time has passed. A tap on the bathroom door from Cecelia, signals me that it's time to move on to the next phase of my life. Mario's footsteps in the adjoining room usher me along as he and his sister talk quietly. The crisp snap of sheets and blankets touching down on a bed and the shuffle of drawers opening and closing instantly fill me with fatigue. Wearing the clean pajamas, robe, and oversized slippers, I shuffle to the nightstand where a steaming mug of hot tea and a grilled cheese sandwich await me. Mario points to an old steamer trunk at the foot of the bed and smiles. Opening the chest, he reaches inside and hands me a pair of trousers that are at least two sizes too big for me. Sweaters, blue jeans, old shirts and a worn out suit jacket become an assembly line of oversized hand-me-downs. Mario's treasure chest of someone else's past has become my donation. He proudly reveals a pair of outdated, off-white dress shoes with cracked patent leather. I thank him and place the oversized pants next to my waist, shrugging a smile. Mario leaves the room. Cecelia watches her brother as he goes and then turns to me.

"Ethan, you have made quite an impression on Mario. He has kept that trunk closed for years."

"Cecelia, I hardly know Mario." My embarrassment forces me to look down.

"Oh, Ethan, Mario has told me that you are the only one who speaks to him at the salon. He says the others treat him like he's invisible."

"Well, I didn't know that, and…I am so sorry he feels that way." I muse on this information and think how everyone has an interior life that isn't revealed to us unless we take the time to talk to one other. "I guess people at the salon get busy and forget…." I suddenly realize how lame my excuse sounds. "Is this is your house?" I say, trying to change the subject.

"Ethan, you don't have to speak the same language to know if someone is treating you with kindness. How long does it take to say hello?" I slowly nod my head. Cecelia is right. "And yes, this is my home."

She turns toward the door as Mario walks through with a woven brown belt in hand. He enthusiastically demonstrates many ways to double wrap the belt around my waist. His expression is helpful and eager and he looks to me for acknowledgment. I feel my stamina fading as I stare longingly at the sandwich and tea. Cecelia becomes aware of her brother's overzealous attempts to lend a hand and motions to him that they should leave me alone.

Exhausted to the point of insomnia, I eat the sandwich and stare out the French windows. Why did I not insist the fireman grab Baxter? Why didn't I try one more time? Hopelessness accompanies every thought as I gaze above the rooftops. Honey rests on the window ledge and stares intently into unfamiliar space. We sit quietly together, huddled like frightened children waiting for the dreaded moment, morning.

***

The clock radio boldly states 7 a.m. Honey has found her new bed comfortable and watches me as I get dressed. An extra large sweater and oversized jacket drown my frame. I wad tissues in oversized tennis shoes. Quietly cracking the bedroom door, I slip into the bathroom to splash my face. Mario sleeps nestled on the couch, surrounded by an assortment of decorative pillows. I sneak past a closed door, down the picturesque stairwell, and onto the front entryway.

Unremitting insecurities along with anticipation accompany me on the secluded morning streets as I head toward my past. The tennis shoes slipping off my feet are the first anguish of dawn. The smell of bacon, toast, and other breakfast treats permeate the crisp air. Cold morning air surrounds my sleep-deprived body, alerting my senses to the scent of burned ash that floats above the trees.

My heart beats a trepid pattern, accompanying the sounds of fire trucks and police cars that still dominate the scene. City workers are arriving to clear up the remains. A solo fireman tangling with equipment meets me as I zoom in for a closer look. Defeated and worn thin, I recognize the same firefighter who escorted me out of the burning building to safety. An expression of optimism quickly vanishes when he nods his head no, and returns to his last-minute duties.

"The building was lost a few hours ago when the fire swept its way across the polyester carpeting. It destroyed everything in its path." His blue eyes show fatigue. "Everything," he says, taking a deep breath and responding to my questioning eyes. "I am so sorry young man. Go inside and gather what things you have left. I am here if you need me."

My heart sinks into my stomach as I look into the gloomy hallway that is now carved in patterns of ash and charcoal. Burnt shadows and charred wooden planks signal the disaster within. Morning light starts to peek through the building and broken windows, yet seems to fade with every step I take. I stand at the threshold of my front door, plagued with a pounding view of a destroyed room I am not able to recognize. Hanging by a fiber, the ceiling hovers over my queen-size bed, waiting to descend upon a drowned mattress. A scorched curio cabinet located near the breakfast nook displays an unharmed antique vase that is accessorized with an assortment of fallen debris from the apartment above. Sounds of trickling water add to the feeling of abandonment. Perhaps this shadowy tomb of unidentifiable and unsalvageable loss will be my nightmare forever?

Gathering a little courage, I step toward the closet, calling for Baxter. I call again. Silence lingers in the air. Destruction has left its mark in the stillness of this dark room.

"Baxter, please come out. Please! Are you there?"

Grief consumes every muscle before nausea settles inside my stomach. I try to fight back the tears as I concede to my piteous state. I seize my vase, inspect the final devastation, and turn toward the apartment door just as sunlight peers through my broken bay window.

Suddenly I'm held hostage by a conversation I had with Brussels in St. Thomas. As I recall what he said, I shiver at the uncanny scene before me. My footsteps rush about the shattered, beveled mirror on the floor, which is highlighted by seared Chinese-red walls. I can still feel his presence, hear his words, and recall his eyes, but nothing, including this heartache, can dismiss our last conversation.

"You have an Art Deco beveled mirror."

"What?" I blurt out.

"You have an Art Deco mirror surrounded by Chinese-red walls. This mirror will fall to the ground and break into a thousand pieces. All around this mirror, I see fire and ice. There are footprints that go in a thousand directions. Whatever happens, do not...."

"Are you a tenant here?" An authoritative voice breaks my concentration.

"Yes! Why?"

"You need to leave the building for safety reasons. Oh, is this your rosary? I found it on your front doorstep this morning."

"Yes, that belongs to me." I take the blue rosary from his hand.

Turning away from the broken mirror, I leave the cheaply built walls where conversations used to dance and friendships were formed. I nod farewell to the nameless fireman who withered the storm and saved my life. Our eyes acknowledge each other's unspoken words, and I whisper thanks to a man I shall remember all my life.

***

"We have been worried, Ethan. Where have you been?"

Cecelia welcomes me as I walk up the stairwell. Towering over his sister, Mario watches me closely as I step into the living room. He holds Honey, soothing her uneasy behavior.

"I've lost everything except this vase and this blue rosary." Completely defeated and sleep deprived, I stare in space. "What am I going to do?"

Cecelia embraces me, comforting pain that only familiar eyes can recognize. "I know, Ethan, I know. You need rest and you need to eat. Come join us."

"I don't know what to do or where to begin?"

"Come on. You need to eat."

Persuaded by her gentleness, I consent to breakfast and follow her to a sunny room off the kitchen. Pale-yellow-and-white café curtains line the windows, and the morning light fills the room with kindness. Mario stands by my side speaking sympathetically in Spanish, and though I can't understand his words, his kindheartedness draws me in.

He pulls a chair out, extends his thumb up, sits down, and passes eggs, tortillas, and salsa. Barely missing a beat, Mario makes the sign of the cross and kisses his closed hand. "Et'an, jew be...jew be okay."

"You should call someone from work when you finish eating to let them know what has happened." Cecelia folds her napkin, watching her brother devour his breakfast when the phone rings.

"Bueno?"

The kitchen countertop is lined with decorative terra-cotta plates and family pictures. A vase filled with white flowers sits next to a large black-and-white photo of a Hispanic man wearing my recently assigned hand-me-downs. He holds his catch of the day proudly, as two children gaze with amazement at a fish three times their size. Mario smiles at my newfound discovery and gleams with joy as we both stare at the same figure of a man.

"Who's the man in the photo?" I say slowly, as if Mario will fully grasp my question.

"That's Papa!" Mario's eyes glow with pride.

"Oh, I see."

I turn and face Cecelia searching for an answer, but she remains fixed on the telephone. Mario reaches for the framed picture and places it on the table next to my plate of food.

"Mi Papa."

"Yes, I see. What a great picture, Mario. Thank you."

Within seconds, Mario hands me the photo and places it in both of my hands.

"Gracias," I say.

I sit in a room dressed like a paper doll in oversized clothes speaking to someone I don't know or for that matter understand. Somehow this moment belongs to someone else, and yet it is mine. I hold tight a picture of a man I assume is Mario's father. The eggs, tortillas, and salsa sit in front of me. I'm hungry. I whisper help to the gods in my head.

"Ethan, what are you doing with Papa's picture?"

Cecelia glances at me, placing her hands over the phone. Mario shovels food in, ignoring his sister's concern, and pretends that this peculiar moment is customary. Apparently I have committed the first act of insubordination as a houseguest.

"Thank you, Mario."

I stare at the photo briefly and pray that Cecelia forgives me and that Honey and I are not tossed out like used Kleenex. Cecelia finishes her phone conversation, takes the photo away from me, and thumps Mario on the head.

"I am sure Mario gave you the photograph."

"Yes, he must be very proud of his father. That is your father, right?"

"We will talk about this another time."

Cecelia places the photograph back in its sacred place and begins to tidy up.

"One of our friends at the restaurant has an apartment for lease. We should go look at it, okay? When we get back you are going to bed. Mario will stay here."

"Okay," I answer like an obedient child.

The main avenue is lined with sycamore trees that cast shadows on the narrow steps leading up to a complex of brownstone apartments. A freshly painted entry door leads to four brand-new brass mailboxes with matching brass buzzers. Above the winding stairwell, a portal stained glass window glows with primary colors. Freshly painted halls and waxed wooden floors ascend up and around the corridors to a sturdy door with a brass peephole. A large figure of a man inspecting the final results of a paint crew's handiwork motions us through an open door.

"Come on in, Cecelia."

"Hello, Chuck. This is the young man I spoke of on the telephone."

Dark brown hair with bushy eyebrows covers a face that I would wager has seen a lot of whisky. A long-sleeved button-down shirt that extends up over a protruding stomach seems appropriate, and his bigger than life hands wipe sweat from his wrinkled forehead.

"My name is Charles Bier. You can call me Chuck."

"Okay, I'll call you Chuck." I extend my hand to a seismic handshake. "Good to meet you."

"Look around, you two. The walls are still wet and the toilet will be fixed tomorrow, but all and all, it's a great place for the money."

"Cecelia, I can't afford this place," I whisper. "And I don't have any furniture."

"Let's not worry about silly things, Ethan? Take a look around. Chuck and I need to talk about a few things."

"Okay. But—"

"Go on. Take a look at the rest of the apartment. The bathroom is completely renovated."

The white claw-foot tub sits atop an off-white tile floor, while an old sink with separate hot and cold faucets gleams across from it. A small push-window provides enough natural lighting. Giant elm trees that climb beyond the second-floor balcony fill the view through the window. The hallway's entrance leads to floor-to-ceiling windows displaying a downtown skyline still life. Throughout the apartment are arched doorways, and in the kitchen shiny-white appliances and pristine white cabinets with beveled glass contrast with the black-and-green tiled floor. I open the kitchen's back door and peer out from the balcony. In the backyard, is an enormous ornate blue-tiled swimming pool? What is Cecelia thinking?

"Ethan." I hear a burly voice from behind.

"Yes?"

"Hey, Cecelia tells me you've had some shit luck?" Chuck wipes his perspiration from his forehead with a handkerchief. "How much can you afford to pay me?"

"Uh, well…I don't think I can afford this place, and—"

"Ethan, excuse me for one moment. Chuck, come with me!"

Cecelia grabs him by the belt loop and leads him into the living room. He bows his head as Cecelia urgently whispers, jabbing the air with her finger to make her point. "You're right," Chuck admits loudly to Cecelia.

"You know, I was just thinking, Ethan. Since you seem to be a nice guy and everything, I am going to give you a discount. Yeah! That's what I am going to do."

Chuck looks for Cecelia's approval. My eyes lock onto Cecelia's, never breaking concentration.

"Chuck, you don't have to offer me a discount. I can't afford this place anyway."

"Oh, okay!"

Chuck turns away, placing his handkerchief in his back pocket, and races to the door. Cecelia grabs his belt loop again and drags him back to the living room. The negotiations begin again.

"Ethan, Chuck has something he would like to say. Isn't that right?"

"Yeah, well, since you're a friend of Papa and Cecelia, I am going to a give you three months free rent. That should give you some time to get back on your feet."

Cecelia nudges Chuck for the final deal.

"And," he says, staring at her, "you don't have to pay a security deposit."

"We will take it. Won't we, Ethan?" Cecelia relinquishes Chuck's belt loop.

"Uh, well, thanks, Chuck, but I can't do this. Sorry."

Cecelia and Chuck stare at me as though I've lost my mind. The air in the room feels like a sealed jar. Perhaps a strong bang on the counter would bring some sense back to me? Why am I rejecting this extraordinary offer from two complete strangers? Why indeed.

"Chuck, I will call you in couple of hours. Ethan has not slept and apparently cannot think clearly. Do not give this apartment away."

Cecelia bids farewell to Chuck as we descend down the apartment's steps and head back to the car. Somewhere between the ride back in complete silence, and the friendly hello from Mario upon returning, I feel my sleep-deprived body caving in. Warm blankets and closed drapes draw me to the guest room and call my riddled spirit to sleep.

"Go to sleep, Ethan." Cecelia's voice fades as if distant lands separate us.

***

Voices grow fainter and then loud.

"Ethan, wake up. Wake up, Ethan. Can you hear me? Ethan!"

My body feels heavy and my eyes want to open, but the burden of exhaustion keeps me anchored in the blankets.

"Et'an, time to wake up."

Startled and confused I unfasten the weight on my eyelids. I push out from the blankets and meet a surge of brightness. Mario and Cecelia sit on the bed petting Honey as I attempt to regain clarity.

"What time is it?'

"It's 10, Ethan. You've been asleep for almost two days."

"Oh no, that can't be right?"

"You need to eat."

"Huh? Okay. Sure."

"You should get up." Cecelia hands me a piece of paper with a number scribbled in pencil.

"What's this?" Still heavy with sleep I yawn and slip back in the safety of the covers.

"Your friend Nora is in the hospital."

"What? How do you know Nora? Who told you that?"

"Ethan, Mario and I went to the salon and told Mary what happened to you on Monday."

"Monday?" I look at Cecelia with confusion.

"Yes, Monday, yesterday. Mary has been trying to call you since Sunday."

"What about Nora? Today is Tuesday? You told Mary?" I wrestle with the covers and launch out of bed. My mind races non stop. "I have to go to the hospital."

Mario and Cecelia look at each other and say something in Spanish.

"Ethan, you need to eat and then go to St Paul's hospital. Nora's room number and extension are on the paper. Ethan," Cecelia pauses for a moment, "I told Chuck you would take the apartment."

"What? Why did you do that?"

"Someone else wanted to rent it. I told Chuck that you would take it. It's too late for you to say no." She crosses her arms.

"Is there anything else you want to tell me?" I race around the room trying to make sense of all this, slipping on clothes that drown me.

"Yes, there is."

I put on blue jeans that hang two inches below my feet and a red flannel shirt that consumes my entire torso. Frantically trying to dress myself, I get tangled in the over size shoes, socks, and Mario's bigger than life brown belt.

"What is it you want to tell me, Cecelia?"

"Some man called from Brussels. I can't remember his name, but he certainly was unforgettable. He said he was calling to wish you well and that he would call later."

At this news, I sink down in the bed. Could life get any stranger? I sit quietly for a moment to process this new bit of information.

"How did he get your number?"

"Maybe he spoke with Mary at the salon? Ethan, isn't he a friend of yours? Never mind, Ethan. Go eat. Oh by the way, Mario got your car and—"

Cecelia stops in mid sentence and looks away.

"I have to go to work, Ethan. The restaurant will be busy today at lunch."

Realizing how kind Mario and Cecelia have been, I turn and hug both of them. "I am acting like a selfish idiot. Please forgive me. I've been through so much and slept so hard. And the news you gave me surprised me. You've been so kind to me. I should be at work…and now Nora and Brussels. I am overwhelmed."

Mario hands me a yellow rose and bear hugs me as we move into the kitchen. Cecelia follows. In the kitchen, she barely touches her food. Getting ready to leave, she kisses my forehead and makes her way down the stairwell.

"Come on, Mario." She grabs her keys, turns around, and looks up at me.

"Papa went to St. Thomas when we were children. He met a man from Brussels too. How weird is that?"

I am speechless.

***

Withered hands steadily tackle the hospital's shiny waxed floors. Mop and bucket sit by the handyman's side while the buffer he uses adds more sheen to the hospital passageway. Nurses and doctors gather around the reception area, going about their schedules, attending to medical concerns and last-minute preparations. Patients walk about the hallways, passing and avoiding the scuttle of visitors. I look for Nora's room.

"Excuse me; do you know where room 11B might be?"

"Yeah, go around the nurse's station to the end of hall, past the elevators and you should find it. Who are you looking for?"

"Nora Berry."

"Oh, yeah, she's pretty cool. Everyone up here loves her." The intern makes his way into a patient's room, pointing a finger toward the elevators. "Down there."

I follow his directions and come upon a small crowd of older people gathered around the hallway of a patient's room. An elderly lady clad in blue pajamas and matching robe inches her way past an older gentleman who is determined not to let her into the hospital room. A Korean woman runs down the hallway, frantically waving pens and note pads. "I got paper. I got paper," she yells. Prescription pads and fountain pens disappear into a vortex of greedy hands, while walking canes and wheelchairs fight for a closer view of the mysterious person. Could this be Nora's room?

I ponder this moment, noticing several nurses storming down the slick floors wearing faces of frustration. This has to be Nora's room.

"Nurse T, please come to the eleventh floor. Nurse T, go to room 11B," a female voice on the intercom announces.

Sprinting down the hall with my floppy pair of shoes, I make my way to the group of elders who are transfixed on a woman they have deemed Divine Goddess.

"Excuse me. I am a friend of the patient. Can I get through please?"

The old people shake their paper and pens and shout to be picked, ignoring my pleas. I swoop by a large woman and launch myself into Nora's room, sidestepping slippers and pajama bottoms. A beautiful older woman with red hair and pale skin holds Nora's attention.

"Oh, darling, he is a player and does not love you."

The redhead pauses, sighs, and suddenly the room let's out a collective gasp.

"I bet his birthday is in December? Isn't it?" Nora scribbles on paper, muttering to herself as the room leans in to catch every word.

"Yes, Dan's birthday is December the sixteenth," the redhead confesses.

Every woman in the room shouts, "Oh my god! Do me. Do me." I stare with sheer delight, amazed at the one Brussels calls Pied Piper. That she is.

Nora sits in a wheelchair wearing a hospital gown cinched with a designer belt, showcasing her perfect figure. Her manicured fingers and toes glow in tasteful soft pink. Her makeup is natural and flawless; her blonde hair gently groomed to a classic cut and shines every time she shakes her head. Beautiful green eyes look onto the room, smiling at every anxious patient as she proceeds with a communion of optimism for the sick and ailing. A black woman and her teen grandchild acknowledge Nora's every word, shaking their heads, extending palms upward, and quietly singing amen's. I carve my way through a room full of pajamas and stop dead in my tracks when faced with Nora's Christian Dior lace scarf camouflaging her IV.

"Nora," I yell.

"Ethan Michaels, I can't believe it's you?" Nora's eyes are hypnotically glued to my immense shoes. Mine are fixed on her lace scarf.

"You brought me a beautiful yellow rose, Ethan." Nora smells the flower as though to honor the moment of sympathy and hands the flower to the redhead who holds onto to it for dear life.

"What a stunning scarf." I can't take my eyes off the IV.

"Ethan," Nora points at the IV, "this is so repulsive. I had to do something. What do you think?"

Before I can answer, the room shouts out in unity, "Do me. Do me. Do me." The patients chant as bobbling pads and pens bounce like spears before the hospital's resident celebrity.

"Nora, why are all these people here?" I look around the room as numerous eyes gawk back at me.

"Oh, honey, I made a mistake and offered a lady a reading." Nora points to a vigorous woman talking faster than a speeding bullet to anyone within earshot, clutching onto a cocktail napkin with Nora's cryptic notes. "Ethan, I had no idea she was the town crier. I was helping her decide on where her daughter should go to college and the next thing I knew 'Miss Chatty Cathy' sent out an *All Points Bulletin* to the entire floor."

"Nora," I whisper with shock, "you know there's a doctor in your room with his pen and pad too?"

"Dr. Newsome? Oh, isn't he adorable. I told him that coming out to his parents that he was gay would be a wonderful experience."

"Nora, all these people are clinging onto your every word? What's wrong with you? Are you okay?"

The crowd starts to shift its focus from telling tales of Nora to our private conversation. Interrupted by an unmistakable presence, the seas of devotees move quickly aside as a full-figured nurse with an elaborate hairdo woven from skull-hugging braids enters the room. She stands before Nora and I, and a quick scan tells her everything she needs to know.

"Ethan, um, this is Nurse T," says Nora in a low voice. "She's rather strict...."

"...Girl, I know you are not the cause of this disturbance? Doctor Newsome, what the hell are you doing here? You better get on down stairs now. Lord have mercy? And you two, over there in the amen corner? That's right, you two! Girl, your husband is looking for you and your granddaughter. That man is going crazy down stairs." Nurse T grabs pillows and sheets from Nora's bed. "Girl, what are all these people writing down on their pads?" She looks straight through me and signals all of Nora's fans to leave. "All of you get back to your rooms. Don't be acting like a bunch of fools." The fan club trickles back to their dull hospital rooms, leaving the three of us face to face.

"Nora, you better sit still in that wheel chair. We got tests to do today, honey. And what have you done to this IV?! This ain't a Christmas tree. Oh, Lord. And who are you? You look like Tiny Tim, from, *A Christmas Carol?*"

Nurse T stops her tirade long enough to register my presence. She quickly moves to Nora and places one broad hand behind her back and another in front of her patient. Nora grips Nurse T's arm and pulls herself up to a sitting position.

"Never mind, young man, I don't want to know who you are." Nurse T takes in my oversized pants and shakes her head. "I have been here ten years and I've never seen a crazier group of people. Nora Berry, I am busier than life. I don't have time for any more circus acts today. Hear me? Tell Mr. Bo jangles that visiting hours are over."

Holding onto my hand, Nora repositions herself in the wheelchair, and asks me to come forward.

"Ethan, they found a lump in my breast. For the first time in my life I am scared."

"Oh please don't say that, Nora."

A lone yellow rose lays crushed on the floor as Nora is whisked away. Nurse T rambles on with more objections as I watch my friend vanish down the hall. Once again the roller coaster of life clanks up the tracks of no return.

"Bye, Ethan," Nora waves a perfectly manicured hand in a gesture that royalty would have appreciated.

Outside near the covered garage, a telephone booth shares the sidewalk with obscenity-laced graffiti. As the cars leave, my heart feels full and impoverished at the same time. When will these aftershocks stop? As I dig for a quarter and then reach for my wallet, I start to think I've left it at home. What home? What wallet? I scan the sidewalk for loose change.

"Darling, he looks so young. Are you sure he's homeless?' says a young female voice.

"Of course he is. Look at his shoes and those pants. Brigit, he can't be more than twenty? What could have happened to someone so young?"

I stare at the couple wondering what could be so shocking and look around to see who they're talking about. The telephone booth floor is swept clean of dimes and nickels.

"Excuse me, young man. Would you like some change?"

"Thank you. How did you know I needed change?" I say with surprise.

The couple looks at me sympathetically and shakes their heads. "God bless you," says the woman, as they turn toward the parking garage.

"Thanks!" I wave good-bye to the strangers and immediately call work to let Mary know what has happened.

"Salon, can you hold please?" Mary's voice jumps to the next call. "Hold on one moment. Be right back. Can I help you?"

"Mary, it's me, Ethan."

"Don't go away, Ethan. Hold on a minute." Mary comes back to the line sighing as if she's been racing. "Are you okay?"

"Yeah, I think so. I just came back from seeing Nora. They found a lump in her breast."

"Is she alright? Hold on, Ethan...okay, I'm back. How are you, Ethan? Hold on...sorry, we're so busy right now because of the holiday. Don't forget we close for two weeks for Christmas this Friday. Before I forget, Julie Gautier called from New York. She wants to bump up the meeting with CBS for next week."

"What? Shit. I don't have any clothes, Mary. I lost everything in the fire."

"Ethan, I know," she says softly. "I called all your clients and told them you would be out until after the holidays. I'll send your pay check and some extra money home with Mario. Hold on, Ethan. Never mind. Call me later this afternoon, Honey."

As I drive back to Mario and Cecelia, I notice the Christmas decorations that seem to have appeared overnight in all the store windows. Christmas Hours as follows: Closed for two weeks. Open January 2nd. Sadness consumes me.

A realtor tussles with a for-sale sign in the front yard as Cecelia makes her way up the front stairs. "Good afternoon," says the agent. I nod my head as I follow Cecelia up the stairwell. I have a feeling that everything is not as it should be.

"Cecelia, everything okay?"

"Ethan, I'm going to make some coffee. Would you like some?"

Real estate contracts cover the tabletop. I shake my head and sit down. Cecelia stares at me intently, grabs the picture of Papa off the kitchen counter, and places it down in front of me.

"What do you see in this picture, Ethan?"

I study the picture. "I see Papa on a dock holding a large fish for display. And—"

"Do you recognize anything in the picture? Look closely."

"There's a small fishing boat." I pause looking for Cecelia's approval.

"And, what else do you see?"

"A tall white-haired man is standing in the background with you and Mario? I can barely make him out, but it looks like he's wearing khakis—?" Before I can finish my sentence, a chill goes through my entire body.

"Ethan, do you know this man?" Cecelia's eyes swell up with tears. "You know this man? Don't you?"

"Yes, I do." I say.

"Ethan, before Papa moved to Texas, he went to St. Thomas on holiday with our family. While there he met a man who changed his life forever. The man from Brussels is in this picture, isn't he? All Papa did was speak of this man after his trip, yet he never remembered his name."

"Oh Cecelia, the same thing happened to me."

"I know."

"How do you know this man from Brussels?"

"Papa died this past Easter in St. Thomas. Before he passed, he made me promise to keep his word to this man he met in Brussels. I was told to rescue the *eagle* that was bathed in *fire and ice*. Shelter and nourish his spirit and bring him to the *place of sycamores*. There, the wounded bird would learn to fly."

"What?" I look puzzled. "That sounds just like that old man with his silly riddles."

Cecelia shakes her head and somberly taps a finger on the table. "Those riddles are not silly, Ethan. Come with me. Get Honey and all of your belongings."

"What? Why?"

Placing the picture of Papa back on the counter, I note a small toe ring made of silver hanging on the side of the wood frame. Could this be Brussels' doing? Walking into the guest bedroom and feeling even more confused, I gather a small heap of clothes from the old chest at the foot of the bed. Cecelia follows me, opening drawers and closets.

"Here, you will need these blankets and sheets. Please take this bathrobe. I will get Mario another one when we get to Mexico."

"Mexico? Why are you going to Mexico?"

"We're moving there for awhile to be with family. I will sell my house and buy something else when we return." Cecelia fights back a teary reply. "We'll spend the holiday with Papa's remaining family and find a place to live after the New Year."

"Cecelia, I don't understand. What about your restaurant?"

"Chuck and I are business partners. He'll run it until I come back. Come with me, Ethan. It's time to go."

Honey's wide eyes stare through the car window, while I sort my remaining belongings on the back seat. Sidewalks lined with empty flowerbeds circle around my new home's old iron gates. They must have been impressive years ago. Brownstone apartments with sandstone steps and green awnings wrap around the inner courtyard, and I can't help but think of summer barbecue parties and beer when I see the pool again. Old wood deck chairs are evenly placed around the surrounding tiles.

"Stay here for a moment." Cecelia has a brief conversation with Chuck at the leasing office. He never takes his eyes off of Cecelia except when he places the keys to the apartment into her delicate hands. She turns to meet my curiosity.

"Come with me, Ethan." Cecelia motions to the rear entrance of the structure.

I grab a handful of clothes as Cecelia reaches for Honey.

"Do you notice anything familiar, Ethan?"

"No? Why?" I look around me, confused at what I'm supposed to see.

"Look at the sign by the back entrance."

"Sycamore Place!"

None of what Cecelia has told me makes sense, but given my confusion and the surreal quality of my life lately, I'm starting to accept these odd coincidences. We make our way up the stairs to my new apartment. As I look up at the stained glass window overlooking the stairs, I notice something new. A red and blue stained glass window lined with gold lettering displays the name, *Saint Thomas.*

Honey jumps from Cecelia's firm grip, and runs inside to inspect her new home. Cecelia leans against a window in the living room and stares at me.

"I heard a small bang in the kitchen the night of your fire, Ethan. I got up to see what could have made the noise and noticed that Papa's picture had fallen on the kitchen floor. And then I heard the fire trucks. Mario and I got dressed, walked outside, and followed the sirens to your place. We saw you racing in and out of your apartment complex, and Mario said to me, 'That's Ethan, that's Ethan.' He ran home and got shoes and blankets. By the time we got back, you were huddled on the ground with your cat crying. Ethan, at the time, none of this made sense to me either. The night you came to my home I drew you a bath. Do you remember?"

"Yes."

"After you finished your bath, I took your burned bathrobe and tossed it into the trash. I noticed the *eagle* on the front pocket of your robe but didn't think anything of it. Well, at least I didn't think anything of it until the man from Brussels called. Then it all began to make sense. Papa always thought he would be the one to find you."

"Cecelia—"

"Ethan, I know this is hard to follow but try. "*Rescue the eagle bathed in fire and ice? Bring him to the place of sycamore?*" The fire and the ice storm that took place that night? Your bathrobe had an eagle on the front pocket. The name of this complex is *Sycamore Place.* Is any of this making sense, Ethan, or do you think I'm crazy?"

"Let me think. And no you're not crazy? It has to be the same man?"

I tell her of my conversations with Brussels in St. Thomas, how crazy I thought he was, and how much he seemed to know about me. I told her how I dismissed him at first but was drawn to him at the same time. As I tell her the stories, she nods her head slowly and then enthusiastically, recognizing a link between us.

"I was a teenager when Papa met the man he called '*The Messenger.*' We would go to St. Thomas on Easter, when Papa had some extra money, and look for the messenger. Papa would sit on the beach at Magans Bay, talking for hours to his wise new friend. All Papa could talk about was this mysterious man. No matter where we were on the island, the man would randomly show up. Papa never questioned that peculiarity. I did. I suppose he spoke to you about the shift?"

"Well, sort of. He spoke more about past histories and the awakening of the feminine consciousness. Some of it made sense, other times I couldn't understand what he was saying. Why do you think he chose your father?"

"Truthfully Ethan, the only thing that makes sense to me is that Papa was a simple man with a good heart. The Messenger saw that Papa was kind and lived his life with honesty. He helped Papa to recognize his authentic purpose. Papa spoke of owning a Mexican food restaurant in Dallas. When we came back to Mexico one trip, Papa decided to move to Texas. Mama, Mario, and I would stay behind until Papa found his destiny. He came to Dallas during the middle of a winter storm, walking the streets daily knowing that a man would take him in. That is where he met Chuck. 'You crazy man, how come you are wearing sandals and a short-sleeved shirt in the middle of winter? Get inside here.' This is where their friendship began. They couldn't understand each other, but

Chuck could see that Papa was a good man. Chuck taught him how to wash dishes, clean and set the tables, and speak English one word at a time. Papa saved his money and bought the restaurant I own today. Ethan, you did the same thing with Mario. Human kindness flowed from your heart just like it did from Papa. Each day, Mario would come home and tell me how kind you were to him. You would always smile at him, help him move the plants, clean up the spilled water, and you did not care that he had a learning disability."

"I never knew."

Cecelia's tears began to flow again. "Does it really matter, Ethan? It is how we treat another human being that matters? That's what Papa learned from the Messenger."

"I don't know if that—"

"Does it matter that we come from different countries with different backgrounds? Does it matter that we speak a different language? Does it matter that Papa was an illegal immigrant, and that we came from poor beginnings? All those things don't matter, Ethan. Always be kind to those around you. And never judge the one who looks like he has nothing. That is what Papa learned from, *The Man from Brussels*. That is what Papa passed onto Mario and to me."

I look at Cecelia, astonished. Yes, these are definitely the words of Brussels. Though I never knew Papa, the spirit of Cecelia and Mario fit like a key to a door that opens to a room full of kindness. It is Brussels teachings of kindness that matter.

"Ethan, I must go. Take these few belongings that are dear to Mario and use them. I will come by before we fly to Mexico and wish you a Merry Christmas. You were brought to our lives for only a moment, but I'm glad I could help for a little bit."

I extend my arms around her petite body.

"Cecelia, you will never know how indebted I am to you. I wish I could have met your father. What was his name?"

"His name was Pedro. Chuck called him the *Fisherman*." She turns to the door, reaching inside her pocket. "Take this money and buy some groceries."

"I can't take anymore from you, Cecelia. You have done way too much for me."

"*Allow someone the joy of giving to you*, Ethan. The happiness you have brought Mario in the past few days has been priceless." She touches my cheek. "Besides, it would mean a lot to my father. He would have been thrilled to meet the *wounded eagle*."

As she reaches for the door knob, she turns again and smiles. "Thank you, Ethan. Thank you."

"Thank you, Cecelia, for everything."

As the afternoon sunset brings tiny rays of light through the stained glass window, I notice how the gold letters spell out Saint Thomas so brilliantly. Moving to the living room window, I watch people walking across the street, cars lined up with drivers impatient to get home. Cecelia stops to look up and waves good-bye. I wave back, filled with a feeling of peace for the first time in a while. I turn to look at my vacant apartment, still smelling of fresh paint, and notice the newly laid carpet covering the room. Honey claims the far-left window ledge and stares into the branches of a giant sycamore tree.

Suddenly realizing I might never see Mario and Cecelia again, I wonder what the future holds for them and what knowledge Brussels shared with Papa? Did Papa feel the same void I feel now since our paths never crossed? What would he have shared with me? How many others have spoken to Brussels? How many listened? Are we pieced together one stitch at a time until the tapestry is ready for all to view? I have come to recognize some truth within this so-called implausible experience. Cecelia and Mario have carried this information for years, never losing their faith in their father or Brussels words. Perhaps my lesson should be to take the *road of blind faith?*

Nightfall comes and the market across the street blinks with Christmas lights. Holiday pastries stare through the windows of the corner bakery. I notice a Christmas tree securely tied to a car full of noisy kids singing carols. Honey purrs her own holiday song. Perhaps now is a good time to go to the market, buy groceries, come home, and make a makeshift bed on the carpet. Tomorrow I'll attempt to take one small step toward my new beginning. Somehow I must have faith in my new life. Hopefully the noisy street below with the hum of cars and buses will lull me to sleep. Maybe my cat will nestle under my arm, finding safety in our new home as we both snuggle on a make-believe bed.

***

I wake to the sound of a loud bang on my front door. The sun isn't even up. Is my watch correct, 6:45 a.m.?

"Hold on!"

I wrap the sheets around my waist, walk into the bare living area, and notice that Honey is standing at the front door meowing. Knock, knock! The door pounds loudly.

"Hold on!!"

I undo the deadbolt and unfasten the chain lock. As I open the door, I can't believe who stands before me.

"Good morning, my dear boy. How absolutely wonderful it is to see you."

"Brussels?"

Message

Chapter 8

Early morning light filters through my windows, while birds sing their morning chorus. Brussels, this mysterious old man, holds a large cardboard box and stands smiling in my doorway. He is dressed in his customary pressed khaki slacks along with a lightweight taupe-colored jacket that seems to emphasize his piercing blue eyes. A mane of white hair swoops across his tan forehead. He greets me with a grin like a force of gentle waves crashing onto a sandy shore. I don't know why he's here. But I'm sure I'm about to find out.

"Good morning, my dear boy. What an absolutely brilliant day. There is nothing like the dawn of a new day to make men feel alive. Wouldn't you agree, Ethan?"

"Do you know what time it is?" I say, sarcastically.

Brussels grabs my wrist and turns it to check my watch. "Dear me, twenty minutes behind schedule. Thank you so much for assisting me with that. Come and let me in."

"Are we about to have another one of those intense conversations?" I say, closing the door behind him.

"Of course we're not, Ethan." Brussels says, with wink. "We have already had those conversations."

"Good, because, what—"

"We have other conversations that need attending to this morning. Let me put this *small* box in your kitchen. Do you mind?"

I point to the kitchen door and feel myself losing patience. "Make yourself at home. What's in the box?"

Brussels places the box on the kitchen counter and rummages in a cabinet for god knows what. Maybe he brought a book on the turning of *nothing into something*. "I would offer you something to drink but I—"

"There is no need to worry, my child. I have brought us teas, fresh croissants…let's see…oh yes, some jam."

"I don't want to sound like a jerk, but just in case you haven't noticed, I don't have any cups or plates or even silverware. Look around, man. Do you see anything?" My charade is obvious.

The white-haired stranger breaks for a moment, strolls around my empty apartment, observing every corner, and humming to himself. Honey follows him as he scrutinizes the walls, floor, cabinets, even opens the closet doors, like a prudent building inspector.

"Ethan, what a lovely apartment you have."

"You're kidding?" I say with a confused tone.

"Perhaps you are seeing something I am not seeing, Ethan. Would you care to help me with this?" His eyes shine with amusement at my irritableness.

"Does the word *nothing* mean anything to you?"

Brussels' ponders my statement and chuckles. "Did you say nothing? Is that correct, Ethan?"

"That's right, nothing!"

"Ethan, perhaps your thoughts are creating an emotional block that makes you think you have nothing?"

"What? You are kidding me? Let me catch you up to speed, just in case you overlooked something in this room. There is *nothing* in this room. I came back to Texas, poured myself into the entertainment business only to be treated like a loser. I met the woman you call *Pied Piper*, but you forgot one tiny thing—she might have breast cancer. We've become friends, but now she is dealing with her own struggle. And in case you have not noticed the *nothing* part, there is nothing in this apartment. No clothes, well, some hand-me-downs that belong to a man you just happen to know? No furniture. No pots and pans. No bed. No towels and blankets. I lost everything in a fire!"

I pause for a moment, realizing I am becoming angrier by the minute. "And let's not forget the famous fire and ice riddle. Remember? And as far as my thoughts go, major new flash—nothing!"

"Ah, a fire represents *a new beginning*."

My head feels like it's about to explode, and my hands are shaking. Brussels pauses for a moment and takes me by the shoulder.

"Ethan, you think you have nothing, therefore you see nothing. I will teach you how to see everything. Let us begin now."

He places his hands on my shoulders and gently steers me to the living room, where he points to the floor. I sit down and wrap the sheets around my waist, trying to calm my frustration.

"Let us begin by understanding the way one thinks. When your thoughts are misguided you create emotional blocks, creating behavioral choices that allow you to feel insecure. Negativity diminishes the presence of peaceful thoughts. You think you have nothing, Ethan? I see quite the opposite, my friend."

"What? Oh, brother—"

"If you feel ungrateful for what's in front of you, of course you will look around and *see nothing*. However, if we come from a place of *appreciation*, we can look at the same situation and see *abundance*." He joins me on the floor, stretching out his long legs, and points to my bathroom.

"Ethan, please describe in detail your bath parlor from the old complex?"

"Seriously, describe my old bathroom?"

"Yes."

"Well, it was really gross. The sink and toilet gurgled every time I ran the faucet or flushed the toilet. Roaches came out from the wall at night. Let's see…oh yeah, hot water sort of came and went. Ug—"

"What about the kitchen, Ethan?"

"It was horrible. Talk about roaches."

"Did you like the old apartment?"

"Where are you going with this?

"Answer me please, Ethan."

"No."

"Ethan, close your eyes and tell me about this new apartment."

"You're kidding?" I say, losing my patience.

"Please consider what I'm asking of you."

I shut my eyes, feeling absolutely ridiculous, but have the tiniest feeling that Brussels is about to make me eat my words.

"Well, the walls are glossed white. Umm…there are lots of windows. Oh yeah, the kitchen is really cool."

"Ethan, keep your eyes closed."

"Okay…the bathroom has a cool pull window that allows you to see the elms in the backyard. The hallway leads you to a bedroom with floor-to-ceiling windows that have a great view of the city."

"Which of these apartments do you prefer?'

I open my eyes and look straight into Brussels' eyes.

"You are kidding?"

"Answer me, Ethan. Which of these apartments do your prefer?"

"This apartment is the one I prefer."

"Exactly! You chose better surroundings over ones that were not so good.

"Yeah, I guess."

Brussels moves in, eyeing me like a cat toying with their prey. "You had all your things in a place you did not like? And now you have a place you like with no things? Is it possible that a *pessimistic outlook* is allowing you to see nothing? When we feel we have nothing, we see nothing, Ethan."

He pauses, letting me digest this latest piece of wisdom.

"Close your eyes again, Ethan.

"The other apartment was not to your liking I gather? The toilet gurgled and there were roaches in your kitchen. Correct? Would you have stayed if not for the fire?"

"Well…no? I would have eventually found a cool place."

"Perhaps you need to be grateful for your new place now? *Eventually* may never come. The more you appreciate, the more peaceful your state of mind. When you are at peace, you are more likely to accept the current situation as a blessing rather than view it as an obstacle. Wouldn't you agree?

"Well?" I look at Brussels and feel foolish. Do I want to admit he is right?

"Ethan, are your thoughts leaning towards disappointment before you have a chance to fully appreciate the miracle before you? Perhaps your emotions, thoughts, and feelings are creating an emotional stumbling block? Throughout time, man has never appreciated the power of thankfulness. He continues to ravel in a *lack consciousness*, sabotaging happiness before it has a chance to get out of the starting gate. The power of one's thoughts, if connected to higher purpose, will expand the source of manifestation. *Ask and* you *shall receive* doesn't mean, *I want*, what *I want, when I want it.*"

"Let me get this straight. You are saying I should be grateful every day? Even with nothing? Get my shit together, I mean my thoughts, feelings, and emotions?"

"Indeed. Learn to appreciate the smallest of blessings. Begin each day with thankfulness. When we operate within the integrity of our emotions, thoughts, and feelings, we are in direct line to conversations with our higher self. In essence, we are having a *moment-to-moment conversation with God.* Therefore, be aware of the inner conversations within your mind. You will receive according to your intent. *Whatsoever a man thinketh,* is more powerful than you have been taught?"

"How do I do that?"

"Stand up, dear one. Come with me."

He guides me to my front window and places my hands on the window ledge.

"Begin each day at your window. Bless every situation that occurred the day before. Bless every encounter; every conversation and every conflict. *Everything!* Honor God for all the daily blessings, that are about to come your way. Elementary as this may seem in the beginning, I ask you to walk through these steps until you begin to see the results of manifestation. Honor the blessings of what comes your way, and more will come."

"Okay." I say, doubtfully. "This will change my outcome?"

"Yes, Ethan, if it comes from *pure* intent. Accept everyone and everything as a blessing in your life, and do so unconditionally."

"What?"

"Be patient with the cashier at the pharmacy when she is having a busy day. Thank the speeding driver who races ahead of you, allowing you to pull into the next lane, so you may avoid an accident. Acknowledge a kind smile from a stranger. These are your opportunities. Bless each outcome, every situation, each day. Once you honor these bylaws, you will attract *all that is and ever shall be.* I say to you, my dear friend, *bless and you shall be blessed.*

He places my hand on my heart and gently pushes in.

"Place your hand over your heart when you recite your gratitude list."

"I need to use the bathroom. I'll be right back."

Brussels nods his head and sees through my phony getaway. Who is this old man? Are his philosophies out there? Am I naïve? Why is he telling me all this? Why is he here? I can't stop my troubled thoughts. I can hear him rustling in my kitchen, as I splash my face with cold water and brush my teeth. Maybe he will finish this charade and leave me to my poor-pitiful party?

"But suppose he's right? I better listen to this man," I mumble.

"Ethan, do you prefer jam on your croissant, or would you like it plain? Would you care for some hot tea or milk?"

How the hell is he going to make hot tea? I guess I better get back to the second *act of wisdom.* God only knows what else will come out of his mouth.

"I'll be right out." I open the bathroom door and go into the living room.

The morning brightness fills every window in my apartment. Brussels continues to putter in the kitchen, as the buttery scent of warm croissants consumes the room. Slipping on a pair of Papa's blue jeans, I wander about my apartment, thinking of what this old man has said. Sycamore trees seem to lean toward the windows, extending their branches as if to salute my mysterious guest. A teakettle whistles, and the sound of silverware clinking against plates hastens my curiosity. Brussels has draped a white piece of cloth over the beat-up brown cardboard box in my empty dining area. Plates, bowls, flatware, and teacups are lined up on my kitchen counter. Napkins are neatly stacked on top of a breadbasket, while marmalade and strawberry jam sit in small jars next to it. And off to the side, tennis shoes, socks, sweatpants, and sweatshirts.

"Ethan, do you prefer cream in your tea?"

"Where did all this come from?"

"What do you mean, Ethan?"

I point at the counter. "The tennis shoes, socks, sweatpants and these dishes?"

"Oh, yes of course? They came from the small box in the dining area. Ethan, be a gentleman and place the croissants and tea on our makeshift table. The jams are my favorite so I hope you enjoy them. Come on. Stop hesitating. We have much to cover and I want you to be alert."

"How did—?"

He chuckles loudly. "Let's not worry about things that come in and out of boxes. We have greater concerns that must be discussed. Sit down and enjoy the time we have."

My mood is somewhere between annoyed and intrigued. "Why are you here?"

"Ethan, I appreciate your question. But perhaps you should ask yourself, why you are here? I know why I am here."

"Why can't you explain anything in simple terms that I can understand?"

"Sit and we shall continue. Ethan, I see that you are concerned? I understand these concepts are new to you. But are these concepts that unusual? I share these beliefs with you because they allow you some insight as to why you are here. Everyone has a destiny. Somehow, purpose has been eclipsed by your misguided thoughts. Part of our talk is to help you understand how to turn loss into gain by merely appreciating what you have—a simple concept, yes? When I am sure you understand this, I will give you a lot more information that will assist you in achieving the next stage of your journey."

"What does that mean?"

Brussels reaches over and taps my hand. "Ethan, look at me, as someone that is assisting in rebuilding your life? Perhaps your first blessing of the day should be *acceptance*? Allow yourself the possibility to accept something that will transform your life. I will answer everything that concerns you. Please sit."

I stare at this old man, his mane of white hair, clear-blue eyes, and calm manner that pervades my empty apartment. I don't know why I just don't throw him out and get on with my life. His kindness overwhelms me, but what he says tugs at my spirit. Is it just because I'm needy? Or is my response coming from a deeper place? Whatever it is, I decide to play out this visit and see what happens. And I'm hungry— jam, croissants, and hot tea are tempting me—and the way my life has been going, who knows? Maybe listening to Brussels is a small price to pay for enjoying breakfast in my barren apartment.

Brussels sits elegantly; his ramrod posture and tilted head indicate another lecture is on the way.

"Ethan, let us begin our morning with a moment of silent appreciation. Find the significance of this day. Go inside and discover the blessings that have come your way."

"Um, okay."

I watch Brussels, anxious to follow his lead. I really don't have any idea what he wants me to do.

"Ethan, close your eyes. Now, that is much better. The last several weeks have been challenging for you, my child. What are you most grateful for during this time of difficult transformation?"

With eyes shut, I attempt to go inside and discover what it is that I must be grateful for. My thoughts zoom in every direction. Minutes seem to add up, and then suddenly a thought. A voice speaks inside me. "Mario and Cecelia must be thanked." Another voice says, "Thank the fireman." Thoughts begin to flow like a running faucet. "Don't forget Chuck, who was kind enough to help you." My body begins to feel lighter and the pressure of the last several weeks dissipates the pillar of doubt I have come to know. "Thank you, God, for this odd stranger who has come to share his food and wisdom." I open my eyes to look at Brussels. A golden light seems to outline his body. Legs crossed, hands extended, the gold light triangles from forehead to right hand to left hand and up into my ceiling. I close my eyes immediately.

"What the hell just happened?"

"Open your eyes, Ethan. We are ready. Please eat."

Brussels smiles kindly. I must try to listen carefully, so I can remember what he says. Please don't let him ask me to recall our conversations in St. Thomas. Please.

I take a fresh croissant; put a mound of jam on top, and bite. Where did these treats come from? I'm not a fan of hot tea, but the flavor is extraordinary.

"How do you know Pedro," I ask.

"Ah, you want to know about the fisherman? I will explain soon enough. But first, do you recall our conversation in St. Thomas? We spoke of energy."

Great, here comes the pop quiz. I turn to Brussels with my mouth full and ask, "Which one?"

"We had dinner upstairs in that wonderful café?"

"Oh, yeah, sure, I remember that café upstairs."

"We spoke on the effects of energy. I am about to merge energy, along with emotion, thoughts, and feelings. I will include peace, and choice!"

Here we go. Maybe I should be taking notes.

"Emotion, thought, and feelings can create certain possibilities—or choices—which lead to action. The actions we take create circumstances in our lives. If we come from a place of peace, our choices will create harmonious outcomes. If we come from a place of fear, we create less harmonious circumstances. These three components are combined with the law of energetic attraction. Every action we take is fueled by emotion, thought, and feelings. In other words, you manifest according to your inner thinking. You mentioned you have nothing. Perhaps you are right? Or perhaps you are wrong? Tell me what you are most appreciative to have before you today, Ethan."

"Umm…I am thankful for Mario and Cecelia. A nice man forfeited my security deposit. Let's see? Oh, a fireman saved my life."

"Ethan, these are amazing things to be grateful for. Perhaps these *things* are more important than the *nothing* that was mentioned when I arrived? What good is it to have belongings if there is no house to place your things in? What good is it to have belongings in a house you don't like? Finally, what good would belongings do if you had sustained severe injuries and were hospitalized? Learn to honor what is in front of you *now*, Ethan, rather than later. I understand that one of the biggest fears is losing what we have attained, but perhaps we need to focus on what has been given to us rather than what we think we don't have. This is *gratitude*. Recognizing this brings you inner peace. Do you understand the energy put behind your original thought? It was fear. And fear created a feeling of lack in your mind. Consequently, rather than seeing something beautiful, you saw *nothing*. Let us move on. There is much to cover, and I don't want to spend a lot of time on uncomplicated things.

"You are kidding? This is not simple. It's complicated."

"Ethan, I am trying to encourage you to supervise your thoughts. Once you gain the balance of your thoughts, emotions, and feelings, not only will you be able to overcome fear, but bring about the necessary changes that lead to your authentic purpose. Now let us move onto the power of energy that is accelerated because of choice."

My appetite fades away. These words—thoughts, choice, fear, peace,—echo in my mind. Who is the bigger nut case—me for listening to this stranger, or Brussels for having confidence in my ability to somehow make a difference in my life.

"Let me put our dishes away, and we can continue this conversation," I say. Honey is cuddled in Brussels' lap, hypnotized by his gentle stroking.

"Ethan, I am glad that you chose to respect a healthy body. The more attuned to physical exercise, the more aware the mind. How wonderful. You must be proud of this physical accomplishment?"

"Thank you. I took your advice." Grinning with self-assurance, I feel like a proud student who scored high points on his exam.

"You had a choice to modify your behavior and focus on a physical change that would bring about more self-confidence. Do not bring vanity into the equation. The body is to be honored with self-respect and not self-importance."

"Oh?"

"When we agree to a choice, let us understand the effects of our choice. Perhaps we should be thankful that we can reform our body, rather than focus on how many pounds we lose or gain. Misinterpretation of this thought can create a spinning wheel of ups and downs on the scale, creating subconscious sabotage. Pounds become the focus. Ego becomes the addiction, and we create lack once again within the spiritual system. The effect of this choice lands many men and women back at the starting line. If we come from a place of peace, even before weight loss, the mind will accept the physical body as it is. Simply put, it is not about how much weight one loses but rather how one comes to be at peace with how one looks. Honor thy body, mind, and spirit and discover *the fountain of youth.*"

"I know," I say eagerly, feeling like I finally have something to contribute. "I got hung up on the scale. Every day I was either happy or upset about how much I weighed."

"Ethan, everyone on the planet operates with choice—from the smallest choices to life-changing choices. Each choice made creates a new reality. Every personal choice you make affects everyone. *Everyone!* Learning to connect to this wakefulness raises the energetic vibration. Imagine a choice made by a collective group of people who honor peace and cooperation? Then imagine choices that are made from those who abuse their power and create choices that destroy *Mother Earth* and the progression of mankind? This is why I have come to speak to you."

I run hot water into the sink, place our dirty dishes in it, and think of how capable this old man sounds. Not only does he bring intelligence to the table but dish soap. What else is in his care package?

"I knew there had to be a reason why you came here," I tell him. "Something you are about to share with me must be pretty radical, right? I can't imagine a more unusual conversation than the one we're having."

Brussels' mood becomes serious. His facial expression changes quickly. He leaps to his feet and walks between my living room and dining room, his flow of thoughts seems to be driven by concern.

"A great crisis speeds to this country. History has demonstrated that the downfall of the greatest kingdoms has been because those in power yield to corruption and greed. This I tell you; *the son, of a son of a son, will steal democracy like a fox in the night. Beware. Nero returns playing a fiddle of words while the New City cries out. The towers will shatter and war will follow.*"

"What?" I turn from the sink and head for the living room, suddenly overwhelmed by this brainteaser. "You can't expect me to understand this riddle? If it weren't for Cecelia, I would have never figured out fire and ice. And speaking of Cecelia, are you going to explain Pedro? This is Cecelia's father. You know that?"

"Ethan, please let me continue." He stops pacing and turns to face me. "*Broken sentences flawed with incompetence are this leader's discrepancy. Heed the black general that rides on the elephant into the ancient city. Man has one half-hour before the eleventh hour strikes. Wise men will be summoned in order to discern the truth.*"

"Okay?" I was really hoping for a less complicated…less nutty, less…crazy conversation. Is he insane? Maybe the best thing is for me to let him continue?

"What do you want me to do? Some of this stuff is pretty weird. And some of this stuff makes no sense, a black general riding on an elephant into an ancient city? What?"

"Ethan, you and others, will awaken to the exactness of these forecasts. Truth always carves its own path. You will accept or decline whatever does not make sense. However, I do ask that you share this passage with Nora. It is in this friendship that you will flourish. Your quandary will become Nora's mission and contribute to her own resurrection of health. Tell her everything, Ethan. *She will reveal the hidden like a panther leaping on its prey, seeking what is veiled in the old taverns of the elders. Her gift to you: higher learning, higher purpose, higher education.* Nora will be quick with her lessons. Listen carefully. Time accelerates after the convergence of the 11:11.

"What? So, Nora is going to be okay?" I fidget, uneasily.

"Ethan, you and Nora have an exceptional blessed path to discover. Your *soul agreement* exists for the purpose of completing higher obligations, not just for the two of you, but also for other kindred souls. The *rings of soul agreements* continue living for many lifetimes for many reasons. This is considered to be one of the strongest energetic frameworks within a spiritual community. Soul mates can come back as husband and wife, brother and sister, parent and child, or rescuing neighbors. When there are two or more gathered within the same sphere of soul agreements, the effects of higher thinking creates collective shifts in consciousness. New ways of thinking becomes a *New Age of Information.* An explosion of new information creates a new reality, allowing humankind to welcome progress into the collective consciousness mainstream.

"Do you follow me?"

"I'm trying. I really am."

"If humanity used this energy of like-minded thought for the betterment of mankind, rather than for self gain, they would begin to grasp the teachings sent to us from its greatest teachers. Teachings from the Christ Man, the Shaman, Hopi, and Buddhist priest are but a few blueprints for mankind to learn by. Yet somehow, humanity never goes forth with its lessons. Mankind continues to traverse the same path of fear-based thinking, because man always *wants more stuff,* therefore creating *more lack* in his life. The very thing man selfishly pursues is the very thing that creates his downfall. Ethan, rather than coming from a place of gratitude, man continually selects the same overture. It is this one elemental thought that dissolves the spiritual evolution of man. It is *greed.*"

My eyes wander, catching a squirrel sitting on the window ledge. I've never heard a single person speak like this. And I feel something stirring inside of me. What Brussels says rings true in a way. Greed makes me feel selfish, and no doubt I can think of times in my life when it has motivated me to make certain decisions, decisions that haven't always played out the way I wanted them to. I have certainly felt lack in my life recently. But I *do* have things to be thankful for. Somehow I feel like this conversation is just the thing to warm the emotional iceberg in my brain. Are my thoughts thawing?

"Let me get this straight," I say, "Energy, thoughts, and emotions are like voltage? Everything we think, say, and do has energy behind it? Am I getting this? And we are here to serve a purpose? And greed is what prevents us from moving forward as a collective whole?"

"Indeed, Ethan. Take baby steps every day until you are able to run with the truth. But, yes, you are seeing a new way of thinking. Though these passages are simple, the test is to initiate these thoughts into your daily life. Man cannot recognize the choices he cannot comprehend. Therefore know this. *A lesson only repeats itself until the lesson is learned."*

"I think I now understand what you are saying. Are we addicted as a nation?"

"Indeed. A century ago, land was the compulsion. This next decade oil will become the compulsion. Soon water will replace oil and become the new shiny penny. More! More and more! Never enough! *Rise and Fall* seems to be the reoccurring theme for every empire? Soon highly developed technology will be the new wrench tossed into the equation."

"Oh, shit. You mean technology will be the new addiction?"

Sighing, Brussels leans in, grasping my hands tightly.

"Yes, Ethan. Unfortunately my time runs short. I must leave. However, I mentioned earlier in conversation that you have a choice. You can accept these words, or you can ignore them. Pedro was a simple man whose choice was to acknowledge our conversation. Blind faith brought a poor fisherman to the United States. Imagine the courage it takes to leave your family behind and venture off to a foreign country? Certainly the odds would be against you? Add a harsh winter. Of course, I dare not forget shoes that came from a thrift store. Yes, Ethan, the tattered clothes and shoes you have on, are from a *fisherman.* I would only hope that you wear them proudly. Grow to be a great *fisherman* like Pedro. Never fear crossing turbulent waters and put a little blind faith in your back pocket?"

I look around at my vacant apartment and feel somewhat ashamed of my attitude when Brussels first arrived. My failure to truly recognize the gifts from Cecelia and Mario humbles me. The early afternoon light sifts in from every window, illuminating my understanding that I have many things in this bare room. I don't know who this man is or why he has taken the time to be so kind to me, but a change stirs in me.

"What is your name?"

Brussels stands up with a grin and embraces me. He says his name, but it fades from my memory as quickly as he says it? Should I ask again?

"Never forget these lessons, Ethan. When times are difficult, ask your self, do I honor the shoes of a fisherman? Begin your every day with gratitude. Go to your window and ask God for peace within."

"Okay? Let me put on some warm clothes and I will walk you out."

"Hurry along, Ethan." Brussels moves to the front door quickly, but turns as his hand reaches out for the doorknob. "*Your next teacher looms on the horizon. The lesson of celebrity is a harsh one for her. Watch only. Do not become.*"

"Yes…okay." I look confused. However, I won't question these jigsaw riddles anymore. Instead they will become my guiding light. Fire and ice allowed me to walk across a rickety bridge to the other side of gratitude. Energy, emotions, thoughts bottled with greed and lack are my clues to a lost treasure map outlining new horizons.

Brussels' final words sound prophetic. "*Listen with your eyes, my child, when you walk through the corridors of political influence. All around you will be former kings and queens who have come to balance the laws of power from their past lives. Do not listen to their words; instead watch their feet. Do they wear the shoes of fishermen, or do they wear false crowns? Transformation knocks at your door yet again. I say eleven by eleven is your time of resurrection. The hand of the elder brings comfort.*"

I stare, utterly bewildered.

"Come and wish me a wonderful journey, Ethan."

Brussels reaches for the door and makes his way down the stairwell, calmly examining the stained-glass window. I follow closely, noting his every move, memorizing every moment. Ambulance sirens vibrate in the distance, pedestrians walk past naked elm trees, and crowded buses stop and go. Brussels walks toward the city market and smiles. "*The miracle of Christmas is at your feet. The man you see is the man you have come to know. Never doubt the strength of your compassion, though many may sway you to leave. In his eyes you will see truth. In his eyes you will find you.*"

I watch this tall man make his way toward the busy market. He whistles a familiar tune. I know what it is—"*California Dreaming*" by the *Mamas and the Papas*. How funny. Where is he going? Are there others he wants to share his knowledge with? Do they live nearby?

"Hey!" I yell out. "You forgot to tell me about Mama Cass, and *The Mama's and Papa's?*"

Brussels yells back to me. "What a dear soul *Mama Cass* was." Brussels smiles at me with a wink. "I *will be there when you reach for the light.*"

"Okay, sure, whatever you say, Brussels…Merry Christmas."

Did I expect a different kind of response? I jog past my visitor, clueless to what lies ahead. Instead the spirit of Christmas feels me with self-assurance. The scent of gingerbread from the bakery and fires warming homes makes me think of the new people I have met who have showered me with their kindness. It occurs to me that this is the first time I've smelled fire and not thought of my utter devastation. I turn to whistle at Brussels, but he has disappeared into a maze of shoppers.

Where is he going? Did he hail a cab? Oh well. I will jog around the neighborhood and go to the market.

Rushing back with a few groceries, I climb the stairs and find a legal envelope tacked to my apartment's front door. It's from Cecelia.

"Sorry we missed you. Your phone will be turned on next Tuesday, love Cecelia and Mario." Inside the envelope is another note along with my paycheck. "Ethan, here is some extra cash from all of us at the salon. Merry Christmas! See you in two weeks. Julie called from CBS. She has scheduled an appointment with you to meet at 1 p.m. next Tuesday, at the San Marcus Building, downtown. Hugs and kisses, Mary."

I can feel my confidence slipping away. How can I meet CBS in thrift store clothes? This paycheck will cover only necessities. Hopefully Julie will understand? I reach for Honey and cradle her in my arms.

"We will be okay, Honey."

I put away my groceries and walk around my apartment with Honey in my arms. In each room, I say thank you for whatever occurs to me—what a beautiful city view, a clean and safe home, friends who care about me. The day finishes with me sitting on my living room floor, Honey in my lap. "Thank you God for my new beginnings."

***

Cold air snaps through the vacant apartment, magnifying a clinking sound that seems to bounce off the window ledge alerting me to open my eyes. Honey yawns, still buried in a warm pillow, as I reach for my watch. Clink. Clink. Clink. What is that tapping sound? Where is it coming from? Rising up from my makeshift bed, I go to the window. Clink. Clink. An icy snow descends on the building and bare streets.

Pale clouds block the sun, and Christmas morning feels complete. The windows are full of frost, and snow begins to paint the neighborhood white.

My visit with Brussels is foremost on my mind, and I say thank you for waking up to this transformed morning, or should I say transformed me? First things first, a shower, food, and figuring out how to spend this day will be my priorities. Honey walks along behind me, following me to the bathroom, where she perches on top of the old-fashioned toilet seat. The hot water streams from the showerhead and feels heavenly. Breakfast will consist of leftover tea and warm cereal with raisins and bananas, sprinkled with cinnamon. Brussels' dishes sit in my glass-paned cabinets, as do the pots and pans he brought. I put on Papa's clothes, his worn shoes that squeak on my floors, and my new red sweat shirt. They fit as best as possible—what a lovely Christmas gift.

Standing by the window, still damp and watching the snow flurries, I honor the man whose gifts could not have come at a better moment. Thoughts of gratitude continue inside me, only to be interrupted by a nagging thought to take a drive and explore my new neighborhood. I listen to this inner voice without delay. What better time than now to uncover the holiday spirit in my area?

"Stay here, Honey. I'll be back shortly." But her attention is captured by a bird signing on an Elm tree branch.

The old Toyota barely starts but slowly crawls forward as I tap the accelerator. My windows are icy and I wait for the heat to melt them. I close my eyes for a moment, concentrating on which way to go. Ah, that street with all the lights and decorations displayed in yards the size of football fields is my clue. I feel absolutely fascinated by this simple journey I'm about to take, and each home fills me with delight. Santa

Clauses and elves and giant snowmen seem slightly incongruous in front of homes with carefully selected sandstone driveways and massive wooden doors. Holly winds around gas lanterns that are accented with red bows, and giant Christmas wreathes that cost more than my car, hang in windows. Through French windows I can see gilded and heavily ornamented Christmas trees. Who lives in these houses? What feasts will be served today?

I continue north, weaving in and out of streets lined with houses that become larger in size with each passing block. I turn on the radio, rolling the knob for hits of Christmas past. Static rock and roll dominates the airwaves this morning, so I pull over and find a station with Perry Como and Andy Williams singing songs of Christmas cheer. This works for a while, but I long for something a little more youthful. I absentmindedly twiddle the knob as I drive. Suddenly, "*All the leaves are brown, and the sky is gray; I've been for a walk on a winter's day,*" resonates from the radio. Is it coincidence that Brussels was whistling this tune as he walked away from me? An old man rakes leaves, stashing his clippings in garbage bags. Before him is a large stone cathedral, Christ the King Catholic Church. Jaguars, Mercedes, and BMWs congest the church's parking lot, and worshippers file up the stone steps and through the massive, carved wood doors in their Sunday best. Should I go inside? No, I better drive on and forget this coincidence? But "*California Dreaming*" plays on with its' haunting words—"*Stopped into a church, I passed along the way; Well, I got down on my knees and I pretend to pray.*"

Just as I pull in front of the church, my Toyota stalls. Immediately someone begins to honk behind me. Because of the icy streets, they can't pass me. "Oh, shit" I whisper, as I try to restart the car. Finally it lurches forward, and I land a spot near the entrance of the church.

"Okay, Mr. Nice Christian Man," I say to the honker, "You win." I pull in listening to the song's finale: *"You know the preacher liked the cold. He knows I'm going to stay. California Dreaming', on such a winter's day."*

Shining brass doorknobs on the heavy oak doors catch my eye as I wander through the church's doors. Beautiful marble floors are topped by ornate pews, and men in dark Armani suits and women in Ralph Lauren dresses and hats, talk quietly with each other. High end hairdressers, personal shoppers, chauffeurs, and various other professionals of the rich, were encouraged to disburse special attention to the parishioners attending today's High Mass. Statues of saints whose names I recall from Catholic school stare into the rectory, while white flower-and-holly arrangements with enormous red bows line the altar. Marble pillars stand like massive trees and enormous crystal chandeliers hang from copestone ceilings. The wealth in this room is intimidating.

"Sir, follow me." A balding usher in a dark-gray suit nudges my elbow.

"That's okay. I am just looking." Now I feel stupid. What am I doing? Buying a sweater from J.C. Penney? "I'll stay here. Thank you."

'Sir, you can't stand here in the entranceway. Come with me." The usher grabs my elbow securely. "Follow me."

Struggling with as much class as I can muster, I tell him I will stay right where I am in a slightly louder tone of voice. Hats of all sizes, suits fragrant with cologne, and a pew of nuns rotate in sequence. Curious eyes see a young man dressed in a large red sweat shirt, a pair of blue jeans that hang inches below sea level, and a pair of Papa's ragged shoes. In the distance I see another usher motioning to my usher to bring me forward immediately. The priest's motions the usher to escort me to the front.

This can't be happening to me? Every face is looking my way. I don't know how to leave without creating a scene? I feel humiliated. The usher leads me by the elbow to the front of the sanctuary. The only sound that can be heard is coming from Papa's shoes squeaking on the newly polished marble floor. This is awful. What do I do?

My personal usher guides me to a pew at the same moment that every head turns to the back of the church to witness a new arrival. I turn to see a homeless man entering the cathedral, clad in clothes that aren't unlike what I'm wearing. Yet again, Mass is delayed, as the balding usher darts to the back of the church. Every person, including me, takes in this decrepit-looking old man. He wears a battered hat, which he immediately grasps in his hands, and an old, holey tweed suit and limps forward with as much strength as he can muster. The usher escorts the bearded old man to the pew in front of me.

Every man, woman, and child gazes at the two of us. I imagine they're wondering if we know each other. A stout woman to the right of the homeless man reaches for her purse and scoots down the aisle, making room for him. The man on my right abruptly copies the same movement as I kneel down to whisper the "Hail Mary." Recalling my Catholic teachings I then begin silently reciting the Act of Contrition. The priest's glance rests upon me and the homeless man in front.

Hands folded in prayer position, the old man kneels down. The entire congregation then stands tall. We both remain on our knees.

"*The Lord Be With You,*" says the priest.

"And also with you," the congregation responds.

"God, our Father, Lord of the world, we thank you that through your son you have called us into the fellowship of your Universal Church. Hear our prayers today."

"Amen."

Oblivious to the Catholic ritual of up and down, the old man recites his own prayer, tears streaming down his withered face. Hands wrought with adversity, the man clings tightly to an old rosary that has witnessed many harsh days. His words are audible only to me. "God, why did you take my only friend away?" The priest begins his sermon, speaks of the brokenhearted and aiding those in need. My heart weighs heavy as tears stream down my cheeks, and the man in front of me breaks down. Somewhere between the present and the past, mankind has neglected to shine some mercy his way. The lady in heavy perfume moves further away from the old man, turning her head with an expression of repugnance on her face. The old man's plea to God reduces me to a quivering state, and tears wash down our faces in complete synchronicity.

I reach inside my large jeans and discover the cash that the salon gave me for my hardship. I reach over and quickly place my folded cash inside his hat while he bows his weary face on his hands. Brussels' riddle suddenly comes into my mind: *The man you see is the man you have come to know. Never doubt the strength of your compassion, though many may sway you to leave. In his eyes you will see truth. In his eyes you will find you.*

As the final words of the sermon come down from the altar, every person stands to face the priest. Completely consumed with my own fears, I immediately realize that the old man may turn around and notice my donation. Avoiding another display of public attention is first on my mind, so I turn to make my escape before the communion procession begins. The old man reaches for his hat and makes his exit at the same time as me. Standing face-to-face, tear-to-tear, the old man opens his hat to place it on his head and notices the cash neatly tucked inside it.

"Oh, my God, my dear God," he says. "Oh, my God, it's a miracle!!"

His cries of joy render me helpless to leave now, as the church members make their way to the communion altar. The elderly man turns around to meet the eyes of an annoyed priest and shouts, "Merry Christmas. God just gave me a miracle!"

I run out the front doors just as someone taps my arm.

"You forgot something, young man."

Trembling from the cold, or from realizing Brussels prediction was spot on, I turn to face a young nun.

"You forgot your keys." She hands me my keys along with a candle. "Please take this candle and light it tonight. Kindness deserves kindness."

I stare with disbelief, wiping tears from my eyes. "What are you talking about?"

"I saw everything. Please take this candle from the Sisters of Hope."

Her face is young, her smile gentle. She hands me a vanilla votive. "Blessed are those who bless others. Have a Merry Christmas, young man."

"What is your name?" I ask.

"Sister Theresa. What is your name?"

"Peter, Ethan Michaels. My friends call me, Ethan."

"What a beautiful name. Thank you, Ethan. You brought the *miracle of hope* for someone in need. God bless you."

Sister Theresa goes back into the church, her black shroud rustling. She turns and waves good-bye to me, as the doors close behind her.

I start my engine and wait patiently for the heat to circulate throughout the car. Church bells have begun to chime as people start to exit the cathedral. I am determined to find a radio station that plays traditional Christmas music. Within moments, Johnny Mathis' angelic voice dominates the airwaves. A car door slams beside me, breaking my moment of glee. The honking impatient driver from this morning glares into my foggy glass windows, determined to be first in line to exit. Sometime it is best to let negative energy dissipate. Ah, Brussels would be so proud. Johnny sings a Christmas lullaby as heat finds it way to my feet.

I drive away from the cathedral, looking to my rearview mirror to make sure that Mr. Nice Christian Man has passed me. I watch the happy faces of the churchgoers as they chat animatedly with their friends and families. As I stop at a crosswalk, the homeless man makes his way across the street. I reach for the driver's window, roll it down, and shout, "Merry Christmas!"

"Thank you, sir. Have a Merry Christmas and Happy New Year!"

The old man smiles as he disappears into a life that I would have viewed with incomplete eyes, before my visit from Brussels that is. In one brief instant, a simple act made a homeless man find hope. I feel proud of myself for bringing joy to someone who has so little, and in some small way I feel that maybe I am *thanking* those that have helped me through such a hard time. Though the old man will never know where his special gift came from, all that matters is that it came from pure intention—*kindness*.

I drive forward, thinking of those men and women whose lives have been marked by different circumstances. *We are each others teachers.* Learning to appreciate that Brussels' riddles come precisely when I need them is something I can count on. Often, reality is fraught with insecurity. My lesson of blind faith becomes my Christmas gift from a white-haired old man who has taken the time to teach me about gratitude. Today I will begin to honor his words. I could easily be that homeless man, hanging on by a thread of despair. I look at the roads lined with so many different trees. Oak, elm, and sycamore trees decorate the streets that bring me back to my apartment. Each tree has a purpose. Each house has its own example of circumstance inside. So do all of us.

I dart up the apartment's steps anxious to demonstrate this feeling of love in my new place of residence. Barren sycamore trees greet my view as I race up the stairwell. The stained-glass window seems more colorful today than usual. At the top of the stairs is a large brown box shoved against my door. The note reads: "Open Tuesday Morning. PS: Remember to open Tuesday morning only." There is no name. Meowing through the other side is Honey. I'm sure she is anxious to hear about my journey. "I'm coming, Honey." Who would have sent such a large box? It feels like a TV. No one would buy me a TV for Christmas. Honey purrs around my legs, excited to see me. I pick her up and press her close to my face. "Merry Christmas, Honey." I use all my strength to place the box inside my apartment and stare at the note.

Lighting the vanilla candle, I make my way to the kitchen. Canned cat food for Honey, and tuna garnished with pork and beans are on the holiday menu. I look out the living room window and watch the snow come down. Blue-violet clouds on the horizon add more color to the gray skies. Traffic has picked up, along with kids playing in the park across the street. Parents' faces shine under the streetlights, as the work of children progresses: throwing snowballs, making snow angels, and rolling balls into snowmen. I watch my Christmas candle illuminate my bare room. Tuesday morning must be a special day? But so is today. I go to my living room window, stare at the snowy streets below, and quietly whisper.

"I am grateful for all those wonderful things that have come my way."

"In all things, give thanks."
Thessalonians 5:18

Resurrection

Part II

Flat line

Chapter 9

"**Mr. Michaels,** are you okay? Can you hear me? Are you in pain?" Shadowy figures in blue hospital scrubs move in and out. I can feel someone breathing on my face. Conversations I can't follow take place over me. Am I on a gurney? Someone counts to three, and gloved hands that feel dry on my skin, lift me. Two faces wearing oversized glasses bend close to my face. I look down. The front of my gown is dark red. Why? An excruciating abdominal pain strikes my left side. Nurses seem anxious, their faces wrinkled in patterns of distress and immediacy. Time pushes forward with every second, yet the medical staff seems frozen.

"Nurse, where is Doctor Johnson? Who lanced these lesions on Mr. Michaels' butt? How much blood has he lost?"

All of a sudden the figures begin to panic. A pounding urgency fills my brain and I can hear a mysterious dripping sound.

"How long has this patient been sitting in the emergency waiting room?" says a nurse?

A loud knock disturbs me. My sheets are soaked from perspiration and feel cold. I touch my face and my hand slips across my forehead, slippery and wet. Another knock alerts me. Honey frees herself from my hold and meows quietly. Another knock more than concerns me, stronger this time, demanding my attention.

"It was just a dream," I repeat quietly. "It was just a dream."

"Southwestern Bell," a voice shouts. "Anyone home in there?"

"Just a moment," I shout back. "Hold on. I'll be right there."

I throw a pair of jeans on and race to the front door. A frowning telephone repairman stands in the hallway.

"What are you doing here?" I ask, still groggy and disoriented.

"Are you Ethan Michaels? Is this apartment 205?"

"Yes."

"I'm here to install phone service today. If this is a mistake, I can reschedule," he says, rushed as he examines his clipboard.

"Oh yeah, I'm sorry. I forgot today is Tuesday. Come on in."

The repairman adjusts his belt and tucks the clipboard under his arm.

"Make yourself at home. I need to clean up. The telephone jacks are in the living room and hallway."

Still half asleep and disturbed from my dream, I make my way to the bathroom. A sharp pain in my left abdomen stops me in my path, and I flash back on the bloodied hospital gown in my dream. I rinse my face with cold water and catch a glimpse of Honey in the mirror. She sits on the bed, smelling the sheets.

"What are you doing, Honey?" She never looks up. Perhaps she has found a roach. Oh god, not that again.

"Oh, shit. Where did this blood come from?"

The white sheets are stained with a circle of blood about the size of my hand. I fetch a small towel from the bathroom and try to dab the sheets clean. The technician walks freely throughout the apartment, unaware of my dilemma.

"Mr. Michaels, I'm going outside to check on the phone lines. Your hallway jack is not operational."

"Sure," I say, relieved that he is leaving me alone. "Make yourself at home."

I see my face in the medicine cabinet mirror, my mind runs riot with anxiety. Is this my blood? If it is, where did it come from? Never mind, I don't have time for this.

A shower, then cereal and juice will begin my day. I stare at the enormous box and walk toward the front door. Now is as good time as any to find out what this holiday mystery holds for me. I can barely move the box into my vacant living room. Cutting through the layers of tape that cover it, I wonder who could have done such a thing. As I pull back the top flaps, I feel humbled. Inside my gift box are dozen thoughts of love. Socks and two pair of shoes complement sweaters and slacks. A queen-size blue electric blanket rests on new sheets and a bedspread. Button-down shirts lay next to colorful ties. Pajamas and underwear are still in sealed plastic covers. New slippers match a gray flannel bathrobe. I sit on my floor, surrounded by so many gifts. Taken by surprise, I find an envelope securely taped to a telephone answer machine. It reads:

"Merry Christmas!! We hope you enjoy this gift? Signed; the salon and your clients."

"Looks like someone is having a late Christmas?"

The technician walks into my apartment, his utility belt hangs loosely on his torso.

"Yeah, it looks that way. Here is my new telephone and answer machine."

While handing my phone to the tech, I notice another envelope at the bottom of the box. It is a gift certificate from the White Elephant Antique store.

Perplexed by yet another mystery, I sit in the middle of my vacant living room staring at my new belongings. If Brussels were here, he could see how thankful I am.

"Sign here, Mr. Michaels."

The technician hands me a yellow receipt, then calls out to me as he walks out the door.

"Your new telephone number is on the purchase order. I will call you in a few seconds to verify."

"Thanks," I say, enthusiastically. "Have a good day."

***

Umbrellas and raincoats line downtown's busy streets. Cab drivers fight rush-hour traffic as buses filled to capacity lurch down the street like elephants. Tall buildings rise above the trees. Various venders hustle their goods along the curb while ordinary people go inside to meet their daily jobs. Windshield wipers on my car tackle the rainy downpour as I search for the CBS Complex. Parking lots on every corner advertise a variety of day rates. I look for an empty lot. A man wearing a yellow raincoat with newspaper in hand waves me down.

"Looking for a parking space?" he shouts.

I roll my creaky window down and shout back. "Yes, how much per hour?"

He comes to my window with cash wadded in his fist. "Its five dollars for a half day, and it will be nine dollars for a full day."

"Here's five dollars." I hand the attendant my keys as he jots down my license plate. "Do you know where the CBS Complex is?"

Impatient brown eyes frown at me, tired of the frigid rain. "Over there."

I take a quick glance at the passenger seat before I race across the slippery street. Papa's shoes lie inside a cardboard box. I wonder if he walked these same winter streets hoping to meet his destiny. Who is this mysterious woman named Julie at CBS? How does she know me? Perhaps Papa's lucky shoes will bring me a fairy-tale ending? I must stop this thousand and one questionnaire that dominates my thoughts. Okay, Ethan. Get your thoughts and emotions in order, I repeat in my head. The patter of rain stops as I enter revolving doors.

A hushed silence commands the lobby floor, making one forget the sounds of the city. Heavily waxed parquet floors echo my footsteps.

Gold elevator doors open and close, releasing businessmen wearing unadventurous dark suits and reading folded copies of the *Wall Street Journal* as they find their way to their office suites. An arrangement of purple tulips sits in the middle of a contemporary glass console next to a tasteful sign-in sheet. Hot coffee, freshly squeezed orange juice and muffins disappear from a matching glass table opposite. As employees exit through the elevator doors, new arrivals take their places. Colognes and perfumes fill the crowded cabin as we speed to the top floors. Hands of all shapes and sizes play tic-tac-toe on the elevator's floor panel.

"Would someone push 21 please," a nameless voice whispers.

An older woman dowses herself with cheap perfume right before she enters the elevator. Everyone's eyes are immediately drawn to the floor. A slightly exaggerated gasping sound behind the perfumed lady elicits a snicker. More coughs. Then throat clearing. Add a fake sneeze. Behind the lady, a portly man grabs his neck as if he is dying from perfume affixation. They all suppress their laughter. Bing! The doors open, and several people exit wearing grateful expressions. A lady enters wearing a tasteful business suit and immediately pushes the next floor. Eager hands also push the button for floor 22. Doors slide open and a mass exodus of the intoxicated stammer out for fresh air. I watch the lady reach in her purse and add more perfume just as the elevator makes its final approach. Bing! A view of a busy newsroom already in progress with today's headlines drowns me with nervousness. We both exit.

"Good morning, Mrs. Sharp." The lady never acknowledges the polite greetings. Instead, she disappears into the frantic buzz of the room; applying blood-red lip color to her mouth.

"Can I help you?" asks a sweet voice.

"Uh, I, uh, yes, I have an appointment with Julie Gautier."

"What's your name?" The receptionist flips through a heavily penciled daily calendar.

"One o'clock. I mean, uh, Ethan Michaels." I can feel my stomach twisting with embarrassment.

"Mr. Michaels, your appointment is scheduled for—"

"Hi, Ethan, do you remember me?"

A blonde, petite woman wearing a tailored Ralph Lauren red-and-blue pinstripe suit extends her hand. "Okay, I guess not? You helped me one busy Saturday morning with a cosmetic purchase. I asked you a million questions, and you volunteered your makeup services free of charge." Julie's eyes wait for my recollection.

"Um, maybe, let me think a moment. I try to help a lot of clients on Saturdays. Oh, I think I remember you?" My stomach growls louder than a hungry lion.

"Well, you're not supposed to be here until this afternoon, but I was just about to call you to ask you to come in earlier. Mark will be leaving on assignment for D.C. and won't be able to see you until weeks from now. I have had to call, cancel and reschedule you due to my hectic schedule. Follow me."

Julie leads me down a hallway as I ponder whether I should have told her of the events of my recent past. Men in pressed shirts wearing an assortment of conventional ties circle the newsroom shouting cryptic fragments of conversation that only their ears appreciate. Assistants on busy typewriters pound away at lightning speed. Telephones continually ring. Faces stamped with pressure skate in front of Julie, avoiding a collision course that would certainly scream termination. A cloud of cigarette smoke looms throughout the office. Glass windows give way to pristine views of the entire city. Inside a small office, a young man talks impatiently on his phone, propped in a chair that is swiveled toward the magnificent view.

"Ethan, would you like a bagel and some juice? Wait here for Mark. He'll be off the phone in a sec." Julie leaves the room.

Jitteriness loops inside my stomach like an airplane waiting for clearance to land on the runway. The noise from the busy staff outside the room seems to magnify my nervousness. What am I doing here? Maybe they want to offer me a position as a staff writer? Why would they do that? What is Julie thinking? Who is this man, and why is he so unaware of my presence in his office? My hands begin to sweat and confidence runs out the bottom of my feet. An anonymous intercom voice speaks through the telephone.

"Mark? Mark! The chief editor from the *Washington Post* is on line three, and Lesley Stahl is still holding."

Oh shit. I repeat silently in my head. Lesley Stahl and the editor from the *Post*—I am in the wrong room. Nerves suck the moisture from my mouth, prompting a silent cough. Good. He didn't hear me.

"Ethan, what are you doing standing there?"

Julie hands me a bagel with cream cheese and orange juice.

"For goodness sakes, sit down. Mark, get off the phone now," Julie demands. Without hesitation, she picks up the blinking line.

"Who is holding? Oh? Hello, Lesley. Mark is on another call, of course, and has one holding. And we're about to go into a meeting. Where are you? D.C.? He'll have to call you back." Julie places her hand over the receiver. "Ethan you don't have to sit by the door. Come sit here." She points to a chair in front of Mark's desk and picks up the next call. "Who is holding? Oh, well, they must have got tired of holding."

Mark hangs up the phone and immediately greets me.

"What a pleasure it is to meet you, Ethan. Julie has told me great things about you. Sorry for the crappy weather, but hey, it could be worse. You could be in New York where it's snowing and 14 degrees."

I stand up and extend a handshake to Mark, feeling like I may have met a new friend. His warmth and enthusiasm dissipates my worry.

"Thanks for taking the time from your busy schedule to meet with me."

"It's my pleasure. By the way, the call on line three was the chief editor of the *Washington Post.*"

Julie smiles and winks at Mark. "Ethan, the reason we called you in was to conduct an interview with you."

"Oh, I don't have any journalism experience." I say nervously. "Although I've been told I should become a writer, I probably won't qualify for the position. I do enjoy reading the *New York Times* editorial section, if my schedule permits. I thought about keeping a journal? What about you? Do you write?" Realizing I have lost control of my tongue, I shut up. Both Mark and Julie stare at me.

"Oh, you're funny? Good. You'll need to be." Mark shuffles through his pile of papers. "Julie, does Ethan know why we called this interview?"

Julie sits down and smiles.

"Ethan, the 1984 GOP convention is being held in Dallas, and we're looking for a chief makeup artist for network personalities. This would entail long hours and would require a low-key personality to be in the anchor room working alongside Dan Rather and Lesley Stahl. Diane Sawyer is the hottest anchor with CBS, and she'll need an on-camera makeup artist for various interviews. Of course, we are conducting other interviews across America for this position. I have watched you work at the salon for many months and have been impressed with your one-on-one client skills"

"Um, well, gosh. I'm flattered, but I want to focus on becoming a special effects make-up artist in film. I don't think I would be right for this." I hear these words tumble off my lips and want to kick myself. What am I doing?

Julie zooms in closer to my chair, eyes wide with inquisitiveness. "Ethan, we have already interviewed 60 makeup artists across the nation. Not one choice comes to mind except you and a lady in San Francisco. I strongly suggest you consider this. Do you know what this will do for your television career? Are you aware that joining the union will be necessary if you become a special effects make-up artist?"

"Apparently not," I say, foolishly.

"Once approved by the network and given a pass by security clearance, you will be permitted to work with many CBS personalities." Julie leans back in her chair and looks at Mark.

"Ethan, you will get the chance...no let me correct that...the privilege to work with Dan Rather, Diane Sawyer, and Lesley Stahl." Mark folds his hands patiently on his desk, grabs a pen and pad, and begins to write something down.

Julie leans into me, softly stroking her hair. "Bob Schieffer and Walter Cronkite will be there as well. Starting in the fall we have two CBS specials lined up. One of those morning shows will pay tribute to Academy Award–winner Greer Garson"

My eyes widen and my throat has become even drier. I stare blankly at these two individuals and am speechless. "You guys are serious?"

"Absolutely," Mark says, handing me the piece of paper that he has now folded in half. He presses the intercom button calling the nameless voice. "Can you have Mrs. Sharp come in my office please?"

Still trying to overcome my nervousness, I stammer, "Jody, I uh, I mean Julie. I don't know what to say. Wow! Uh—"

Before I can finish my stammer, a fragrance I am familiar with glides past me. Holding an assortment of papers and an envelope is the perfumed woman from the elevator.

"Hello. I'm Erma Sharp." The lady with blood-red lips stares through me. "What is your name? I don't think I got it while in the elevator."

"No, you didn't." My joy slips away. Maybe she'll realize that I wasn't one of the people making fun of her in the elevator.

"My name is Ethan. How is your day going so far?" I take the envelope she is thrusting toward me.

Julie and Mark watch the exchange between Mrs. Sharp and me. Not sure where this charade is going, I regain my composure. She moves closer in and winks at me.

"What a lovely gentleman you are for asking how my day is going. Fill these papers out and give them to me before you leave." She smiles and walks out of the office.

"Ethan, Mrs. Sharp has been with CBS for 25 years. She is Mark's personal secretary. If you need something and I'm not here, ask for her. Now, if you're interested, we'd like you to complete these papers, and we will start the process. But that's only if you're interested."

"Of course I... thank you both."

"Ethan, Mrs. Sharp or I will contact you within the next several weeks. Assuming all goes well, I think you ought to know that Ms. Sawyer prefers to work with female makeup artists. So please be aware of that when you meet her." Julie motions to Mark that our meeting is over.

Mark shuffles papers in his briefcase and looks up at me. "Ethan, I hope this works out. We'll be in touch with you." He bids good-bye to Julie and I and runs out the door.

Julie extends her hand and smiles. "Thanks for coming in, Ethan." She walks me to an empty office and points me to a chair. "You can put the papers on Mrs. Sharp's desk when you finish. Oh, I forgot to mention, I will make sure that you are accepted into the union." And with that she hustles down the bustling hallway.

Down the elevators and out the building, I feel a sense of luck. On the street, I reach inside my pocket for my parking ticket. A small piece of paper from Mark shows a hefty salary. Perhaps CBS is what Brussels was referring to, in terms of my new journey? Sunlight peers through the downtown skyline, promising a beautiful day. Pedestrians in business attire fill the city streets, and smells of pizza and hot dogs from sidewalk stands compete with bus fumes. A window cleaner clings to his pulley, unaware of the hustle below his feet. I shuffle my pockets hoping to find a quarter to call Nora.

"Richard, its Ethan Michaels. I'm calling for Nora. How is she doing?"

A strong cough trembles through the phone. "I'm on my way to the hospital to bring her home." A slight hesitation in his voice leads me to wonder what he is not sharing. Would I be out of line to ask or should I let him volunteer?

"I hope everything is okay?"

"Ethan, why don't you call a little later? See if Nora is up to conversation. Okay? I'll tell her you called."

What is he not telling me? It must be hard for a man to be married to such a beautiful woman as Nora. With all of her admirers, Richard seems to take it all in stride.

"Please tell her I have great news and can't wait to share. Have a good day, Richard."

I reach for another quarter, call Mary, and watch the sun play peek-a-boo with the clouds. The skyscrapers reflect the city's radiant light. An unrecognizable voice softy answers the phone.

"Is Mary there?" I ask.

"One moment please. Mary the phone is for you. Hold on for a second." The receiver is muffled and a familiar voice answers. "Hello."

"Mary, its Ethan, I…"

"Ethan, I was about to come over to your new place." Mary says with urgency.

"That is so nice—"

"Ethan, can you rush over to MPS Studios? Now! The makeup artist for *PM Magazine* is sick, and they need a replacement right away. They're taping a new segment for next week's show."

"You're kidding? What's the address? Who's the contact?' I ask.

"Someone named, Leeza Gibbons. I'll call the studio now. Do you know Regal Avenue?"

"Yes I do. I know where it is. I'm on my way. Tell them I have to go to the salon and get my bag, and I'll be there in 20 minutes." The phone clicks.

Rushing traffic and busy intersections claim the drive. I walk into a studio of organized confusion. Cables snaking along the floor lead to a soundstage where the production crew huddles in small groups over cameras and lights. The cameras surround a set that is decorated with club chairs and fake plants. A thin woman in a black-and-white T-shirt rushes to the crewmembers and speaks in a commanding tone. "Hurry" and "Now," she says.

She turns in my direction and yells. "Are you the replacement?"

"Uh, well…Mary told me to—"

"Get over here. What's your name? Oh, never mind. Sound, can you mic him now?"

What the hell is going on? What am I supposed to do? Who are these people? I start to feel confused, but something tells me to suck it up.

"Lady, what do you want me to do?"

"What do you mean?" Her bloodshot eyeballs stop wandering and focus on me. "Oh, for god's sake, did anyone clue this guy on why he is here? Well?"

A man on my right extends his hand. "My name is David. Follow my lead." A blonde woman with a classically beautiful face smiles at me. "This is Leeza," says David.

"Hi, I'm Leeza. Thanks for getting here so quickly. We'll do a brief walk-through."

"Leeza, David, on set. You too," the slim woman says.

Genuine chemistry ignites between both hosts of *PM Magazine*. Their silky dialogue becomes a fluid expression of perfection. I take note of their ease with the camera while following each melodious step. I can do this. Cameras disappear from my view, as does the production crew. Feelings of familiarity settle in, their charisma goes on autopilot, and I begin to dance the waltz of on-camera presence. Apparently luck has called my name as we finish the last take. I feel like an understudy sliding in on opening night to receive my first standing ovation.

"We got it. Great job, you guys," a voice shouts from behind the camera.

David extends his hand and congratulates me on a job well done. Leeza smiles and is immediately surrounded by her assistants. This day has been astonishing, but a hungry cat at home needs my attention. Before leaving I rush to the bathroom, hoping to relieve a sudden pain in my abdomen.

"Great, Ethan. You did a wonderful job. This show will air next Tuesday at 6:30 p.m." David shouts to the bathroom door. I huddle near the washbasin grabbing my left side. I must have food poisoning from the cream cheese and bagel? Maybe I should take some more pain pills. Is that blood on my slacks?

***

Humidity hangs heavily on the azaleas as the remains of the red blossoms dangle loosely before the true summer heat arrives. An abundance of yellow-and-white butterflies glide through the courtyard. I sing praises for the warm skies. Sycamore trees crammed with green obscure my view of the city. Blue jays chitchat loudly, warning the other birds that nuisance is the name of their game. A letter from Mario and Cecelia joyously relates their happy times in Mexico and how anxious they are to visit me. In less than 48 hours, CBS's coverage of the GOP convention will begin. My nervous thoughts move like a tennis match inside my head. Did I make the right choice to accept this position? Surely this decision will speed my special effects career along rather than chain me to politician's egos and empty promises? I wonder if Brussels will visit soon.

"Hey, Nora, it's Ethan. How are you feeling today?" I look at my watch and wonder if I can beat the traffic to her house.

"Are you coming out today?" Nora's voice shines on the other end.

"I'm on my way. Depending on traffic, I could be there in 35 minutes."

"Great, honey. Maybe you can help me with this wig. You would think by now that my damn hair would start to grow. Our appointment with Madame Rosario is at 7:30 p.m. Let's go grab a bite to eat and then we can go to her house."

"See you in a few."

I hang up, swallow a round of pain pills, and jump in my new car. Nora's recovery from surgery seems like yesterday. Ironically, it was her tapping at heaven's door that made solid choices for us both. Leaving the salon and going freelance with CBS was a good decision. Nora's pilgrimage to decode Brussels' conversations in St. Thomas has become her mission. Madame Rosario comes highly recommended, but will she be able to shed light on who Brussels is? Nora seems confident with this psychic, but like many before her, it leads us down a path of nowhere. "Each step we take will get us closer to understanding Brussels' messages," Nora says, continually. I can only hope.

I turn off the car engine and stare through the passenger window. Elaborate weeping willows surround a Spanish stucco mansion. I stride up the walkway, past impeccably landscaped flowerbeds, to the two colossal front doors and see Nora standing in the doorway wearing a giant smile. I pretend not to notice her thin hair.

"I guess the traffic must have been heavy, Ethan? We won't have time to go to dinner. Come on in. I'll make us a sandwich."

Nora leads me through the front entryway. The airy rooms are made more so by the high ceilings. On the taupe-colored walls are paintings and antique tapestries. Off-white shutters cover the windowpanes, allowing enough brightness to illuminate the entire house with daylight. Crystal vases filled with flowers mingle with bronze statues. Nora escorts me down a wide hallway that leads us to the conversation room. Blue Willow pottery is displayed on beautiful walnut consoles that accent this formal room. Neatly tucked away in a corner of the parlor stands a baby grand piano with a swatch of sunlight splayed across its top and a bronze vase filled with fresh flowers. A Persian rug lies underneath a cast-iron coffee table with claw legs. On it sits an ornate silver tea set on a matching silver tray. Books filled with exquisite collectibles are stacked next to a small bud vase containing a single miniature yellow rose. Nora's home speaks volumes about her character.

"Have a seat, Ethan. Can I get you something to drink?"

"Yes. A soda will do."

Nora whisks away into her French provincial kitchen and returns with two Coca-Colas. "Would you like a lemon with your soft drink?

Oh, enough with the small talk. Aren't you excited to see Madame Rosario?"

"Well, uh—" Nora scoots back into the kitchen. The crashing of pots and pans allows me a moment to gather my thoughts. "Perhaps this clairvoyant will be better than the last few?" I say quietly.

Another crash of pans seizes my attention. "Oops!" I can hear Nora chuckling. Cabinet doors and the bang of a refrigerator door closing, add to the sound of flatware falling onto the floor. "Don't worry; it's just a silly accident."

Seconds later, Nora carries a rattan serving tray topped with a small white flower. Pressed linen napkins and covered dishes conceal the banquet. Complementing my secret dinner is an ornate serving bowl filled with potato chips.

"Well?"

Nora's smile captivates me. She places the tray in front of me and waits for my approval. Looking up, she offers a quiet prayer. Her words catch my attention.

"God, I hope Ethan enjoys this dish as much as I enjoy the second chance you have given me. Amen."

I enthusiastically lift the lids of the silver bowls, expecting something marvelous. Stacks of white bread oozing with strawberry jam are packed to overkill with crunchy peanut butter. I look up at Nora as she laughs.

"Hurry up, Ethan. We have to get a move on," she grins, munching on her potato chips. "Don't forget to take your pills."

"I already took mine. What about you?" Nora nods, but I sense the obstacles she must face daily are much more challenging than mine.

Nora finishes her half-eaten sandwich and returns to the kitchen with her plate. "I'm going to put on a hat and freshen up my makeup. Hurry up, darling. I'll meet you outside by the garage.

"Okay, Nora."

Thick balmy air sticks to our clothes as we make our way into Richard's restored 1965 yellow Cadillac Fleetwood 60. Heavy doors with gleaming wood panels and individual curved ashtrays that overflow with cigarettes make the car feel like a beloved toy. Restored to perfection, perforated, tan leather cushions extend from the driver's seat to the passenger's side. A thin chrome steering wheel highlights a sleek dashboard that proudly displays an elaborate speedometer. Nora puts the key into the ignition and navigates this large car out of the driveway. One sturdy hand applies a coat of lip color, while the other shifts the automatic column.

"Ethan, we have less than twenty minutes to get to the other side of town."

"Nora, are you sure about this meeting? I would much rather spend time learning about numerology with you." She taps me gently on the hand. "Mrs. Briggs tells me that Madame Rosario is amazing. She told her that her husband was coming into a windfall. Ethan, what do you think happened? Guess!"

"I suppose a windfall?" I shrug my shoulders. "Who is Mrs. Briggs?"

Ignoring my question, "Honey, when we get there, remain open." She hits the accelerator. "Mrs. Briggs told me that Madame Rosario is a little theatrical."

"What do you mean?"

Nora reassures me with a gentle squeeze to my cheek. "Oh, never mind."

A sudden jolt tosses me to the passenger window. I become conscious that my unfastened seatbelt is buried in the cushion. Wrestling with all my strength I try to release the tan belt that has probably remained inactive since 1965. Bump! Another jolt throws me to the side. Did Nora hit the curb? Realizing that the road has become unstable, I reach behind my left hip and grab the thin belt and place it around my waist. Whack! Why is the road so bumpy? I grip the seatbelt. Within seconds the view tells me the story. A red-and-white baseball uniform belonging to a 12-year-old boy appears out of the corner of my eye. Thump! A softball slams into the front windshield scaring the jeepers out of Nora and me. High-pitched voices from stadium benches stare at this 1965 yellow Cadillac racing just beyond second base and center field. Little League tryouts come to a screeching halt as we pass a group of boys who are tickled by the classic car tearing through their practice game. A chubby boy stands over home plate wearing a look of shock while an assortment of Wilson baseball gloves are tossed at the Cadillac's ornate hood. A coach remains at a standstill completely engrossed with this classic automobile sending excitement throughout the field. Laughter, cheering, and yelping support Nora's right of passage. I now know how Moses felt at the parting of the Red Sea. Nora rolls her window down shouting, "I am so sorry!" and "Please don't hate me," which only seems to arouse more excitement from the team of red-and-white uniformed boys. Even at Nora's worst moments, she is met with applause and admiration. Dust covers the entire Little Leaguers' inside field as we speed past third base. I catch a glimpse of a young boy running alongside Nora's window and yelling, "Come back, hot lady. Come back!"

"Ethan, that boy should be reprimanded." Nora returns to her concentration and slams the accelerator. I am overwhelmed.

Luck eventually shines down on our voyage, allowing every green light to glide us to our final destination. A circular drive leads to a bland two-story red-brick home, a fitting place for this dull suburb. A friendless crape myrtle bush in the front yard begs for attention. The sidewalks need repair, and the yard needs to be mowed. We look at the address on Nora's day planner and double-check the address when a stranger appears in the front door and waves to us to come in while she stares at her watch impatiently.

"Come on in. You must be Nora? And you must be Eddie?"

Nora sizes up our greeter.

"I'm so sorry we are late. Traffic was a bear, honey. And his name is Ethan, by the way."

"My name is Jane Doe. Please don't call me honey." Nora pauses, and then turns to me. "I will bring you to Madame in one moment. Please place your money in this black box, and I will inform Madame that you both are finally here."

"You go do that, sweetie." Nora and I try not to break into laughter.

Ms. Jane Doe disappears into a long hall that is void of pictures, furniture, and, for that matter, any form of life. The sound of her low heels reverberates throughout the foyer, reminding me of detention hall back in St. George's Catholic School. We can hear hushed murmurings from behind the closed doors.

"Nora, I'm getting a weird feeling. What about you?"

Sighing with a half smile and frown, Nora blurts out, "Well, let's see what Madam Rosario has to say."

Ms. Doe signals for Nora and me to come forward. Our footsteps rebound off the spotlessly clean floors as we make our way to an open door.

"Go inside. Speak only when you are spoken to."

Nora and I nod our heads in unison.

We walk into a large room with brown-wood paneling and small windows lined with pull out bars. Plastic cords line the walls, encircling the bare room and leading to a small microphone that sits on a metal receptacle in front of us. We stand in a spot on the floor marked in the shape of an X with black duct tape. Jane Doe reenters the room through a side door and motions us step up to the microphone. Behind her is a large blue bedspread draped over who knows what. With one sturdy pull of the coverlet, Ms. Doe reveals a large woman sitting in lotus position on a group of purple pillows. Her eyes are shut, and she begins to whisper a language I can't make out into a small microphone she clutches in her large hands.

"I am Madame Rosario. I come from a faraway place called Pleiades. Please close your eyes, join hands, and allow me to discern your secrets."

Confusion, bewilderment, and astonishment come to mind. Madame Rosario sits on her stack of pillows, continually moving each finger as if she is playing a musical instrument. Nora and I stare at each other, open mouthed.

"Venus blesses you both. Do you lovers have any questions before I go off into the astral plane to uncover your spiritual assignments?"

Nora and I quickly glance at each other. Neither of us can speak.

"The gods want to bless this union—"

"Oh, Madame," says Nora. "We aren't—"

Madame Rosario continues her babble.

"Honey…Honey…please. Can you stop for a second?" Nora's voice gets a little louder.

"It is in this progression of earthly love that the two of you must—"

Nora grabs the microphone, pulls it close to her mouth, and speaks.

"Honey, are you there!? You need to stop. Ethan, she can't hear me." Nora begins tapping on the microphone. "Hello. Miss Rosario. Stop for just a moment."

Ms. Doe pops out from behind a closed door. She shakes her head and claps her hands once and leaves.

I reach for the microphone on the card table. The on-off button is unfastened.

"Let me see if this knob will work now. Can you hear me? Hello, testing, one, two, three, testing!"

Nora and I wrestle with the on-off switch. The cord seems to have a loose connection.

"Nora, all I have to do is put this here, and it will work. Does that make sense?"

"Of course, oh, yes, Ethan, is it on yet?"

Our voices are amplified throughout the empty hallway and onto the driveway, beyond the sad crape myrtle bush. I imagine that the Little League game has been interrupted by us yet again, and this time by our loud voices. Ms. Doe's heels smack against the shiny floors as she makes her way to Nora. Clap! Clap! She smacks her hands even louder.

Madame Rosario moves about on her purple pillows and seems to have come out of her trance. In fact, her eyes squint, roll and blink every time Jane Doe's hands clap. Once again, clap, clap! Jane Doe moves closer and gives Nora a look. Clap! Clap! Why does she keep clapping at Nora? Are we supposed to clap back? I start clapping and look at Nora, who follows my lead. Clap! Clap!! We look at each other and clap as loudly as we can. Jane Doe begins clapping. Nora and I look at each other and clap repeatedly! Our clapping sounds ricochets through out the empty house. Jane strolls up to me, gives me a strange look, grabs the microphone and turns it off. Her angry frown tells us that our time with Madame Rosario is over. With sullen faces, we look over to Madame Rosario, and make our way back to the Cadillac.

On the drive back to Nora's house, we remain quiet. Once there, I hug Nora good-bye, thank her for a wonderful day, and watch her slip through the front door. Ending this day with silence doesn't feel right. I sit in my car with my thoughts. Another five minutes goes by. Go inside and tell Nora that everything is okay. Richard, already alert to the situation, greets me at the door and politely points me to the atrium. I walk past the formal room and find the atrium with Nora staring at the night sky. Her head upward, cigarette in one hand, and a face full of tears, Nora turns to me.

"Ethan, I am so sorry. All I wanted to do was help."

"Oh, Nora, what a wonderful day I have had with you. Forget about, '*Woman who Sits on Pillows*', with her side kick, '*Woman with Clapping Hands*.'"

Nora lets out a belt of laughter. "You are so right. Come here and hug me."

Leaning inward for a hug, I see that Nora's feet and ankles are covered in dirt. She speaks unassumingly. "I needed to ground myself before I went to bed."

"Okay." I remove my shoes, socks, and roll my pants up, and plant my feet firmly into the ground. We stand there, dirt to our ankles, and gaze onto a starry night. I reach for Nora's hand. "You are one of the most amazing people I have ever met."

***

I am walking the corridors of the Dallas Convention Center lost in a maze of mobile homes all displaying the three major television network symbols; NBC, ABC, and CBS.

This is it! The 1984 National Republican Convention has arrived.

All around me is the energy of fast-moving figures, racing to meet scheduled deadlines and all glad to be inside, escaping the hotter-than-normal Texas heat. Everyone seems to know where he or she is going and what he or she is doing. Secret Service agents are abundant, and security is so tight that I feel I might be whisked away for looking at someone the wrong way. Luckily, I find the newsroom and am greeted by the assistant producer with, "Thank god, you're here!" and "Forgive us for issuing the wrong security floor badge." This apology melts my frustration about the delay caused by this oversight.

I am immediately immersed in the symphony being created by numerous busy typewriters. My arms don't even feel the strain of my 55-pound makeup case. As I walk through the hum of the newsroom, I catch a glimpse of Dan Rather preparing for the telecast. It is captivating to see so many energies working together with such speed. I catch myself daydreaming, wondering what Lesley Stahl is like, and think of her CBS

Sunday morning show, *Face the Nation.* I wonder how I will act when meeting First Lady Nancy Reagan or former First Lady Betty Ford. Walter Cronkite's black eyeglasses sit low on his nose; while he listens to Bob Schieffer report on his weekend activities. This mystical moment is short-lived as Michael Huddle, Diane Sawyer's personal hairdresser, ushers me into the makeup room. "Diane, this is Ethan Michaels."

Ms. Sawyer sits behind her typewriter, a pencil between her teeth, and hair pulled away from her face. Her skin is free of makeup. I am about to recreate the famous CBS morning persona that America loves. Her uneaten sandwich lies to the side of her desk and reminds me of my missed lunch. She extends her hand.

"Your name is Ethan?" Her clear eyes reveal a warm personality.

"Yes," I say, shyly.

Someone squeezes my shoulder from behind.

"Good, you've met Ms. Sawyer. Michael, please escort Ethan to the anchor booth and introduce him to Lesley Stahl as quickly as you can."

Julie Gautier gives me a quick hug and rushes Michael Huddle along.

"Please tell her we're sorry for the delay." Julie walks into an adjacent room already buzzing with organized perplexity.

Massive television cables edge along the mobile homes that crisscross the convention center's cement floors. Michael's long legs move quickly through the labyrinth of journalists to get us to the anchor booth that will become my temporary dwelling. Connie Chung greets Michael with an affectionate hug as we near the metal black stairwell that leads up to a control room.

"Connie, this is Ethan."

"What a pleasure it is to meet you." I stammer like a schoolboy.

Connie extends her hand. "You don't mind if I ask Michael a personal question, Ethan?"

"Oh, please do." I am impressed. She actually said my name.

Michael points me to a secluded corner. "I'll be right back."

The view of the arena is surreal. Within hours empty seats will be filled to capacity. A large American flag, GOP banners, and red balloons decorate the main auditorium floor as policemen scour the bleachers. Sound technicians and camera crews ignore a handful of local newscasters who mull about the main floor checking out the major network control rooms. Secret Service men are scattered in strategic locations talking into their hands. Michael calls to me, "Let's go meet Lesley."

Up the black metal stairway we go. I hear boisterous laughter bellowing from the newsroom out to the empty convention hall. A policeman with an intimidating face demands our floor badges, opens the door, and grants permission to enter. The staff room desks are empty except for a group of men in suits and ties that are laughing hysterically with a woman wearing a traditional gray skirt and cream-colored blouse. Michael shuffles past the team and shouts, "Hey guys, this is Ethan. Ethan, this is Mark Shields, Jack Kemp, Senator Dole, and Lesley Stahl."

"Good afternoon—"

A woman enters from another cubicle wearing an impatient expression.

"Hey, Ethan, I've heard great things about you. Michael, we've had a change of plans. I am going to start Lesley and if you can take Ethan to Dan Rather that would be great. Mrs. Reagan is going to address the GOP Convention Wednesday night, and Dan wants to do a personal interview. She'll need a touch-up. Ethan, it's nice to meet you."

She disappears down the stairs. I feel my stomach clinch into a knot as we are instructed to exit and go to the primary anchor booth.

Dan Rather approaches the booth, lights a cigarette, and turns his attention toward the empty arena. His black suit, white shirt, and square shoulders make him seem like a solid man. Secret Service men comb under the stairwell, clearing the area before Nancy Reagan arrives. Two Secret Service men at the top of the stairwell stand like giant pillars. I follow Michael's lead, gather my confidence, and climb the stairs. A familiar pain to my left abdomen begins to throb as one of the Secret Service men searches my body and makeup kit. Damn! The pain medications have not kicked in. The sweat hanging from my upper lip surely must signal unease, but my admittance reassures me that I am just feeling insecure. Michael nudges me quietly, whispering, "When you finish Mrs. Reagan's makeup, politely excuse yourself, and one of the secret service agents will escort you out of the control room. You are not permitted to stay."

I take a deep breath and whisper, "Okay."

At the bottom of the stairs I see two more Secret Service men on either side of Mrs. Reagan. Both men wear Johnson and Murphy wing-tip shoes and dark business suits. Their short, parted hair and conservative ties seem at odds with the Smith and Wesson 352 revolvers that hang in their holsters. They lean their heads to one side, having conversations via small wires that appear from the back of their shirt collars.

"What is your name?" One of the agents breaks my concentration.

Before I have a chance to answer, Michael Huddle breaks in.

"This is Ethan Michaels. He's with CBS." Huddle reaches for the security badge around my neck and shows the agent. "I'll see you later, Ethan."

I am escorted into a control booth of technicians committed to TV monitors and sound equipment, oblivious of my presence. Instructed to stay positioned until Mrs. Reagan enters, the agent returns to his outside post. A small group of men wearing dark suits surreptitiously lower their voices. Distracted from their conversation, a gray-haired man wearing an expensive blue suit looks up and tosses me an agitated glance. "Who is that?" my voice asks. I stare down at my shoes, pretend not to listen, and disappear into my thoughts. I feel a chill shiver down my body as I observe the man with gray hair. My fretfulness is quickly lifted as First Lady Nancy Reagan enters the booth with two towering agents, Dan Rather, and an assistant director

The assistant director shakes my hand and says, "Mrs. Reagan, this is your makeup artist."

Extending my hand to the First Lady, I say, eagerly, "My name is—"

"Mrs. Reagan, what a pleasure. Welcome to Texas. We are honored that you will be speaking to the GOP Convention Wednesday night." The man in the blue suit interrupts my introduction.

"Thank you," says Mrs. Reagan. She extends her hands to me. "What time is my interview, Dan?"

"When ever you are ready, Mrs. Reagan." Dan Rather excuses himself politely, exits the control booth, and enters the soundproof anchor room to prepare for his interview.

"Gentlemen, can we let Mrs. Reagan have some private time?" The assistant director moves us both to a quiet space. The three men return to their private conversations.

Mrs. Reagan's small frame is perfectly suited in a classic dark-blue skirt and blouse. A red, tailored mid-waist jacket and red belt complement her tiny figure. She has a sophistication and authenticity that many attempt and few actually have. Her eyes are gentle, fraught with years of life's curves and aware of an inner beauty that she has earned. I gently apply her makeup, taking care to bring out the wisdom I see. As I finish, I notice the three men in the control booth. My uneasiness returns quickly. Are my thoughts justified? Why are they talking about future elections and Iraq? Their concerns should be the Soviet Union. Who are they?

"Mrs. Reagan, are you ready?" the assistant director asks, politely.

"Thank you, Ethan." The First Lady does a quick glance in the mirror, squeezes my hand, and waits for the sound tech to prepare her microphone.

I hug her like an adolescent schoolboy, pack my belongings, and proceed to exit the anchor booth. "What a nice lady," I say out loud. The news crew whispers as I advance through the door. I am unaware that my hugging is inappropriate protocol.

"Sir, can you please stop." An agent moves to block my exit.

"Oh, I'm sorry. Oh, I'm not supposed to touch her...and, I forgot to wait for your escort." I say with embarrassment. "Am I in trouble?"

"Please go back to the anchor booth. You can not leave yet." The agent's voice is firm.

"Oh, shit," I say slowly. I turn around and make my way back through the control room and into the anchor booth. Dan Rather is sitting at his desk, and Mrs. Reagan is seated in the guest chair. The assistant director approaches and leans in to me.

"The First Lady has asked that you stay," he says.

I detect a note of surprise in his voice. I look to Mrs. Reagan and meet her eyes. She motions me to come forward.

"It would be nice if you stayed for my interview." She summons the assistant director over and asks for a chair so that I may sit out of camera view.

"Whatever you think is best, Mrs. Reagan." The assistant director looks at me and grabs a chair. "Sit here, Ethan."

"Five, four, three, two, one, and we are on…"

***

Somewhere between the benevolence of CBS, Julie Gautier's unwavering faith in my artistic ability and Mark's forethought into my developing charm, my long awaited dream has become the prize. My telephone rings nonstop with eager offers that I take on. Hours become days, days become weeks, and weeks become months. I learn the art of agent protocol over the phone, return every call to every client, accept every appointment no matter the fee, and become media mindful. I balance every penny, collect late payments, and invest my limited precious time with Nora. At sunrise I awaken to a two-hour workout, come home, study Nora's notes on metaphysics, and devour a meticulously prepared meal. By 9 a.m., my appointment rounds consist of the homes of the social elite, on set with another perfect face for the coolest fashion magazines, or on an airplane to anywhere. My hands touch the face of many powerful women, including Mary Kay

Ash, from Mary Kay Cosmetics, Linda Gray, Miss USA, Courtney Gibbs, Martha Teichner, and Academy Award–winner Greer Garson. They all come through CBS. These women, with their bigger-than-life personas, give me self-confidence and melt my inner bashfulness like an apparition that fades with the bright light of morning.

Cecelia and Mario visit each December, celebrating a friendship I cherish for many reasons. I learn the ways of the fisherman with every visit and share old conversations about a man I call Brussels. Mario sits on the floor like a small child, listens to my stories of the rich and famous and applauds. Cecelia smiles, finds joy in her brother's excitement, and speaks about their life in Mexico.

We are coming to Dallas in November instead of December. Mama has passed, and I want to look for a place to live. We are finally coming back, Ethan. Let's meet *November 11* for your birthday dinner, Cecelia's writes in a letter. I am thrilled.

My blessings are many, but none are more gratifying than the light of passage that Nora brings me. Her fondness for numerology is my daily addiction. Nora's gentle guidance and sophistication saturate me like summer rain, inspiring me to new awareness I never knew I had. We sit in her formal parlor, laugh, and chitchat, make fun of each other, and listen to soft rock. Nighttime is our medication-gossip hour, and before I travel back to the city, we pop one of our many pills and berate the doctors for prescribing such toxins to our gentle spirits. The steroids and anti-inflammatory drugs alongside the painkillers seem to calm my intestinal cramping, yet the doctor's lack of knowledge about my condition sheds little understanding on this chronic disease. The sudden weight loss and fatigue is overshadowed by my hectic schedule. Nora's concern seems to have no limits.

"Promise me you will look into finding a specialist," she repeatedly warns me.

"I will, Nora, I will."

As I drive back into the city, I reflect on my empty promise to Nora and feel guilty. I climb up the stairs, pass the Saint Thomas stained-glass window and notice the latest headline in the evening paper on my doorsill. "*Aids Epidemic Spreads Though out America.*" Fatigue has overtaken me tonight. I pop another round of pills and throw myself down into a soft bed. Have I been exposed to AIDS?

A gentle paw swiping my cheek, followed by a sweet meow, informs me that morning has arrived. Honey sits on the pillow next to my head. I must rise and greet my day. I turn to pet her, feel wet sheets, and quickly spring out of bed. A dark pool of blood stains my comforter. I yank the crimson-covered sheets off the mattress. Blood is everywhere. I run to the bathroom and stare in the vanity mirror. Brown spots have suddenly appeared all over my stomach. How? I make my way to the kitchen. Nausea sets in. I pour some cat food in a bowl and listen to Honey's meow. It seems to forewarn of a day that will go down like a collapsed bridge. The first ring sets the day.

"Hello," I answer, bothered by this interruption.

"Ethan, this is Doctor Fisher's office. Can you hold for the doctor?"

"Sure," I say.

"Ethan, this is Dr. Fisher. The results of your test are in. Can you come down to my office this morning?"

"Well—"

"This is important. Your blood count is extremely low for some reason. Is there something you are not sharing with me? Son, we need to run an upper and lower GI test on you immediately." Doctor Fisher's voice is uncompromising.

"Let me see if I can rearrange my day. I have a production party tonight. I need to be at the hotel by 5 p.m. Can we try midday around 3:30 p.m.?"

I'll have Nancy work you in this afternoon. If you no show again, this time I am charging you double. Understood?"

"Yes," I say ashamed. I place the phone down and look in a mirror. My eyes are drawn and two small brown lesions are on my neck. I can see a small lesion on my right cheek. The phone rings.

"Hello."

"Ethan, this is Julie. I have some good news. TJ Lawton arrives today, and I think it would be great if you two met. Lindsey Collins is crossing over from Cover Girl to feature, and he feels she is about to become a huge star. I told him about you."

"Oh my god…you are kidding?"

"Can you pick him up at the airport today around 4 o'clock and take him to the hotel? This will give you a few minutes to get to know each other. Are you still driving the same white sports coupe?" Julie puts me on hold for a few seconds. "Ethan, say yes. I have to take this call. He arrives on American flight 1111. Call me later."

Exhaustion is all over my face. You're just tired, Ethan, I try to convince myself. These medications will kick in soon, and the pain in my abdomen will subside soon. Perhaps if I get more sleep I'll feel better. This is a huge opportunity. I can see Doctor Fisher tomorrow. I lay a new set of sheets on the bed and fall back to sleep only to be awakened by the telephone again.

"Ethan, its Cecelia, we are here. Can we see each other this afternoon?"

Shit. I silently say to myself. "Cecelia, is there anyway we can meet later tonight? I have a client meeting and production party. Hey, why don't you meet me at the Crescent Hotel at 8 p.m.? It will give me a great excuse to slip out."

"Ethan, you don't sound like yourself. Is something wrong?" Cecelia's voice wavers with concern.

"I'm fine. I am tired. Meet me in the lobby at 8 p.m. I can't wait to see you and Mario."

"Okay, Ethan, Happy Birthday." Cecelia's voice fades away.

***

A bold wind has crept in during the afternoon, bringing with it an unpleasant drizzle. The temperature takes a dive, leaving me chilled to the bone. Taxis, shuttle buses, and rental cars are jammed at the airport pickup lane. Passengers jog to their families anxious to flee the congested intersections. Policemen's whistles scream, warning unaware passengers of the pileup of automobiles. TJ was to meet me outside of baggage claim 30 minutes ago. Where is he? I can't keep circling the airport looking for TJ. Hands waving recklessly get my attention. Windshield wipers graze my windows. I see a yellow raincoat belonging to a police officer. Is he waving me down? He motions me to roll my window down.

"Yes, officer, I'm sorry to be driving around in circles. I am looking for—"

My mouth drops to the floor hitting the brakes.

"This man is inebriated. Get him off the curb or I am hauling him to the county jail downtown. Understood? Open your back door now!"

The officer is pissed. He tosses a very drunk TJ into the back seat of my sports car, luggage included. Angry honking horns encourage me to make a quick getaway before the policeman changes his mind. Slurring his words, TJ begs me to slow down so he can vomit. Changing gears, I speed away in my sports car, with its fresh smelling leather seats, while Michael McDonald croons, "Taking it to the Streets," on the radio.

"Please don't throw up in my car," I yell. I pull to the side of the road to let TJ vomit.

"Let's get out here." In the back of the car, I pull TJ to the curbside.

TJ looks at my clothes with bewilderment. "Why are you dressed like that?"

"I decided to wear some hand me downs, due to the rainy weather. Can I change into my suit at your hotel when I drop you off?" I avoid telling TJ that I am bleeding. Once we arrive, I'll use the men's room to change, and stuff my underwear with toilet tissue.

"Sure, no worries," TJ covers his mouth, trying to prevent the inevitable.

Excruciating pain pounds my abdominal muscle. I lean to the backside of my car and topple to the ground. TJ vomits uncontrollably as I huddle in a fetal position, blood saturating Papa's slacks. Passing vehicle lights become spotlights to a scene that has become ill-fated. The pain has become unbearable as I beg TJ to help. I feel my eyes' closing as the rain covers my blood-stained body.

***

"Mr. Michaels, are you all right? Can you hear me? Nurse! Nurse! Take this man and get him prepped for surgery." A stranger's voice loops in my ear. "Mr. Michaels, how long have you had these brown contusions on your stomach?"

Florescent lights above my head are blurry. A male nurse pushes a hospital gurney that secures my body in and out of a narrow hallway. He swiftly passes a man with a gunshot wound who is surrounded by police officers that point to a woman in the adjoining room. Doctors frantically speak to one another as the woman lies lifeless on a hospital bed. From the corner of my eye, I can see a family crying hysterically as a father cradles his small child in his arms. The hallway's desperation seems never ending. We twist and turn, making our way to a secluded cubicle with blue curtains that partition a single bed. The medical staff floats from room to room, assisting with each patient's trauma, laboring to rescue the sick and dying. The nurse looks down at me with a fear that is beyond measure, wiping perspiration from his face. He boosts my body onto a single cot that smells of death and quickly returns to the frontlines of duty. Blood continues to spew from my anal passage, saturating the sheets. An intern looks at the brown lesions peering out from my hospital gown. He immediately exits the room. Outside, doctors deliberate the exact identification of my illness, unaware that I can hear every word.

"This young man has brown lesions on his lower torso?" A male voice says with concern. "We should not be in same room with this patient?"

"Who is that man that came in with Mr. Michaels? Someone get him sober!" An authoritative voice shouts.

"Doctor, that man is TJ Lawton." A female voice responds. "Administration discovered Mr. Michael's day planner and three prescriptions. They have already contacted his doctor."

"That is TJ Lawton?" You're fucking kidding me? Someone get Michaels' doctor on the phone now. Nurse, page Doctor Johnson immediately."

The intern pokes his head through the thin curtains with a look of nervousness. Nurses and ER staff argue outside my room, refusing to come inside. An annoyed female voice speaks. "He is still a human being! We are medical doctors and nurses for god's sake."

"Well, Sullivan, then you go inside and prep him for surgery. I'm not going to put my life at risk!" This man's voice thunders in the background. "Are you insane? Look at him. He's homeless! His blood has spilled all over the cubicle floor."

I crunch over to my left side, both hands cradling the agonizing pain in my abdomen. "I am not homeless," I try to talk. Why is the medical crew so afraid of me? A middle age woman enters my room, clean sheets, mop and bucket in hand, holding a fresh hospital gown. One of the nurse's yells from behind the drawn curtain "Put some damn gloves on Sullivan. And cover your face! Don't expose the rest of us to AIDS, because of that homeless man!"

Ignoring her coworkers, Nurse Sullivan addresses me.

"Honey, this might hurt a little, but I need to clean you up. Can you hear me? If you can, roll over for me."

I nod my head, mumbling, "Where am I? Why are all these people afraid of me?" I roll over into a pool of blood. "Someone needs to feed my cat."

"Sullivan," one of the ER doctors calls. "Get out of there, now!"

Nurse Sullivan gently washes my torso, comforting me with kindness. "Don't you worry, honey? Everything is going to be okay as long as I am here. Your friend Nora is on the way," she says. "We'll get someone to take care of your cat."

Nurse Sullivan wipes me down, making sure my blood does not touch her skin.

My thoughts sink into a sea of anxiety. What a horrible state of affairs for TJ Lawton to be introduced to. What will Julie do when she finds out? Oh, my god, Cecelia and Mario must be worried sick? Nora is going to freak out when she gets here. I feel my eyes becoming heavy. Everything goes dark. A small white light begins to crest over me. How can I see this light? My eyes are closed? Once again, everything becomes dark. Nothingness takes over. Voices come and go.

"His veins keep collapsing, and his hemoglobin level is below 8, Doctor," Nurse Sullivan shares. "He needs blood desperately!"

"Get him into the OR now! And find a way to keep that IV in him." A nameless doctor disappears back into the ER room.

Distorted imagery plays havoc with my alertness. Doctors and nurses enter through doors that swing back and forth. A handful of patients are dispersed outside of operating rooms. I can see uneasy faces staring at me. Concentrated blue-white lights shine down on my bed preventing clarity, yet somehow, these illuminations call an inner prompting for me to turn to my left side. Struggling with every scrap of strength, I follow the voice that gently directs me to an African American woman whose bed is parallel to my own. Radiant blue eyes, white hair pulled back, a smile that shines clear. Peace seems to emanate from her being. Her ageless face has a majestic kindness. I reach out for her hand.

Instantly, the room becomes still. White lights spiral all around us creating a funnel cloud, projecting a calm storm of peace within my aching body. Transparent cheerful individuals stand at the outer edge of this sphere of light, sending a sign of welcome. Who are these people? Why are they here? Why are they smiling? Within seconds, I realize these are souls that I knew life times ago. A gentle nudge to my hand engages me back to the woman, allowing me a closing revelation. I struggle to shift my body on the bloody gurney. The African American woman has vanished, and before me is a familiar face. Sulivia takes my hand and squeezes it with a loving gesture. Luminous white lights surround each patient's bed, creating a beautiful abstraction that fills the narrow corridor. Vertical strands of light ascend from each patient's solar plexus climbing through and past the ceiling. Hallucinations waltz in my head until a masculine voice gets my attention.

"Its 11 o'clock. Has Michaels' doctor arrived yet? Where is the anesthesiologist? Mr. Michaels, are you okay? Can you hear me?" Blue orbs circle my gurney.

"Where is Dr. Johnson? Who lanced the lesions on his buttocks? How much blood has he lost?" An indistinguishable tone of voice roars like a ghostly phantom to a surrounding staff of medical crew. I know this nightmare.

I turn my head to acknowledge Sulivia, her calmness and smile embracing me, remembering Brussels' message from former days.

"Transformation knocks at your door, yet again. I say 11 by 11 is your time of resurrection. The hand of the elder brings comfort."

This memory gives me hope at this dreadful hour. Reaching out for a final squeeze, I lock onto Sulivia's hand, and witness the same orbs just as before. "Don't be afraid," her voice speaks inside my head. But her lips never move. Her lustrous face watches with steadfast affection as my gurney slips into the operating room. I look around to say farewell to Sulivia but she is nowhere to seen.

"Mr. Michaels, can you hear me?" A young doctor stands above my hospital gurney.

I nod.

"How long have you been bleeding?"

The OR goes dim. Voices disappear into a void of nothingness. The pain is more than I can tolerate. Dizziness spins me like a merry-go-round. A sudden forceful strike evaporates the oxygen all around the room, similar to a vacuum circulating around my body. Instantly, the pain vanishes. Blue-white orbs float at the north corner of the room, gliding past the ER crew. Ethereal sounds of hypnotic notes play like a skilled symphony, serenading the blue-white lights. A portal of white light fills the room, I see beyond the bed that holds me. Outside the ER room, down the hospital corridor to the admissions desk and into the waiting room, I see Nora sitting next to TJ. Conversations vary from small talk to heavy subjects as Nora thanks the admissions clerk for a pen and pad. TJ is transfixed by every word from Nora's mouth as she introduces him to his life purpose through her gift of numerology. Her warmth and compassion fill his heart, allowing him a life of many possibilities.

"Your addiction will destroy your life. We all have choices. We can learn by *sorrow* or we can learn by *happiness*. What's its going to be for you, honey? Surrender this addiction to your higher power and give your life new direction," Nora continues as TJ chugs on his coffee. My vision continues, taking me to the elevator and up to the seventh floor. A stout man is handcuffed to his hospital bed while two police officers sit on chairs outside his room. His heart is cold from a torrid past. He blames his father for his miserable life, yet the very person he blames is the person who encouraged him. This man's ears remained closed to his father's words all throughout his life. I wonder if he can hear his father's spirit communicating words of love. I can. Up and down, throughout the hospital, I witness death and witness new life. Each cycle of human life begins with light and ends with light. How precious and how fragile is this light?

"Peter, Ethan Michaels! It is not your time to go. Do you hear me?"

Nora's teary petition brings me past the elevator, down the hallway, and back to the waiting area. TJ comforts Nora, embracing a new friendship whose compassion and love will change them both forever. I see the frantic faces of doctors and nurses as I am guided back to the OR hospital table. Whatever this group of medical experts is discussing weighs heavy with complication. I look down upon this familiar body, watching Doctor Johnson repetitively pummel my chest. Nurses move in and suddenly away from my limp body, avoiding pools of blood on sterile floors, making room for doctors who must perform the resurgence. I look to my right. A large digital clock shows, 11:11 p.m. I look to my left. The rotating white light has returned. A familiar face, stands at the opening. Mrs. Bellamy, my third grade teacher, smiles and waves me towards the circling light. But she is young and beautiful? Not the teacher I know, who is on the cusp of retiring? David, a young boy I played with in my backyard, smiles and summons me forward. Over and over familiar faces from my past, smile, waving me towards a revolving tunnel. Sound becomes unsound. Like a black-and-white silent movie, this drama plays out to an audience that feels every moment.

A large cord of golden light exits my stomach, climbs past the ceiling into an atmosphere tinted with thousands of other illuminated lights. Ready or not, I feel my soul yanked from my body, hoisting me upward, almost like the top of an amusement park ride. The roller coaster climbs the wooden track one rotation at a time until the edge of the plunge is visible. Spiraling down the tracks at top speed, sound returns, with hues circling the table. Melodious sounds slip into a vacuum of continual light, thrusting me onward and upward. Orbiting at speeds beyond understanding I see other lights entering Mother Earth and exiting simultaneously.

I seem to understand that these illustrations in yellow-gold brilliance are souls discovering purposeful understanding to this mystifying passage we call life. Up and beyond, past all other lights, a large empty space awaits my arrival. Beautiful musical flutes sing of Native American folklore. Echoing soft drumbeats accompany me as I make my way toward a young Native American man. Howling coyotes sing alongside female voices that are hypnotically haunting. The Indian extends his hand, pointing to a corridor that takes me to red rock valleys, up majestically serene mountains, and vibrant blue skies. A *red-tailed hawk* climbs the panoramic scope, circling above my view as the Indian man follows behind. *Buffalo* and *mountain lions* sit side by side with *bears* and *coyotes.*

"Come with me." The Indian man persuades me to join him as we walk along the desert floor.

"Why do you wear those *Keys* around your neck?" I hear my thoughts played back to me. "We have met before?"

"Yes."

Key Master

Chapter 10

Clay red mountains push upward toward vast turquoise skies. Valleys that lead to a green meadow are brimming with yellow wildflowers. An Indian flute dances over a babbling creek that overflows with harmonious female voices and serenades my ears. The song of crickets vies with that of a crying coyote. I am filled with an inner peace and am in awe of this vivid fertile canyon taking place in my imagination. The smell of dogwood overwhelms my senses as I try to adjust to the young Indian man's shimmering aura that radiates around him in a triangle shape. Hypnotic melodies tunnel past the mountainous range, captivating my senses. I float toward a giant oak tree. Shining dark hair hangs past the young Indian's chiseled shoulders. He motions me forward toward a funnel of multicolored winds. Purple, green, and pink lights loop around my head, filling my brain with a feeling of stillness, as if I have suddenly learned the secret to serenity. A rush of cobalt-blue waves crashes at the base of my collarbone, flowing down a body I can no longer perceive. Numerous white lights flutter around me, guiding me toward the oak tree. It is bound to the land by muscular roots. Dusk begins to settle as a warm breeze seeps through the tree's regal branches. The Indian man summons me to the top of the impressive oak, as I hover just above the ground. Old-fashioned keys bound to a leather band hang proudly around his neck, clanking with every breath he makes. Why are you wearing keys around your neck? I hear those curious words, but they are only in my head.

Mother Earth revolves before me as though a cinematic screen has been placed front and center for my viewing. The entire atmosphere, beginning at the foothills and continuing up and beyond, as far as the eyes can see, is like a full-screen theatre showing images and events of my life. The Indian guides me to sit upon the oak tree, as my every sense races full speed ahead. All knowing, hearing, understanding, tasting, and smelling are secondary to the emotional connection I feel with the universe. Heavenly knowledge saturates my intellect, permitting *14 rays of golden light* to descend from the solar skies. Recognizing that I have come to this junction, I feel humbled before a greatness I cannot describe. Mathematical formulas coupled with sound vibrations and color blueprints to music I have never heard fill me with awe. I am mesmerized by visions I can only attempt to comprehend. My soul is housed with so much energy that mankind couldn't contain the vocabulary necessary to decode such a gift. A drum beats inside my thoughts as operatic voices echo a bursting light; its energy launching itself downward to earth. White-gold light, in the form of cone-shaped cylinders, pulsates like seismic waves, locating various cities within countries. Exploding energy fields spiral into homes at every hour, consuming each person during and after sex. These light fields burst inside and all around the human body like transformers to a breaker box. My vision allows me to witness my youthful parents engulfed in their own individual radiant-energy patterns. Golden-yellow, pink light surrounds their united bodies just before a pallid light explodes inside my mom's inner womb. Thousands of light rays speed inside my mother's female organs, overflowing throughout her entire being as we reconnect our soul-pattern energy for the second lifetime as mother and son. Momentous karmic lessons begin immediately as our souls try to instantaneously adapt to every split second of each other's prior lifetimes hurts, accomplishments, and challenges. Connecting onto my father's energy gridiron permits another karmic bond encompassing obligation, accountability, and honor, while striving to value various lessons of commitment to relations. This analogous relationship cycle repeats itself in different forms for several lifetimes until all parties are balanced with self-love, broad-minded thoughts and principles, and kindness for all of mankind. In turn, the framework of love, respect, and honor between male and female energy fields passes onto the next genetic energy code. Like a pot of simmering stew, each ingredient that is added, allows for the continuation of the soul's perfection. Bound to earth to discover new purpose or meaning, I realize that consciousness stops and begins simultaneously.

From a distant corner, a distressed voice interrupts my magnificent revelation. "His pressure is dropping. He is going into V-tach. Give him one amp of Atropine now!" I observe the doctors panic. "Okay, clear the table. Stand clear!"

Conversations between the OR doctors bob wavelike as I survey the gurney that holds my body. Floating beyond the bed and in-between the staff seems natural. Staring at my motionless body, annulled from emotion, I observe the medical crew perform a critical surgical procedure. Pain is absent from my physical being, but tension weighs heavy amongst the medical staff. "We have Asystole! Give him another amp of Atropine, Attempt to cardiovert him now. Clear the table. Stand clear!" The OR staff looks to the monitor.

A loud snap! Large white-gray horizontal energy currents devour the room. Blankness. Nothingness. Soundless. Total blackness. Another loud snap! Immediately, cone-shaped funnels take hold of my awareness, speeding me through an entryway filled with glowing colors I don't recognize. Translucent images call my name as they appear near a portal opening, rotating in a circular motion near the tunnel. This powerful wheel of watery color summons me to enter. Melodious tones hypnotically propel me near the opening as past, present, and future merge as one. Wisdom beyond the mind's eye fills my head again, but this time hundreds of rays of light descend in and through my light being. Universal knowledge consumes every aspect of my consciousness, allowing unconditional acceptance to observe not only my inaccuracies in life, but mathematical equations, theological edits, masterpieces of creative work that lay dormant because of someone else's opinion dissuading their initiation. This back order of collective intelligence surrounds Mother Earth's atmosphere pulsating during peak REM cycles. Hopes, wishes, prayers, creative genius, are the sacred treasures of our planet and float above, waiting to be sent back for our next incarnation, if we only trust in the *power of love*.

Colossal solar systems outside of *Earth's* galaxy transfix my mind. Sound vibrations pleasantly harmonized to color fill my being as I revisit the massive mental screen that displays my entire life. Thousand of seconds do a play-by-play of my youth as I witness the actions of my past. I am able to make a distinction between right and wrong as early as the age of 4 when I disobey my parents and play with the next-door neighbor's child. Forbidden to be friends because of our parent's ill-conceived narrow-mindedness, I slip out the bedroom window on a hot summer morning and meet David, my first Hispanic friend, outside of my house. Punished and scolded for this act, the image allows me to understand the balance of correct choice verses authority. Distinctive inner promptings recommend the right choice of action. Learn to listen to your heart rather than to the influence of prejudice. This forbidden friendship instilled a sense of self-truth as I come to appreciate that our early days of someone else's opinion influences our future actions. Flash to the next illustration; I witness the caring connection between my sister and me as we walk side by side to our lockers inside the school hallway. "I love you" are words I could have spoken if I had only known my sister's last days were concluding that same evening. Our parting hug plays in slow motion, allowing me a simple reminder that *love* must be shared and spoken *daily*.

A new image plays. I look upon a group of high school boys ridiculing Mike, who struggles with his grades in the special education class for slow learners. I am able to hear my selfish thoughts magnified on a loudspeaker as I pass Mike, feeling sorry for the behavior put upon him. Unfortunately, my punctuality takes precedence over human kindness. Devoured by the continuation of this forgotten episode in my life, I watch a distraught family embrace their handicap son, reassuring him of his specialness. Permitted to look at this situation from an all-encompassing understanding, I quickly gather that this is a valuable landmark to universal law. When we gain knowledge of any wrongdoing, this knowledge demands an immediate response to stop the continuance of negative acts before it becomes a threefold consequence of *collective disregard*.

The next powerful depiction plays like a daunting 3-D movie, jolting each scene to a full-bleed border. Images play throughout an immeasurable stratosphere, and I am sitting front and center in this gigantic auditorium. Speeding to a late appointment, I stare down at my watch, grab a piece of chewing gum, unwrap it, place the gum in my mouth, and toss the silver gum wrapper out of my car window. Like a zoom lens on a camera, my eyes follow the tiny wrapper over the guardrail and into the river below. An inconspicuous little silver wrapper descends into the mighty waterway, making its way downstream, passing neighborhoods and various communities and trash thrown out by other polluters. I was an oblivious person. And so were the others. Within a split second, I am witness to one-million wrappers creating five-million toxic, irreversible landmines to our rivers and oceans. Rotted tree branches nestled along the banks host numerous fast-food paper bags, cola cans, garbage, refinery overflow, all producing a coat of slimy contaminants over the water. Dying birds and dead fish they travel the river's current while young people skinny-dip in the same river. Empathy fills every cell in a body that I can no longer see or feel. My conscious mind should feel a sickening display of shame, yet somehow an all-inclusive compassion crosses the threshold of my intellectual awareness. Objective insight into every good deed, achievement, thought, neglectful act, and selfish inclination permits a continuous perspective of truth. The strongest link to everything we do, say, believe, and act upon is one law—*love!* When we operate within the province of this emotion, the gift of universal greatness is guaranteed. *How can I stay in this inclusive compassion?* An inward celestial voice answers my thoughts: "Wholeness begins with *gratitude.* Listen to the *language of your heart.*"

Flashes of my recent Christmas holiday show my donation to the homeless man during Mass. I am reminded of the homeless man leaving the church as our paths cross at the intersection. "Merry Christmas," he shouted as he passed my car. Unaware of where he was heading, I am forwarded to the next scene. Money in hand, the homeless man makes his way to a 7-Eleven and buys cupcakes, milk, bread, and toothpaste. I am spellbound by the next image. A small gathering of destitute people huddle under a bridge rejoicing with thanks. Giving gifts to one another, they speak of their holiday encounters of passing citizens who kindly gave to them. *"Listen to the language of your heart,"* booms throughout this cosmic display of my life. Immediately, white-yellow sunbeams plunge onto each person that gives to those in need and magnifies twice the light to those who receive. *Totality begins with gratitude* and changes the *electrical* rate of return within each of us. This universal law of love, once understood, governs the immediate change within the nature of man. Daily, we are given a choice. Each decision guarantees a cause and an effect. We are all connected to continual *energy currents* that burst into tiny flames of light every hour, every second of every day. If choices are amplified by a loving attitude, then the outcome of our lives displays an *external* brilliance, I come to understand as, *Eternal Light.*

The sound of running water falling off rocks draws me into a new image. Native American flutes dance with male vocals that call nature's essence. Distant, shadowy figures lay hands to drums, creating subtle beats to call forward ancestors of the past. The young Indian beckons me to the oak tree once more. His hands turn to the setting sun, as I witness a montage of mankind's foibles. These visual fragments show me countless injustices. Socrates' bitter fate lies in the hands of those who disregard the most. A man whose truth became his demise chills me to the bone: The next image is of Thomas Becket's murder at Canterbury. Then I see senators and Brutus surrounding Caesar, delivering him to death. This is cut short, by the atrocious massacre at *Wounded Knee.* The battle at *Red River* shows more bloodshed and sends me to my next vision. I look upon a past *World War ll* image of the tired, frightened faces of men, women, and children, who seek underground shelter during the bombings of London. *Civil Rights* demonstrations then play, creating another new consciousness, yet the deceitfulness of government policy sends another wave of activists rallying against the *Vietnam War*. German concentration camps hide atrocities; the Armenian genocide warns of future evils if the laws of love are not applied. Over and over, historical misguided choices dance across my bigger-than-life screen. Those who dare to destroy the towers of freedom that Abraham Lincoln constructed are the very same political leaders of today's opposition who overshadow America's *Equal Rights* Movement. This message of social equality dies on the *Senate floor*, and the *misuse* of *political power* continues to darken the spirits of generations to follow. I come to appreciate that mankind is always prepared to blossom with *New Age* initiation, but throughout time, we are cut off from our spiritual evolution, and a boomerang effect of recurring lessons takes place. Mankind falls, rises between the fractures, igniting new thought consciousness, and produces from out of nowhere, men and women of substance. Somehow self-indulgence eventually casts shadows on our collective progress as we favor gluttonous men of power, war, planetary abuse, apathy, profit, bigotry and the annihilation of the animal kingdom. This poisonous impression is stamped on the very foundation of which all civilizations *rise and fall*.

Seconds turn to split seconds, and within each frame of a second another chronological story is shared. The past becomes now and then becomes soon to be. Thoughts rocket at such momentum in my head. I am amazed at my ability to digest this wisdom. I become aware that my inner voice always provides me a nudge that reveals if certain actions are the right choices. It is during this tennis match of disheveled thoughts when the battle of *free will* verses *inner knowing* becomes the cause and effect of choice. Global intelligence explodes inside me every time I comprehend any human error and the balance of personal rectitude

I choose to follow. It is not about what we have done, though this is significant, but how fast we make amends to those we have wronged because of *bad* choices. Moments of human life are like a vaudeville act, granting every false performance another audition. Perhaps each dress rehearsal leads us to another opening night and the opportunity to excel.

My next installment of apparitions allows a brilliant kaleidoscope of new events that seem to accelerate beyond what is in front of me. White transparent figures surround the screen as another group of figures encourages me to step into a new area. Beings that are familiar call me forward to a new doorway. I go beyond the white figures and feel my spirit being vacuumed into a sea of sepia-toned funnel clouds, spiraling in various directions. Historical visions roll out like a showcase of men creating, perpetuating, negotiating, and engaging in conflict. Saxons, Romans, Greeks, Muslims, Turks, Israelis, Catholics, Protestants, Germans, Japanese, and Americans bring forth aristocratic conquerors, determined to govern human life, seize and destroy land, and introduce values that are unnatural to the flow of the *Holy Spirit*. This fast-forward spinning circle shows a series of ill-fated governments throughout history rising and falling to the trail of one principle: *greed*. I stand in a vast gallery of stars, and I am persuaded to view Mother Earth through an untainted lens, agreeing to a neutral perspective of man's wrongful struggles. I answer the call.

In the name of God, man brings forth change through an obsession with progress. Carrying the symbol of the cross over his shoulders, man introduces a new willpower that changes the course of civilization. Deceptive theology serves as a smoke screen for Christ's perfect teachings, and what was pure becomes an adaptation of the truth. Marching across kingdoms, villages, and distant lands, they carve a path that dissolves freedom. Fear replaces tranquility and liberty is yanked from the hands of peaceful men, taking away their lands, replacing their divinity with a new God, called progress. Sadness stirs inside my soul with every image I witness, from the *Inquisition* to the *Civil War*, the horrors of bloodshed painted across *Normandy,* to the killing fields of *Vietnam.* I cry out, "Stop. This is not what *God* asks of us." I hear my words again. "This is not what *God* asks for." Did I say the word, *God*?"

Above, a red-tailed hawk guides me to the *Trail of Tears.* I witness the deaths of thousands of innocent men and women because of government policy. His crimson wings take me beyond Death Valley into an isolated part of the desert where Japanese Americans rush a United States government military post, demanding their freedom. Their tears, like many atrocities in America, are forgotten. No country is free from the stains of its past wrongdoings. In fact, every massacre, every evil act committed by man, is recorded onto a *Matrix Energy Grid* made up of electrical currents, leaving a residual of its past on the site where the atrocity occurred. Those who came before us leave their personal *frequencies* recorded on the land while future civilizations build new structures, high rises, grocery stores, and condo's, forgetting the sins of the past.

The Indian returns, hand extended beyond the galaxy, and points west. He waves me through a large entryway that loops with translucent images of beings that are no longer living. They stand facing me, these people whose past actions are filled with compassion, and choose new soul purpose as they descend to Earth. Luminous gold light hurls at lightning speed, transfiguring these fully developed images into light rays, locating parents that have been chosen by the balance of their fate. An unknown soldier chooses to balance his karma and come back as the soul of Gandhi. The plight of poverty-stricken India becomes his predestined battlefield. Perhaps he will create a foundation for global peace? I look upon Dr. Martin Luther King's spirit as it is propelled to a small town in Michigan to a single mom who struggles with financial woes. Boys and girls ostracize a fair-skinned green-eyed boy because he speaks clearly of Civil Rights subjects they don't understand. He is called to become part of the *Savior Generation* in future years.

There is one vision that outshines all the other visions. A red-gold light in a triad shape consumes every part of my inner self. *Women of power* illuminate my big screen, showcasing female *spirits* that are purified at such a rate I can't begin to comprehend. A black woman born in Mississippi selects a family of abuse, poverty, and discord and becomes one of the world's greatest media global leaders. Lifetime after lifetime, her soul advances through hardships, as she holds fast to spiritual ideals that will become Earth's greatest lessons for *womankind.* A petite woman from Houston speaks to a small crowd in Santa Monica, California, tapped into a collection of lifetimes, sharing profound messages of *New-Thought* reality and an awakened consciousness. This undersized group of followers multiplies tenfold as this *Speaker of Truth* sprouts spiritual wings and speaks to millions. A new image forms. A cosmological wedding ceremony predestined for a princess. She walks through the landmines of hardship wearing a *Crown of Hearts* for her fellow nation. Click. I am lead to another image of a sea of flowers lining cobblestoned streets, while millions of onlookers wear grief-stricken faces. Time comes to a complete standstill as humanity pays homage to one of their *Chosen Workers of Light.* Who is this woman whose light has shined for centuries as the sovereign of the people?

Images of *female spirit beings* are thrust upon the earth, move rapid-fire in front of me. Female rock-and-roll icons bounce into the entertainment world with their contemporary music, raising the collective consciousness. They are joined by writers, actors, ministers, as well as moms, all cocooned into *feminine souls* destined for purposeful missions. For centuries, enlightened womanly compassion has remained dormant, eager to address its new worldwide mission. Each female soul speeds through this *assembly line of fine-tuning* and is outfitted to meet an advanced earthly objective. I see male spirits, but the blemish of a war mind-set congealed with greed, delays instantaneous departure. Sprinkled in the hundreds, however, are *Masculine Souls* that are solid with spiritual intellectual wisdom from their past errors? They join the feminine departures to support their mission of global uplifting.

As this arena of participants prepares for their worldly assignments, scholarly radiance fills me. A feeling of wonder migrates through my entire being slowly, guiding me to my center, supplying my soul with abundant brilliance. An all-knowing supernatural being radiates gold light through my crown chakra, refining my thoughts and emotions into a triangle configuration of father-mother-child. This trinity is a winding path to an all-purposeful destiny. I accept, I think to myself. I am made aware that every mountain that greets the sun is our divine daily reminder of greatness. We are one flower, one bird, one river, and one person on this one planet, all connected to one almighty being. We are no more than the orange butterflies that fly from flower to flower in a spiritual garden. No less than the lakes, rivers, and oceans that journey effortlessly, destined to hit the shores of our intention. We are one. And when one of us uses *free will inappropriately*, the overall effects of this vibration can create a hurricane of damage within a soul structure that is already fine-tuned to perfection. The realignment of this toxic choice can take centuries to balance, especially if that soul is in a position of power and authority. This lack of understanding, of the world's framework has consumed, destroyed, and imprisoned love, which is the infrastructure of *All* civilization—God's gift to all, is to be great, but yet humble.

Lifting my soul upward, golden-white lights blind my visibility as a strong tug snaps inside my solar plexus, pulling me forward. Immediately, all goes still. Complete blackness. I see nothing. I feel nothing. Seconds pass. Still, there is a void of nothingness. The sound of my heartbeat thumps in the far-off distance. Louder and louder, I feel an inner presence near me. I feel my spirit. My breathing joins the melody of heart pounding. It's as if a stereo woofer surrounds every corner of this galactic space. Snap! A vertical white line appears changing from straight to zigzag. Complete blackness again. A proverbial voice echoes on the other side. "Ethan, do you want to return?" I am frozen. I try to answer, but sound is unsound. I hear it again. "Ethan, do you want to return?" I cannot feel or see my body, but I try to reach out to the voice. "Yes, I want to go back." I verbalize, but darkness consumes my response. A small ball of light launches itself toward my space. "Then, it is time to return." A white light appears again, allowing a split second to view my caller. Is this brightness I am blinding by, God? Is this being of absolute love and peace, God? A *Divine* presence consumes my spirit as I look downward. A Hispanic man wearing tennis shoes stands side-by-side with Cecelia and Mario. "Are you Papa," I call out. I see Cecelia radiant in a cobalt-blue sphere holding his hand. A sudden darkness takes over.

***

"Oh, Jane, what a beautiful stomach he has. Come over here and take a look."

"You are kidding me. You're such a dirty old lady. Get away from that young man. He is old enough to be—oh my, pull the rest of that sheet back. If someone catches us staring at him, we are in trouble. Go take a watch at the door."

"No one is there." Jane peeks down the hospital corridor. "How old is he?"

"He's too young for you!" Joanna stares at my motionless body. I feel her breath on my face, and her red hair smells freshly shampooed.

"Well, if your ass were any bigger, we'd have to toss tokens at your toll booth to get onto that turnpike." Jane snarls with a quirky smile and stands at her post by the door.

"Speaking of tossing coins, apparently they ran out of bloody funds when they offered half-price boob jobs for the likes of you. Oh my god. He's got a ring on his left foot. Come take a look." Jane dashes over, lifts my bed sheet with her right hand, allowing a tepee view of my torso. Joanna makes a quick jog to the other side of the bed, tempting Jane with another round of catty conversation. Both heads move up and down under my sheet, unaware that I see every angle of the room.

"I bet he's a runner?" Jane says, testing Joanna.

"I think he's a dancer." Joanna's smug remark challenges Jane.

"You and those damn men in tights. You're just a little too old for that fantasy."

"Speaking of large, how's that diet going?"

A powerful vacuum heaves my soul back into my body. The pain in my abdomen has returned. I open my eyes with a loud moan. "Shit!" Both nurses scream, fighting the bundle of sheets that drape over the three of us. Jumping hysterically, Joanna hits the IV hooked to my left wrist as I let out another bloodcurdling scream. "Fuck!" Dashing in every direction, both nurses hit the table tray, turning rounds of medications into small missiles. Bang! Bang! Clank! The tray table looses its hold and topples downward as Jane makes an Olympic hurdle over the IV. Joanna's instincts kick in, and both nurses fight to save the IV from crashing to the floor. I realize another round of excruciating pain is near as I join the race to fight for my arm. I lift my body up, yelling nasty four-letter curse words, tossing every syllable as if these words will keep me from hitting the floor. As it is, we all go down.

"Ethan Michaels! How are you feeling, honey?" Nora stands in the doorway, wearing the latest Chanel ensemble, flawless makeup, and shoes that cost more than what my insurance company wishes to spend annually on my health care. Nora's entire white outfit seems appropriate for this moment, and she waits anxiously to introduce the new and improved TJ as she stares down at this pile of misfits.

"Ted. Come here, Honey. Look at Ethan?" Nora's motions TJ to enter the room. "You had us all scared to death." Nora's attentiveness on both nurses is priceless.

TJ pokes his head out from behind the door and greets this madcap bundle on the floor. "Hey," he says softly. His eyes open wide as he stares at our bodies clumped over one another.

Nurse Jane stands up, finds her dignity, and puts me back in the bed. Joanna's face is filled with embarrassment. Both nurses regain their professionalism and restore my confidence with their immediate attention. The room is quiet until Dr. Johnson enters the room. Blessed with extreme good looks, everyone hangs on to his every word.

"Good evening, Mr. Michaels. Glad to see you are finally awake. Jane, how's our patient today?" Dr. Johnson notices the IV dangling from the stand and makes a peculiar expression.

"He's doing quite well. We had a bit of an accident and…well… he…let's see…uh?" Nurse Jane stumbles on her words. "Joanna and I—"

"The IV was hurting my arm and I inadvertently—" I say, looking at Nurse Jane.

Joanna joins the lie. "Absolutely, I tried to adjust the IV…well, there you have it."

Nora scans all three of us waiting for the punch line. TJ grins and dismisses our white lie. Dr. Johnson eyes the spilled medications. I rub my face trying to understand why rainbow colors have suddenly appeared over each person's outer frame.

Dr. Johnson's explanation of Crohn's disease is vague. "Another surgery is imperative; however, your recovery is a must for now. Your internal bleeding was due to a perforated viscus." Doctor Johnson's words fade in and out. He looks at me with awe.

"Mr. Michaels, it took four units of packed cells to complete your blood transfusion. Apparently your bleeding went unattended? We removed a small section of the lower intestine, and I am suggesting another surgery in about three months. Unfortunately, I can't guarantee this surgery will be a preventative. There is no cure for this disease. Your hemoglobin count is still very low, and you are anemic. You are quite a lucky man. Doctor Fisher and I believe…"

Dr. Johnson's words fade again, and his sentences become background noise. Colors beam off his outer perimeter as he moves about the room. Nora's golden light radiates all around her head, and TJ spins a green aura of some sort. The room is consumed in numerous shades of bright colorful auras as if they are glimpses into each person's story line.

"Dr. Johnson," I ask.

"Yes." He continues writing on his clipboard.

"Please tell the man in room 702 that his father loved him very much."

Dr. Johnson lifts his expression and shows a face of surprise. He looks over at Jane and makes a startled gesture. She nods her head with astonishment, quietly shrugging her shoulders. Dr. Johnson looks at the eruption on my left cheek and comments. "Well, thank you very much. I will be sure to tell him. I'll make sure you receive new med's for that staph infection on your cheek and some different anti-inflammatory drugs. "You are having inexplicable allergic reactions to your med's?"

All parties watch him leave, and Jane announces that visiting hours have come to an end. Nora comes closer to the bed and kisses my forehead.

"I'll be back tomorrow and we can have a private conversation. Okay? By the way, Ted is staying at your place. Honey is great. Don't worry about anything."

Nora takes TJ's arm as they walk into the hospital hallway. She turns around to say good-bye with a smile.

"Okay, Mr. Michaels. You've had quite a busy evening. It's time for a snack and some medications." Jane motions Joanna to retrieve a new round of medications.

"I'm glad you decided to come over from Southport for a little adventure, Nurse Jane." I innocently comment. "If you had not come over, you would have never left that man."

Jane's face turns completely about as she leans over my bed. "Bloody hell, how do you know about that?"

"I don't know. I just know it." I look as confused as she does. "I'm tired. We'll talk later." I feel my eyes close.

Jane and Joanna finish their duties, staring at me with surprise. Joanna whispers softly into Jane's ear. "It took forever to type and cross him. Don't you find that odd?"

I hear every word.

***

Indigo lights at the foot of my bed pulse in time to the monitor beeping beside my guardrail. A sharp pain throbs where the IV was placed, and this draws my attention to the incision below my stomach. Slow-moving figures in the hallway make their nightly rounds to various work spaces. Nurses come and go to patients' rooms quietly checking temperatures and heart rates. The night is still, and my room is cool. I stare at an Indian man hovering near my bed. His eyes are alert to the medicine tray and never break away from the silver stand. It appears to be a pivotal moment of concern for this phantom being. I want to exchange words with this man, before one of the nurses enters the room with more nighttime meds.

"Who are you? What do you want? Something is wrong?" I ask quietly.

He nods his head and continues glaring at the medicine tray. The image vanishes quickly when a beam of light breaks through the door. A female nurse enters. Nausea grabs me quickly, and I grab the IV stand and try to get up.

"Are you okay?" asks the nurse.

"I'm going to be sick."

I try to make my way to the restroom before she comes closer. The pain in my abdomen takes precedence of the nausea. I lose my equilibrium and fall to the floor.

"What kind of medications did they give me?" I ask, holding my stomach. "I feel sick to my stomach all the time."

Chart in hand, the nurse buzzes for assistance. She reaches for the light switch and reaches down for me just as a male nurse enters the room.

"Let me lend a hand," he says, noticing my swollen wrist. "We need to make this IV a little more comfortable." He leads me to the bathroom, lifting me gently to the toilet. Slightly shutting the door behind me, he comments, "I'll be right here if you need me." I can hear both nurses banter over my medicine as I brace against the toilet seat.

"These medications shouldn't cause him to become ill. He's sick from the anesthesia. He'll be okay." The female nurse peers into the bathroom as I cuddle the toilet seat. "He'll be fine."

"I'm going to adjust his IV and give him some sleeping pills and clean this mess up. If you need to attend to other patients, please do so," says the male nurse, as he says good-bye to the female nurse. "Let me clean your face, Mr. Michaels, with this cloth and get you to bed. Take these pills and get some rest. You'll feel better in the morning."

"Thank you," I say, apprehensively as he steadies my IV. "What are you giving me?"

"This is a new anti-inflammatory steroid. Take these and try and get some sleep. You need to rest, Ethan. Understood? Push the intercom button near the pillow if you need me. I'm on duty until 7 a.m."

He closes the door. I concentrate on the indigo light that has returned. Sounds of drums beat softly.

***

Voices awaken me. The scent of lemon cleaner is more than my morning senses can handle. I open my eyes and a woman wearing blue scrubs is cleaning the floor. "Good morning," she says with a smile. Around her are a crew of interns, a nurse with breakfast tray, and Dr. Johnson.

"Good morning, Mr. Michaels. How are you today?" Dr. Johnson occupies himself with a nurse, taking a quick glance at my chart. "I understand we had a situation last night?"

I try to come back with a reply, but the room bursts with vibrant colors. Green-golden light surrounds Dr. Johnson's shoulders and circles his head. A pale-yellow light sits on the nurse with the breakfast tray and becomes more effervescent the closer she comes. Kaleidoscopes of colorful rainbows bounce in every corner of the room as I try to focus on Dr. Johnson's words.

"These medications are too strong for me, and they're affecting my vision." Before I can continue with my complaint, I hear several conversations playing inside each person's head. Their thoughts are playing faster than their conversations with each other. One of the nurses looks at the infection on my cheek and smiles nonchalantly. The words inside her head tell me a different story.

"I would hate to have that on my face. It looks worse today than it did yesterday." She keeps staring at me.

I can hear the thoughts of the nurse in the blue scrubs, and she is not happy. "I don't know why I am the one to always clean up this shit. And if Joanna talks about her boob job one more time I am going to take this mop...Oh! Doctor Johnson is sexy. I wonder if he's married. If he is, I bet that wife must—what is Joanna doing now? She's trying to put the moves on him. Who does she think she is? Damn, this lemon solution is strong today."

Joanna is crooning with wishful thinking. "I'm going to move in a little closer and graze Johnson's arm with my breast. Why is she looking at me that way? What the hell did she put in that bucket?"

Dr. Johnson looks at the clipboard and makes a funny face. "No wonder this young man is sick to his stomach. This lemon antiseptic is enough to make me want to gag. Good god, Joanna, is your breast touching me?" His thoughts bounce around like a volleyball match in his head

Between the repetitive color extravaganza and the nonstop inner dialogues, I begin to wonder if this medication has side effects that no one has told me about. I can feel, see, and hear everything before anyone opens his or her mouths. Words mean nothing compared to what is being voiced inside their heads. Even though they speak of hopeful possibilities, their thoughts indicate great doubt in my ability to overcome this chronic disease, even with another surgery and a round of radiation.

"Let this poor man eat," says the nurse in the blue scrubs. "He has too much information on an empty stomach." She hands me a small covered tray with a paper cup with more medications and hustles everyone out of the room. "Mr. Michaels, this is a light breakfast so take your time and enjoy. I'll be back in a few minutes."

***

The room is quiet and voices of daytime television coming down the hall make me feel weary. The breakfast tray has come and gone, which means I can have some privacy. I move the IV to the outside rail so I can slide out of bed and use the portable toilet. This hospital gown is ridiculous. How can I slip out of it and use the toilet before the nurse comes back?

"Good afternoon, sweetheart."

"Nora. What a surprise. Listen…I need to…never mind."

"Everyone is asking about you, Ethan. I have tons of questions." Nora looks at me and scrutinizes the small room. "Honey, where are the flowers?"

"What? What flowers?" I feel the urgency to go to the bathroom.

"Where are all the flowers? Has anyone come to visit you today? Never mind, Ethan. I'll be back in a bit. Get some rest." She leaves my room.

I wrestle to remove my hospital gown, and surrender to the fact that the gown is going to drape at the foot of my wrist. The phone rings.

"Hello," I say, wrestling with my gown.

"Ethan, its Mary, we have been worried for over a month. Are you okay? Is this a bad time?"

"Well?" I pause for a long moment. "Yeah, it is. It's been a month?"

"Just to let you know, Chuck is coming by to see you today. Okay? I have to run. Bye." Click. The dial tone bangs in my ear.

How weird. Why would Chuck come to see me? Why did Mary act so strange? I leap forward to the portable toilet, plop my half-naked body on the cold plastic seat, and firmly grip the IV.

"Surprise, Ethan!" Six elderly patients dressed in the latest pajama fashions from Kmart plow into my room dragging their IVs. An old lady wearing a purple happy-birthday crown hobbles my way, removes her prized birthday tiara, and places it on top of my head.

"My name is Rhonda, and I am in room 205." Rhonda takes a puff on her asthma inhaler and introduces her new friends. "Well, I don't know all of your names so introduce yourselves?"

"Hi!" Collective raspy noises from the elders come my way. "I'm Jim. I am in room 207." He hands me a pair of dark dress socks.

Stunned beyond belief, I sit on my portable toilet seat, frantically grasp my hospital gown, fiddle with the purple tiara on my head, take the socks, and watch six old people bearing flowers, candy, and a half-eaten birthday cake that matches the tiara. "Rhonda, I don't think I'm up for company. And besides—"

Rhonda wheezes heavily. "Now's not the time to feel sorry for your self, young man. You got to live. Enjoy life. Take it by the horns." She inhales deeply on her inhaler and begins her next round of life-stimulating words. "You got to believe in miracles, starting today. Hey. Come over here, Lulu, and say hello to…? What's your name, again?"

"Ethan. Ethan. My name is Ethan. I am trying to use the—" I look attentively around the room and see enthusiastic expressions. Who got these old people stirred up?

"You like Godiva chocolates? Well? Do you?" A barefoot middle aged woman wearing a bright-green robe hands me her candy with a card still attached. *Get better, Na Na. We love you.* "I don't like chocolate so you can have it. By the way, my name is Llewellyn. Most my friends call me Lula. My ex husband called me Lu. Can't say I like that name much. Lu, Llewellyn, Lula—which name suits me best, Edwin?"

"Ethan! My name is Ethan."

Standing in the doorway wearing a giant smile, Nora mimics applause with her hands as she lifts the black veiled hat that covers her face. A one-piece black designer dress cinched with a beautiful black alligator belt and matching shoes somehow seems fitting as her elderly fans make room for her. Multiple IV stands squeak as they are pushed across sterile floors to make way for Nora.

"Ethan, is this not priceless?" Nora looks at Lula and calls her by name. "Llewellyn, I mean, Lulu, isn't Ethan the most wonderful young man you've ever met?"

"Oh, he is Mrs. Berry. He is." Lulu reaches for a hankie inside her robe, blows her nose, and never takes her eyes off of Nora. The elders relax and begin to chat with each other. Nora mingles contentedly, completely immersed in their personal stories. I, however, sit on the toilet and surrender to Mother Nature. Talk of Truman and the days of Ike dominate this party just as the sounds of running water trickle loudly down the plastic toilet bowl, halting their conversations. Nora elegantly makes her way to me waving kisses, laughing and admiring the gathering. I continue to pee.

"Fabulous O'P's, just fabulous O'P's." Nora continues smiling and acknowledging the small get-together. "Ethan, they are fabulous!" Nora chokes up.

"Nora. I am naked and I am peeing. I am totally embarrassed. What the hell are O'P's?"

"Oh, Ethan, I've given birth to three kids. I've seen everything. No need to worry, sweet face. I am not embarrassed, nor should you be. What are O'P's? They are old people." Nora leans in close to me. "But don't refer to them as old people. Okay?" Nora takes her black veiled hat, gently places it on my privates, and returns to the room.

"Excuse me." A cough comes from the outer door. A blue sphere lights up the entrance, but all I can see are old people. Another cough is louder. "Excuse me." The blue light shines. The room stands still and time seems to stop. "Ethan," a voice calls. I focus on the door. Chuck, Cecelia, and Mario stand patiently, looking into my room.

"Hey guys, come on in." I call Nora to help me with my hospital gown, but the room is frozen. Cobalt-blue lights trickle around the door's frame as Chuck enters. Cecelia and Mario remain stationary. Chuck's lower lip begins to quiver as the room goes back to normal speed and conversations return. He fidgets with his Cardinals baseball hat and fights tears. Nora catches the emotional weight of this man; she quietly escorts the old people out of the room. All space becomes tranquil again. Where did Cecelia and Mario go?

Hitching up his trousers and fighting an emotional meltdown, Chuck begins to cry. "Ethan. I'm afraid I have some bad news." He comes forward and leans against the wall near my IV. "Cecelia and Mario—" He pauses, tears stream down his plump cheeks.

"Please, Chuck. Please don't say it." I can feel tears building in the corners of my eyes. "Dear God! Please don't say it." Nora is in the doorway, fully becoming conscious of the situation as she wipes her tears.

"Ethan, Cecelia and Mario are dead. They were killed by a drunk driver on the way to the hotel to meet you." Chuck trembles. His tears fall to the floor as Nora races to embrace him. I remain immobile. "That son of a bitch ran a red light and hit them broadside." Chuck cries uncontrollably.

I glance through the hospital door and see that Lulu and her entourage are listening. Their faces are distorted with sadness. I realize at that moment that we are never prepared when loss claims a loved one. Heaviness consumes everyone. I feel numb.

"Mr. Michaels, it's time to prep." A nurse walks in; unaware of the drama that has befallen our room. "Okay, everyone, it's time to scoot. The lab has a busy schedule, and we need to get our young man ready." Nora embraces Chuck and bids farewell to her fans. Chuck squeezes my hand, looks at me with his swollen eyes.

"Ethan, Cecelia loved you. And Mario put you on a pedestal. I wish you could have met Papa. What a great man. He will always be the fisherman—" Chuck never finishes his words. Nora embraces him and asks that he wait for her outside in the hall.

"Nurse, can you excuse us for a moment. We need some private time. Please."

"No, I can't. We're really busy and time is slipping away." The nurse follows her routine by the book. There is a lack of compassion in her tone.

"Honey, I need some private time with Ethan. I'll find you in the hallway when I need you." Nora's voice is firm.

I watch Nora glare at the nurse as she exits. She waits patiently for our hush-hush moment. "Ethan, you crossed over to the other side, didn't you?" She grabs my motionless face. "I felt your soul leaving the night you were in the operating room. Nora puts her arms around me. "Please don't think I am crazy?"

I nod my head. "No, you're not crazy. You told me it wasn't my time to go."

"Yes! Yes, Ethan. Did you see your life play before you?"

"I did, Nora. I saw my past and future at the same time."

Lights flicker all over the room. I suddenly realize that Nora crossed over.

"Don't do what I did, Ethan. I spoke to Ted and he knows of a healer in Santa Fe that can help you." Nora cups my face and looks at my sad eyes. "I am not letting you go through radiation. Do you understand? There are alternative medicines available. We will both do this together." Nora swells with emotion. "You didn't want to say anything because you're trying to explain this away. Blame it on the drugs? You think you are crazy. I've been reading about energy grids on the human body and how they are affected by disease. Tomorrow I will bring you a book called *Heal Your Life*, by Louise Hay. You will love it. Ethan, keep this private for now. Say nothing, especially to the doctors."

I reach for Nora and break down. "Thank you." Nora places my head on her shoulder as I weep. "Cecelia and Mario are dead." Tears continue falling down my cheeks. The pain of their loss overwhelms me. Cecelia and Mario hover by the door surrounded by indigo lights. "Nora?"

"Yes, Ethan."

"How long have I been in the hospital?"

Nora looks up, surprise in her face. "You were in intensive care quarantine for a month."

I look at Nora in shock, fighting tears. "I can't believe Cecelia and Mario are dead. Why? Why them? Poor Chuck. Someone's got to watch over him, Nora. When was the funeral? Never mind. Bring every book you have on crossing over. Nora, in my car is a pair of old shoes. Bring them with the books. Okay? Doctor Fisher told me that another surgery won't—" I look down at my wrist and adjust the IV that has begun to hurt. "Tell TJ, I want to go to Santa Fe." I fight back the tears.

"Mr. Michaels. We need to take you to the lab now." The nurse has returned to the room with another nurse. "If you don't mind, lady, this is a hospital and we have procedures to follow. Leave now! I can call administration and—"

Nora continues to sit on my bed. "Ethan, where are my manners?" Nora never looks up to acknowledge the angry nurse. "I'm so sorry, Miss. Please accept my apology. I have tons of things floating on my mind. Would you do me a favor, Honey?' Nora looks at the other nurse. "Is it possible you could hand me my purse? Please?" Nora points to the nightstand.

Both nurses look perplexed, however, they accommodate Nora and hand her the purse.

"Where is it?" Nora digs in her purse, pushing her possessions from side to side. She stands up, kisses me on my forehead, turns around, and hands each nurse a five-dollar bill. "I love you, Ethan. I'll see you tomorrow."

"This is a hospital, not a hotel, Lady! I never—" The nurse glares at Nora.

Nora looks at the rigid nurse and says in a completely calm tone, "I know, Honey. It shows! Would it be too much for either one of you to call valet?" Nora waves good-bye and says hello to a stranger in the hallway. "Aren't you adorable?"

***

"Can I have your attention please?" the ticket agent commands on the intercom. "Will passengers needing a pre-board please come forward? We will board first-class passengers shortly." An oversold flight to Santa Fe and tension, is mounting among the standby passengers who wait frantically by the ticket counter. An older feeble woman being pushed in a wheelchair by a family member gets the attention of a flight attendant near the boarding entrance. "Can I have some water, Miss?" she asks, in a weak voice. "And would you mind getting some peanuts so I can maintain my strength." The flight attendant responds with compassion. "Don't worry; I'll be right back with water and some peanuts. My name is Pam."

I look at this touching scene feeling miserable as Nora reminds me of Cecelia's post memorial service when I return. "I don't want to be a pre-board with all these old people, Nora. Why do I have to sit in this silly wheelchair?"

"Ethan, we have had this conversation over and over again. What did we agree to? How many times do we have to have this same conversation? Well?" Nora looks at her watch and looks at the flight monitor.

"But, Nora." I sit in my pre-board wheelchair, legs covered with a tasteful Polo blanket Nora got at Neiman Marcus for my trip to Santa Fe.

"Well? Come on. Say it." Nora taps me gently on the hand.

"O'P's, O'P's, never say old people." I say with an evil smirk.

"Thank you. And you are going to save your strength. Correct? Ah, here we go. You're about to board. I will call you from Mexico. Tell Ted I love him and I am sorry that I can't meet Lindsey." Nora seems nervous. She is trying to be brave, but I know she is concerned that I am flying by myself. "Ted will meet you and Lindsey at the Hertz counter. Remember that Lindsey is flying incognito so you may not recognize her immediately. Excuse me, young lady." Nora addresses the flight attendant who is preoccupied with the old lady in the wheelchair. "This young man is very ill and will need some special attention."

"Nora, I'm sure I'll be able to recognize Lindsey. She's on last month's cover of *Vogue*." I glance at the old lady and see murky-gray lights all around her.

"Ethan, when you meet the Shaman, remember everything he says." Nora places a piece of paper in my shirt pocket.

"Okay, okay. What's this?" I reach inside my pocket and discover that Nora has written down contact numbers in case I should get lost or need immediate attention.

"Nora!" I say, embarrassed by her attention. I remove the just-in-case list and wad it up. "I will be okay."

Nora takes the wrinkled paper from my hand and begins to flatten it out. "Peter Ethan Michaels."

"Nora, I am not a school boy."

"You certainly are acting like one. Excuse me, Sir. Can you help me?" Nora flags down a man wearing a classic blue suit.

"Yes?" He gives Nora the once-over. "Would you mind helping me?" Nora says in a sweet yet sexy voice.

"Absolutely," says the predator right before he pounces on its innocent prey.

"Turn around!" Nora's authority excites the stranger. "Ethan, you are taking this! What's your name, Sir?" Nora never lets him answer. "Slightly tilt your back down and face that monitor near the gate. Does that make sense? Don't answer." The man immediately bends down and nods. "Don't take your eyes of that monitor." The man nods again.

"I am a grown man, and I don't need you to treat me like a child." Nora becomes angry. I see the old lady in the wheelchair staring at us, her mouth wide open.

Nora takes the wadded paper and places it neatly on the stranger's back and begins smoothing it out. "You are going to take this. Or? " Nora continues rubbing the man's back.

I twist and turn my wheelchair closer to Nora. "I am not taking it!"

"Yes, you are taking it." Nora begins to smack the paper at rapid speed. "Spread your back a little more, Sir. Lower. Bend your knees." The man spreads his legs apart. Nora raises her voice. "You will take it." The old lady starts to look around to see if anyone else is watching our tit-for-tat argument.

The man in the suit howls, "I'll take it! Give it to me. I'll take whatever you give me, Lady. Please."

Nora stops pounding the man's back immediately. I can't speak. The lady in the wheelchair is waving frantically for the flight attendant. "Oh? Thank you for being such a gentleman." Nora grabs my wheelchair and speeds me to the pre-board gate. "Miss, please take care of this young man." The flight attendant greets me with hello and takes my ticket. "Ethan?" Nora says daringly.

"Yes, Nora?"

Nora takes the almost flat paper and hands it to the flight attendant. "What's your name, Darling?"

"Pam," she says, modestly.

"First of all, Pam, you are absolutely stunning. I bet you spend hours getting facials? I have never seen such beautiful skin." Nora grabs Pam's hands, making sure I see the outcome. "Ethan has someone meeting him in Santa Fe, and they must have this."

"Please don't worry. And it's you who has the beautiful skin. I'll take care of him." Pam places the paper in her jacket pocket as I am escorted down the passageway.

***

"Ladies and gentlemen, even though we have landed, the captain has asked that you please remain seated and keep your seat belts fastened until we come to a complete stop. We apologize for the delay and know that you all have choices. We hope that your next choice will bring you back on American Airlines." A nameless female voices clicks off the microphone.

The clatter of seat belts unfastening ricochets all the way to the back lavatory. Passengers stand up and battle each other for the overhead bins. Tension dominates the stale air as conversations that never occurred during flight suddenly begin with, "Is this your first time to Santa Fe?" or "How long are you staying in Santa Fe?" No one really cares if the stranger answers the nonchalant question; it is a ploy to throw your opponent off track and grab luggage.

"Excuse me, Miss? Where is my wheelchair? I'm ready to get off the plane now." The old lady at the airport who witnessed Nora's slap-the-back incident becomes slightly distressed.

"One moment, please." The flight attendants attempt to bring order to a full flight of passengers who have become rowdy due to overdosing on soda's and peanuts. "Please remain seated until the captain has turned off the seat belt sign."

"I want my wheelchair now!" The old lady suddenly becomes irritable.

"Pumpkin, we need to let the other passengers deplane. Okay, Honey?" Pam oozes with kindness. Bing! The seat belt sign is turned off.

"How come you let me pre-board in Dallas?" The old lady raises her voice with sarcasm. Passengers turn away from the overhead bins and look forward.

Pam, never losing her early years of flight attendant training, comments sweetly. "Well. It's much easier to allow all the passengers to deplane, and it's also for your own safety."

I decide to assist the beautiful flight attendant who seems to be in a delicate situation.

"She's right, you know."

"I want my wheelchair now! Bring my wheelchair to me now." All the passengers go silent as the old lady begins to scream.

Pam comes to realize that rules and regulations that were written in the 1950's must not apply to this particular in-flight situation. After all, we were a much kinder and gentler nation 30 years ago. Pam removes the paper from her pocket and looks at it. "Ethan. That is your name? Isn't it?" She places the paper back in her pocket.

"Yes," I say, proudly, thinking I am about to save the day. Every passenger is focused on the front cabin.

'Would you hand me that red-and-orange pillow." Pam remains calm. "Thank you, Ethan." Pam moves in closer to the old lady. "All right, Honey. When you feel the urge to get out of control, inhale. Be sure and take long deep breaths, place the pillow over your mouth, hold it for a second or two, remove the pillow from your face, and exhale. If you want to rant and scream, and interrupt my flight one more time, I am going to take this pillow and hold it over your mouth forever and take that seat belt and bound you to our first-class section as a reminder for future irate passengers. Do we understand each other? I thought so. Now eat those peanuts I gave you and don't make a sound."

The lady rips open her bag of peanuts and waits for the oncoming crewmembers to open the front-exit door. She glares at me. Male passengers move slowly helping women who are suddenly helpless with their overnight suitcases. The door swings open, and the old lady makes an Olympic dash past Pam and out the exit door. Wow! I think to myself. This is going to be an interesting trip. I've just seen my first miracle happen to a weak and feeble old lady.

***

"Paging passenger, Ethan Michaels! Please go to the Hertz counter. You have a message waiting." The intercom message blasts throughout baggage claim. I hobble slowly to the Hertz counter.

"Sir, there's a message for me. I am Ethan Michaels." I look for TJ in a crowded airport.

The clerk hands me a gray slip and walks away to help another customer. "Thank you," I say to his back.

"Ethan, I have gone to get our car. Find Lindsey and come outside baggage claim near the taxi pickup. Ted."

Oh my god. I can't believe TJ wants me to meet Lindsey without him. I begin to panic inside. "You can do this, Ethan. Come on. You can do this." I whisper. I remain close to the rental car post. I will find

250

Lindsey, be discreet, introduce myself, and quietly escort her outside. That's my plan. Minutes pass. Passengers come and go. The baggage claim area becomes full and empty with people. Where is TJ? Where is Lindsey?

"Paging passenger, Ethan Michaels! Please meet your party by the Hertz counter."

The voice echoes throughout the foyer. I go to the counter and look for TJ. I ask the clerk who made the announcement. He shrugs his shoulders. I look around the chamber hall watching a new wave of oncoming passengers. Where is Lindsey? Where is TJ? I'm getting upset. I march back to the counter and ask the clerk to make another announcement "Can you ask Ethan Michael's party to meet him at the Hertz counter." He rolls his eyes and grunts. "I'm quite busy. Are you renting a car, Sir?"

"No! Our car is already rented. We're supposed to meet here by the counter."

"What does your party look like? Who is it?" he asks, with an attitude. "If your party has rented a car from Hertz, why would you meet here? Did you try the lot?"

I begin to feel my neck tighten up. The agent walks away from me and begins to assist another customer. "Paging passenger, Ethan Michaels. Please meet your party by the Hertz counter now." I scream at the clerk. "That's me. That's me. Where is that coming from? Who is making that page?"

I frantically scan the mass of people that floats between security and flight gates. I don't see TJ in the crowd. Nor do I see Lindsey. Are they at the counter? Nope. I take a few more steps forward hoping for the arrival of either TJ or Lindsey. I take one final glance toward the counter and see the clerk pointing in my direction. He's talking to a man in army fatigues, matching jacket, and combat boots. A large straw hat covers his face as he turns to catch me staring. He touches his dark sunglasses and walks toward me. I can see his eyes popping out. A silver dog tag is wrapped around his neck. Oh my god! Perhaps TJ and Lindsey are hurt and they are at a military hospital? My palms begin to sweat. Who do I call? Oh my god, Nora was right. I do need that piece of paper with all the contact numbers. Damn! Nora, I am so sorry for being such an ass.

"Are you Ethan Michaels?"

"Yes, Sir, I am." This man's cologne is way too sweet. Oh, I get it. He is a she.

"Please come with me."

"Is everything okay? I have been very sick and though I am not fully recovered I can take the bad news. I lost two dear friends over ten weeks ago, and I am deeply hurt. Shit! I don't know how to reach TJ's family—" My mouth won't shut up, and my brain has gone into a deep forest. "I can't tell you who I am to meet. It's confidential. Well," I pause for a split second, "You probably already know who it is since you're accompanying me out of the airport to a military hospital? Is this hospital near Roswell? Oh dear god. Speak. Say something. Please tell me. I can't take the silence." Sweat pours off my upper lip.

"Ethan, I'm sorry for the delay. I switched cars. It wasn't big enough for the three of us." TJ jumps out of the car and opens the trunk. "Let me help you. How was your flight?"

I look at TJ and my masculine-female escort. "Please don't tell me?!"

Lindsey removes her straw hat and dark sunglasses. She tosses the bulky military jacket in the back seat of the rental and introduces herself. "Hi.

I'm so sorry to hear about your friends. Don't you worry? I have a feeling we are about to become new friends." She reaches over and hugs me.

"Ethan, give me a hand. I need to rearrange this trunk. Let's see? If I move this vacuum cleaner over here and put my Dust-Buster over here...hmmm?" TJ moves our luggage to one side of the car and gently places an assortment of vacuum cleaners on the other side of the trunk.

"Teddy. Look, what I got you. It's a new all-purpose vacuum cleaner." Lindsey opens her large suitcase and displays the small red gadget.

"This is fantastic. Where did you get it?" TJ is full of joy.

Screeching tires pulls up next to our rental car. Four teenagers roll down their windows and scream. "Are you Lindsey?"

TJ shuts the car hood. "Ethan, get in the car now."

"What?" I say confused.

Lindsey grabs my arm and shoves me in the back seat of the car. "It's the enemy. Teddy, hurry up. Start the car." Lindsey jumps in the front seat and ducks down. TJ dashes to the driver's seat and starts the ignition. "The enemy's approaching us, Teddy!"

"I can't believe its Lindsey," one of the young girls screams. She approaches the car.

"Teddy, put this car in first and go now." Lindsey rolls her window up.

I sit in the backseat and watch four teenagers race to Lindsey's window, holding pen and paper. TJ puts the car in drive and speeds away leaving disappointed fans lurking in lot C. I am speechless. The look of panic on Lindsey's face is one I won't forget and one I soon come to understand.

***

A pounding headache vibrates from my temple to the back of my neck. Dizziness seems to take over as I feel nausea inside my stomach. The pain pills are useless since I have gone against doctor's orders and cut my dosage in half. The anti-inflammatory drugs serve no purpose, and the bleeding continues. Nora's home remedies of black root and garlic tablets are a saving grace but not enough to combat this disease. "TJ, pull the car over. I'm about to be sick." Lindsey pulls the passenger's mirror downward so she can check me out.

"Hold on, Ethan. We're almost there. Teddy, is he going to be okay?" Lindsey's voice begins to fade.

A Technicolor valley surrounds the desert, and the howl of coyotes in my ears is more than I can bear. Skies burst with turquoise and the brown-orange-taupe Mountains stand in sharp contrast. Yellow auras canopy my view, allowing only small silhouettes of TJ and Lindsey. A familiar pull to my solar plexus tugs at my spirit as the thumping of Indian drums beats in the distance. The uneven road aggravates my nausea, and trails of dust block my view from the back window. The car takes us up a narrow winding hill to a place called Saint Francis Point. Red-and-gold lights swallow the desert foliage, and the sound of drums pulsates in my head. "TJ, these noises are hurting my ears."

"What noises? Hold on, Ethan. We're here." TJ stops the car and rushes to the backseat. "Help me, Lindsey. Please help me."

A strong arm reaches inside and draws me upward. The pain disappears instantly as I am pulled from the car. TJ and Lindsey stand outside the rental car looking panicked. "Is he all right?" Lindsey is near tears.

The sound of keys clinking against a bare torso awakens a rainbow of colors all around the top of the mountain. A red-tailed hawk flies above the powdery skies, calling to the wild.

"Come with me," a gentle voice chants in my ear. TJ and Lindsey watch with wonderment as the Indian man shepherds me to the adobe house. I stand to my feet, breathe fresh air, and see a swarm of hummingbirds circling the young man. A coyote sits near the foot of the hill watching the property. "Welcome to all of you. Come inside."

I look upon the face of a young Indian man and see kindness. Keys dangle from his neck. Red-gold lights hum like young tenor voices in a choir. "Why do you wear those keys around your neck?" I fade away.

Guardians

Chapter 11

The stained cement floors are laced with desert sand. Thick stucco walls with long cracks muffle the footsteps of our party of three. In the corner, a black stove sits. A woven basket filled with hickory wood rests on a small cushioned seat, neatly situated so one can observe the magnificent mountains in the distance. Vanilla incense fills the air. A rug in muted colors, hangs on the walls between crude shelves that display hammered metal bowls and wooden dolls. A glass Mason jar filled with pale-pink sand sits next to a simple white cup that holds long bird-feathers. The young Indian man speaks kindly to TJ and Lindsey while I stare at several hummingbirds that have gathered outside an open window. I lose count of the birds and am startled by the friendly barks of a black-and-gold German shepherd. A large gray cat stretches in the dirt outside. The Indian man says the cat's name is Lincoln. A large pearl-colored cockatoo, its plumage pronounced like a tribal headdress, squawks lazily in the corner. Makeshift bookshelves hold numerous medical journals, books on Native American folklore, and Edgar Cayce transcripts. A sturdy massage table covered with clean white sheets stands in another corner under a ceiling of ancient numerology symbols I have never before seen in my studies.

"You are feeling much better, Ethan. You have a psychic headache that will go away shortly." The Indian man turns his attention to Lindsey. "Come, we have much to discuss on your past." Lindsey is eager to begin. I wonder why these headaches continue.

I nod my head and pretend to know what he is talking about. "Okay."

TJ and I are asked to wait in a private room by the kitchen or in the backyard. I go outside; TJ picks up a couple of books and heads for the small room. Lindsey glances nervously at TJ as he leaves. I feel a new strength for the first time in over a year.

"There is green tea that is freshly made and bottled water, which you need to drink, Ethan. The restroom is next to the bedroom." The Indian man speaks with a soft confidence. "You are looking much better, Ethan. Please enjoy the view."

"TJ, he's right. I feel much better. My head is clear and I don't feel the pain near my stomach as much," I whisper. TJ yawns, says he is going to go read, and is barely able to complete his sentence. He finds the bedroom, lies down on a bed covered in Indian blankets, opens a book, and passes out.

"TJ, wake up." I wait for a reply. "Okay, you rest. I'll be outside."

I walk slowly through the narrow hallway, taking note of the many paintings that hang on the wall. Abstract, geometric shapes in bold reds and greens are slashed with black-and-white lines. I can hear Lindsey asking questions. She sounds nervous, so I exit through the back door to give her privacy and rediscover the view I missed because of my bout of illness.

A large ponderosa tree stands in the distance near a cliff that overlooks a rock-strewn valley. It seems vaguely familiar. Do I know this view? Scanning this tranquil scene, I see yucca plants scattered around, their sword-shaped leaves giving way to woody stems that explode into white blossoms; nature's version of fireworks. Lizards scurry from cactus to rock. I turn back toward the adobe house and notice golden lights ascending to the blue skies. What is happening to my vision? Perhaps the Shaman can enlighten me as to why I feel like I'm on acid. My eyes are playing tricks on me. Just over the foothill and past the empty creek bed, a coyote sits quietly, surveying my every move. I remove a protein bar from my pocket, unwrap it, and swig on my bottled water. Frozen in sand, I come to a halt. Faint sounds of flute play in the distance. Do I hear the voices of children? I shiver all the way down my spine as I recall those convoluted images that played like a Fellini movie in the emergency room. A large sandstone rock looks inviting and offers a perfect view of the valley. I sit and listen to the wind. For the first time, I feel peaceful. Those hours of darkness that took Cecelia and Mario feel far away. The sky transforms from deep blue to shades of marigold orange and violet. The blue sky can be uplifting but can just as easily send me to my knees with its painted glories. A sudden coolness in the air descends, sending a breeze across the desert and sand sprinkling against my tennis shoes.

"Ethan, Ethan." A voice behind me brings me back to the house. "It's your turn." TJ approaches me from behind, his smile anxious and large. "Ethan. He is fantastic. Please hurry. It's getting dark outside." TJ grabs my arm and yanks me forward. "Come on. Come on."

"Where has the day gone, TJ? How long have I been out here?" I look at my watch and see that it has stopped.

A bright star has become visible in the sky as TJ and I approach the adobe home. The early night air has brought a new display of celestial pyrotechnics. I stop at the entrance of the house and turn around to gaze once more at the shiny light that has led so many. "Time slipped past me, TJ." I look at my watch again, shaking it recklessly in hopes of restoring it. "Wow. It is so beautiful out here." I follow TJ inside the adobe house.

"Teddy, Raziel is amazing. Isn't he?" Lindsey strokes Lincoln who has found a new friend in a warm, tender female lap. "Ethan," Lindsey whispers. "Come here." Her flawless face is cradled by the night's light. "Look at me." Another whisper slightly stronger in tone guides me closer so she can speak softly to my face. "We don't know each other yet, but we are about to become great friends." Lindsey's face is a gift from Venus, worn only by a few, and she knows how to honor her beauty by bestowing me with a brilliant smile. "Ethan, all of us will be moving to Los Angeles very soon." Lindsey says with enthusiasm, still whispering.

"Lindsey, don't say anything to Ethan," TJ moves in closer. "Let's see what Raziel shares with Ethan, and we'll compare notes at dinner." TJ huddles the three of us face to face. Like children always caught-up in the throws of mischief, we listen to TJ and nod our heads in unison. "Okay."

"Where is…? What's his name again?" I look around the room, trying to locate our host and still obeying the code of quiet talk.

"Raziel, Ethan," TJ quietly speaks in my ear.

"Is he Jewish?" I ask innocently. I can tell by the response from my newfound friendships, I have failed my spiritual lesson. "I won't say his name then. Okay?" TJ and Lindsey focus past my shoulders, purposefully denying my silly comment. "Well, so when are we are moving to L.A.? Hello?" They keep focusing on the wall behind me. "I've never heard of a Jewish Indian?" I chuckle trying to be cute. "What are you guys looking at?" I turn around.

A large red-tailed hawk sits godlike on the arm of Raziel. A high-pitched girlie-sounding scream falls from my mouth: "Oh my god!" TJ and Lindsey remain still.

"Come and eat a little corn bread before we begin, Ethan." Raziel places the hawk near an open window. I stare at this picture-perfect image of an Indian man. The wisdom in his face is palpable. "You must drink this liquid and eat this bread before we begin."

My eyes keep to the window. "What is it?"

"Ethan, don't question him on this," says TJ, shaking my elbow. "Hell, those doctors plugged you with so many damn drugs; I'm surprised you aren't with me in Alcoholics Anonymous sharing your story."

"When did you join AA, TJ?" Lindsey asks unassumingly.

"I met a very interesting friend of Ethan's," says TJ, but his reminisces are interrupted by Raziel.

"There is a diner at the foot of this hill. Please bring back freshly cooked vegetables and fruits. I will have tea for us all when you return." Raziel's charcoal hair falls over his black eyes as he turns away from us. We have been invited to share supper. This is good.

"Fantastic. That's a great idea." TJ helps Lindsey from the chair and bids a quick farewell. "Ethan, remember what Nora always says when we embark upon something new and exciting?"

I break my concentration from the window where the beast of the sky perches and quietly remark, "Keep an open mind. I guess you know about O'P's too?"

"What?" TJ glances back. "What's an OP?"

Raziel moves across the floor, opens the door to a starburst sky, and gently points to the road. "Go down to the foot of the hill and drive until you see lights on a building." Sounds of crickets and owls linger in the atmosphere.

***

The stove smells of freshly lighted hickory. Candles positioned through out the small room give off a gold light that flickers into the room's corners. Raziel wears moccasins that poke out from faded, worn jeans. Keys dangle every time he moves about, sending me a memory of the man I saw the night I died. Sitting obediently, prepared for mysterious passages, I wait to speak until I am spoken to. I pass the time. Nothing is said. I sit. I fidget. I look. I stare at my wrist and rediscover that my watch is useless. Raziel stares at me, as I squirm on the sofa. I begin to sweat. What is he doing? Why does he sit so quietly?

Finally he rises. Good. Now we can begin. He moves slowly toward the stereo and slides a cassette into it. A female voice that angels have blessed sings quietly. I begin to see colors again, shades of blue, purple, and reds. I'm starting to take this kaleidoscope like moments for granted.

"What are we listening to? This is awesome."

Raziel's eyes begin to draw me in. I try to resist the tug-a-war that has begun. He says nothing.

"Wow, I love this music. I'll need to write down who this is when we're finished. Oh, well, I guess we need to start first, huh…?" My hyperactive mouth is revealing my nervousness. "I guess since we're talking I might as well ask now who the recording artist is. I have this desire to listen to quiet music these days. I don't know why? Hey, tell me about those keys around your neck."

I can't shut up, nor can I make eye contact. Will he react? Silence again. The colors in the room have become larger, engulfing the room. Spiral shapes of red and gold move about like spinning tops. Raziel crosses his legs and shifts his chiseled body into a lotus position. Black lashes graze the tops of his cheeks, and his dark eyebrows frame closed lids that seem to flutter with the music. I see amethyst lights allover the room, dominating the space, and I remain glued to where I sit. Colors in the shape of a pyramid surround this man and seem to vibrate with every breath he takes. The keys rumble against his bare chest. I sneak a quick peep to see if he is alert and witness a past experience that causes me to choke up. White-golden lights start at the center of his forehead and descend downward to his left hand, where they explode into deeper shades, which then travel to his right hand and ascend back to his forehead. A slight breeze ruffles his black hair, causing the candle that sits on the table near the stove to dance. I am spellbound.

"Sanat Kumara!" Razeil speaks to me with his eyes wide-open. All colors break up.

"Nope," I say, confused. "I've never been overseas. I would love to go to London." I look around the room, hunting for the colors that have vanished.

Raziel stands up and stares at me. "You have spoken to the white-haired man with blue eyes from Brussels." I sit on the edge of the sofa astounded.

"Paper and pen rest on the mantle, Ethan." Raziel's eyes remain focused on me.

I rise, go to the mantle and notice two burning candles next to an old photograph of Cecelia, Mario, Papa, Raziel and Brussels, standing on a pier in St. Thomas.

"Do you know the man from Brussels?" I ask with shock.

"Yes, I do. He is the *Key Master.*"

***

Sparkling stars that begin at the base of the desert floor reach beyond the horizon and fill the night sky. Bright high beams from the rental car shine onto Joshua trees that randomly jump out from the mountainous highway. Lindsey is half-asleep in the back of the car, while TJ and I talk.

"Ethan, what happened back there? What did he say to you that has you so quiet?" TJ concentrates on the road.

"I'm still trying to understand, TJ."

"It can't be that difficult?" TJ is tired and irritable from a long day.

I watch Lindsey. She is pretending to be asleep but I know she is listening to us. "TJ, I am starving. I need to eat a little something. What did you do with that takeout? You were gone forever."

Lindsey's face scrunches into a tired smile. "Teddy took the wrong exit. We drove 29 miles before we realized we were lost."

"We're all exhausted from our day. Let's head to the hotel." TJ watches the road.

Shooting stars explode over the mountaintops, but I am too tired to make a wish. The white highway-lane dividers zoom toward the car like lightning rods. All I can think about is what took place at Raziel's place. I hear the call of coyotes as we drive past a small town that seems to be blanketed in slumber. Lindsey curls up and watches the scenery. TJ stares at me and knows I hold a secret. I eat a cold hamburger in an awakened silence, pretending not to notice TJ. Raziel's forecast of my *rise and fall* in my professional and personal life will come in ten years. His prediction scares me.

"Get up, everyone." TJ is full of excitement. "I want you two to come with me to an Alcoholics Anonymous meeting this morning as my guest. It's an open meeting and then we'll drive up to say good-bye to Raziel before heading back to the airport." TJ has breakfast already sitting on the table.

"What time is it?" I am slow to rise as always.

"Who cares what time it is?" Lindsey jumps out of bed, races to the bathroom and begins her less-than-five-minute beauty regime. "I'll wash my face and brush my teeth in the shower and we can go."

"TJ, you realize that if every girl in America saw Lindsey's beauty routines, we would have cosmetic assassins at our doorstep in one hour." I jump out of bed and devour the hot cereal TJ has made. "What are you doing?"

"I'm straightening up." TJ has three vacuum cleaners lined up for a heavy-duty military inspection. Hunting with precise action, TJ finds the outlet and begins to suck away any known particles that may have crept into our non sterile hideout during our brief visit. Lindsey sings carelessly in the shower, gurgling on her toothbrush.

"Come on, Lindsey. You need to hurry. Ethan needs to shower. You know he takes forever to tidy up." TJ yells loudly over the Hoover's blare.

Lindsey scurries out with a towel wrapped around her perfect body. "Teddy, have you tried the high-volt Dust Buster I got you?"

"Yes. It's fantastic. I used it this morning on the interior of our rental car."

I watch these two people who have plunged into my life. TJ, the feature film publicist whose all-American looks work against his genius, and Lindsey, a black, African female who has graced the cover of more fashion magazines in one month than any working model could wish for in their entire career. I wipe the morning sleep from my face and enjoy the vacuum cleaner-bonding episode between my new friends. "I'll be out in a flash," I yell. I feel an inner strength I have never felt. The dizziness has vanished.

We leave trails of dust behind our rental car as we blaze a trail to Saint Francis Point. The midmorning sun has the feel of a heat wave. We open our car doors to bid farewell to Raziel. Hummingbirds flit about the front porch, waiting for the young Indian to greet them. TJ shares how honored he feels that Lindsey and I attended his first out-of-town AA meeting. We could see the joy in his face when he took his 60-day chip. Realizing that the miracles of transformation rest in the lives of those who find the courage to face an incurable disease with the grace of a higher power, it is I who must do the same. These fragile, newly established people welcomed Lindsey and me this morning, finding purpose with every spoken word of *The Serenity Prayer*. Green auras were abundantly visible to me throughout the meeting.

"Good morning, my peaceful three." With a big smile, Raziel jokes around. "I see beautiful spirits today. How are you feeling today, Ethan?" Hummingbirds circle above Raziel as he fills their red containers with water and honey.

"The dizziness is gone. So is the pain in my abdomen." I am determined to understand this mysterious occurrence especially since I have not bled since last night

"I feel fantastic." TJ grins from ear to ear. Humbleness overcomes him.

"Lindsey? What about you?" Raziel waits for her reply.

"I...I...," Lindsey breaks down sobbing. "I can't thank you enough for all you shared with me." Tears run down her face. Raziel embraces Lindsey, watching TJ and I survey the hummingbirds that swarm the adobe's porch. She hands him an envelope and turns to TJ and me. "Guys, this is on me." Lindsey is firm with her contribution. TJ acknowledges Lindsey with a smile. I am humbled.

"Please take these gifts back with you to your destinations." Raziel hands each of us a different-sized package wrapped in brown-paper bags. "Do not open them until you are in flight." We jiggle our heads and accept his generosity.

Boldly I come forward and persist. "I have a question for you, Raziel?" The need to know the why of those keys around his neck consumes me for many reasons. This curiosity is a bigger gift to me than the package I proudly hold. TJ and Lindsey look at me with uncertainty.

"I am also a *Key Master*, the one who helps you open the door to your authentic purpose. The name Raziel means to unlock the hidden secrets of the universe. Does this answer your question, Ethan?"

I stand there in complete astonishment. "Uh…." TJ and Lindsey look stunned as well.

"The man who speaks of the *tinker* will give you the next key. Remember that, Ethan." Raziel walks inside the adobe home and the hummingbirds take flight.

***

"Can you come through security again, Sir," the security guard at the airport says with a sour voice.

I walk through the security entrance, and the buzzer goes off yet again. "Maybe I left my keys in my pocket," I say with an apology.

"Please come over here, Sir." The guard, who looked merely bored before, now has a stern expression.

"What's in the brown package?" Another guard retrieves my present from the conveyor belt.

"It's a gift," I say, but this time with a tone.

"Open it." A stout man wearing thick eyeglasses and a uniform joins the other guards.

"Please take off your shoes." This guard can't weigh more than 140 pounds but his cockiness is huge.

"Now, walk through again, Sir." The stout guard takes the present from my hands and begins tearing off the brown paper. I set off the alarm again.

Lindsey and TJ stand past security looking concerned. "Go ahead, guys. I'll be okay." The security wand goes up and down my body at a slow pace. "I'll call you when I get home."

"Okay, Ethan. We love you." TJ and Lindsey rush to catch their flight back to New York. I stand at attention watching the security man frown. "There is nothing in this box except a handwritten note, a tape cassette, and herbs. Go through one last time, Sir." The guards glare at me.

The buzzer is silent. Thank god. Now I can gather my belongings and leave these men to tend to better moments. "Please give me back my gift," I demand to the skinny guard who jostles my items around. "I don't see anything suspicious. Do you?" I pull myself together, race to the gate with a tattered bag that was meant to be opened during a special moment on the airplane. Six passengers board the plane that is ready to taxi.

"Go ahead and board, Sir. The flight is not full." A stewardess half-speaks to me while sharing a conversation with her coworker about a party she attended in San Francisco. "Let me take your boarding pass, Sir." The ticket does not slide through the slot. "That's weird. Here let me take your boarding pass." The attendant looks at it, asks for my identification. "Go ahead, Sir."

The cabin is wide-open with empty seats. Luck is on my side as I find the emergency exit aisle seats vacant and plop down by the window. I place my carry-on bag on top of the seat next to me and rummage through my gift: herbs I am not familiar with, a piece of paper with odd names and cities. This baffles me. I continue digging through the tissue paper that is now displaced inside my gift box. I look around the cabin, making sure I have some privacy, and begin to read the paper.

"Sanat Kumara" is written in bold pencil next to a drawing of a white dove in clouds. On the left side of the paper is a small drawing of a turtle and the word "right" just above this. On the right side of the paper is an even smaller drawing of ants with the word "left" just above it. "Material" is written much larger than the other words and connects to the word below it: "*Mayan*." I find another piece of paper bearing the phrase "Lady of Undercroft," next to an address, "8383 Isis." "Angel Bath on a Green Moon," makes absolutely no sense, nor does "Ray of Light." "The Lady by the Bay 777," is even more confusing. "Falling Tower," makes a little sense, and the numbers, "333," "444," and "777," are next to "D.C." and "London." Next to London is the phrase, "8 days the world will stop to honor Venus." What is this? I look upon this second piece of paper and notice a reminder of my ten year life change. Neatly tucked away in the bottom of this small box is the cassette tape the security guard found. I rustle through my carry-on bag, tossing toiletries and personals on the seat next to me, trying to find my cassette player. "Where is it?"

"Sir, you will need to put all of your belongings back in your bag. We are about to take off."

"I am so sorry, Miss. I was trying to find something and here it is."

I slip the tape in and wait for takeoff. Baggage men in blue suits throw luggage into the belly of the airplane haphazardly. Food services go about their duties as flight attendants run through last-minute procedures. I tune everything out and reflect on this nomadic journey that keeps unfolding. Where are you, Brussels? Why of all times in my life have I not seen or heard from you?

Suddenly an epiphany takes hold. I realize that, like St. Thomas, this trip has become a turning point in my life. I am living through one of the all-time greatest American films, with four of the main characters put to a contemporary setting. No other movie in our history has had a bigger effect on young and old people alike; moving every generation with its heart-tugging story, *The Wizard of Oz*. Meeting Nora was the first encounter at the crossroads of my life. Just like the Scarecrow's character, Nora's wisdom will keep us safe as we travel down the yellow-brick road of life. TJ's big heart qualifies him to be the Tin Man, leading us back to ourselves when it is time for our tune-up. Lindsey's greatest role is not one from her glamorous career; it's the role of Dorothy. "There's no place like home" will become her motto, or will "Surrender Dorothy" become her epitaph? And last but not least, courage underscores my role as the Lion.

My days lay before me in this odd road map with cryptic codes, locations, and names that will surely make appearances in my life, leading me to places I dare not go alone. Raziel made sure I understood every word, every passage, and every clue so that when trouble came, my foundation was built on solid ground. No one could be better suited to play the Wizard than the Indian man. His gift to each one of us is our destiny, painted on yellow sandstone. We are off to a place called OZ, also known as, The City of Angels, which many in our television industry also refer to as Sodom and Gomorrah. Our task at hand is to find the Wicked Witch of the West and bring back her heart and not her hat. Raziel should have warned us. But if he did, I would not come to know the *guardians* of the city of Los Angeles that will change my life forever.

"What are you listening to?" The flight attendant's sweet smile breaks my private time.

"I don't know, but it is beautiful." I remove the tape from the cassette and look at the black casing. "Enya," I remark.

"I've never heard of that? Where did you get it?"

"It's a cherished gift I will always remember from a special person," I say with a gleam in my eye. "I have a feeling this is going to be a new trend," I whisper under my breadth.

I put the tape back on, smile at the attendant, and look out the window. "Sail away, sail away, sail away...."

"Angels are principally the guardians of our spirits"

Eileen Elias Freeman

Ten Years Later - Easter Weekend

"Paging passenger, Thomas Johnson. Please come to baggage claim. Attention all passengers, American Airlines flight 101 to JFK is now boarding." "May I have your attention please? Would stand-by passengers Gonzales and Marcel come to gate 47?" Numerous voices vibrate over the intercom at a very busy LAX this Thursday afternoon. Hurried faces run to and from their gates in the hopes of getting a head start on a busy Easter weekend, oblivious to the airline employees who have just begun their grueling holiday shifts. Outside the airport, palm trees line Century Boulevard like faded sentries. Families and friends scan the baggage claim area. A loud red buzzer sounds, and claim area C rolls out an assembly line of colorful suitcases. A telephone booth empties just in time for me to call TJ at his office.

"Mr. Lawton, please?" I ponder for a split second as I look down the airport corridor lined with retailers peddling sunglasses and Mrs. Fields cookies. "Tell him, it's Ethan Michaels please," I say to the nondescript voice on the other end.

"Please hold. I'll see if he is in," the voice hesitates

"Ethan, where are you?" Loud voices in the background tell me I have called at a bad time. "Can I call you back?" TJ covers the receiver and says something to his staff.

"Sure, I just flew in from Hawaii. I'm going to catch up on this jet lag. Call me at my apartment later."

"Fantastic. That sounds fantastic. Do you like coffee or tea with your bagels?"

"What?" I say, confused. The busy telephone booths on either side of me are making it hard for me to hear TJ. "Call me later. Bye." The receiver goes dead.

"I'll call Kevin and see what his plans for Easter weekend are." I speak at full volume as though the man in the next booth needs to know my holiday plans.

"Hey, this is Kevin. I've gone to Palm Springs for the weekend. Leave a message." Beep!

Quickly realizing that Los Angeles is about to shut down for the holiday weekend, I decide I better fetch a cab back to West Hollywood, before Century Boulevard becomes a morning of holiday travelers. "How much is the fare to Doheny and Santa Monica? Oh, never mind, just take me there! And don't get on the 405."

"I'll take you down La Cienega. Okay?" Today must be this man's first day on the job. He seems too kind—probably because he hasn't experienced the hunger woes of production crews coming off a four-month film, shooting in a remote village near Zambia and missing good ole hamburgers and bottled water.

"That sounds perfect. Thank you kindly."

I watch the meter zoom into the double digits as we pass Melrose Avenue and make our way into West Hollywood.

"Take a left on Santa Monica and a right on Doheny. Okay?" I catch a glimpse of the time and note that my watch is spinning in the opposite direction. How weird. I hand the cabbie fifty dollars and click my shoes. "Yea, I'm home."

A small magnolia tree fresh with creamy white blooms welcomes me home. A green yard, small enough to entertain a party of two, leads to a brown door that a set designer must have stolen off the lot of Universal Studio back in the 1940s. My cat's meows can be heard from the other side of the door. She's anxious to wrap her fur around my tan ankles. Acorns tumble off the red-tile Spanish roof, just barely missing the exuberant fichus tree. I step into my home, feed Honey, throw my luggage onto the floor, and hit the bed. There is nothing like sleeping in your own bed.

***

"Ethan, are you there. Pick up." A muffled voice is faint in the background. "Ethan, its TJ. …wake up."

I jump out of bed, wrestle with the on-off switch, and shout with my I-haven't-been-sleeping-voice. "Hey, what's up, man?" My watch is still spinning. I need to get it fixed today.

"Ethan, I'm heading to New York for the Easter holidays to meet Lindsey." TJ is alert to my jet lag. "She's filed for divorce. This could not have come at a worst time."

"I called her while I was in Hawaii. She sounds awful. Damn it. I should have flown to New York instead. I don't want to spend the weekend by myself without you guys. It's been ten years since my trip to St. Thomas. I wanted to do something special." I say, hoping TJ will feel sorry for me. "TJ, I'm a little worried. All the celebrities I work with are coming off series that have been canceled or are in their last season. And CBS is downsizing."

"Well, don't worry about it this weekend, Ethan. What can you do about it now? I'm heading out in the next few minutes. I'll call you from New York. By the way, Carl and Chris are heading to Laguna. They aren't the best company, but Laguna should be fun." TJ tries to soften the punch.

"Carl and Chris will be my company?" I think quietly, it's come down to Carl and Chris on this special weekend. That's okay, TJ?" I pause. "If anyone can get Lindsey to cut the ties to that screwed-up relationship, you can."

"I know." I hear guilt in TJ's voice. "Enjoy the holiday. I'll call from New York." TJ blows a kiss through the receiver. "Love you!"

"Come on, Honey, it's time for breakfast and a good workout." Honey squeaks quietly to her bowl. The phone rings. It's TJ with a change of heart, I say, arrogantly, to myself. "Yes, so you decided to get Lindsey to come here so we can enjoy Easter together? I can't tell you how excited I am."

"Ethan, you are a nerd! I don't know why I even bother to call you. Oyo' bro, it's Carl. And no it's not TJ. Why don't you call him Ted, like everyone else?" I hear a whiney voice mimicking the way I say TJ. "Anyway, he told me to take you to Laguna. We're leaving at noon. See you then." Click.

"Damn, TJ. Why?" I rush around, gathering my gym clothes, and head to the Athletic Club.

I can smell coffee brewing through bungalow windows as I leave my place. Homeless people climb from the bottom of Doheny Boulevard and tread aimlessly to the top, arriving near a contemporary high-rise on Sunset Boulevard. Yellow-and-white honeysuckle mingles with orange birds of paradise that seem to take root everywhere. Mercedes, Porsches, BMWs, and Ferraris—all luxury cars—make their way down Doheny to Santa Monica Boulevard and turn into Beverly Hills. City sweepers keep the avenue spotless, while late morning joggers and walkers in their best workout gear pass them. I see a lady wearing a white robe and large hat, as she crosses to my side of the street. I place my Sony Walkman on my head and start my steady pace down the hill. New tennis shoes feel perfect on my feet. The tank top I wear isn't warm enough to battle the morning breeze, and my watch has stopped ticking altogether. I look across the street and see a large garbage truck making the rounds, collecting trash from bins and enraging several homeless people from their morning rituals. A quick thump followed by an electric hum comes from my Sony Walkman. The cassette player opens up and spits out *The Best of Roxy Music*.

"Excuse me? Would you mind petting my dog?" The lady smiles regally, softly caressing her gray-and-white dog. Inside her pocket I can see a white rose.

"You want me to pet your dog?" I look around to see if she is really speaking to me.

"Yes, I want you to pet my dog." Her incredible bright-blue-green-eyes, take my focus away from her larger than life hat. "She won't bite you."

"Well," I pause and look around to see if anyone is looking for this woman. "Okay, there. What a sweet puppy." I pet her dog and say good-bye. "Have a wonderful day." I pretend that my watch is operational and use my get-away excuse, "Oh, wow, time is slipping away."

Your watch is broken." She smiles with a grin. "Why are you covering your hand over your watch?" She looks at the cassette tape on the sidewalk. "Don't forget this."

"What?" I can feel my eyes exploding out of my sockets, hitting the pavement right before they injure her sweet dog. "I...I...my throat is dry. Yes, that's my tape." I have been busted.

"Do you know what today is?" She smiles, never breaking her concentration.

"Friday, today is Friday." I lean in for a closer look to see if she is all there.

"Ten years ago." She pauses. "Now that was a special Easter. Wasn't it?" Her blue eyes tease me.

I pause, look up and down Doheny trying to locate TJ hiding devilishly behind a palm tree. "Oh, it was a wonderful time." Wonder how much TJ has paid this actress. "Wow, ten years ago on Easter. What were you doing?" I'll play along with this moment.

"I was traveling to remote islands in the Caribbean." She leans down and speaks a pretend dog language.

"How wonderful that must have been?" I have no idea what time it must be, but somehow I must disengage myself from this conversation. "Well, I'm on my way to the gym. Isn't this a great day to work out?"

The mysterious lady reaches for my watch. "What time is it?" She looks down at my wrist and smiles.

"I think my watch needs new batteries, so I can't give you the correct time." This should end this silly conversation.

"You seem to have the correct time." She touches the face of my watch and softly taps the small glass cover. The second hand begins moving slowly.

"11:38 a.m. is the correct time." My watch is suddenly working again. "Ah, where were we?" she asks. "Oh, I believe this tape belongs to you?" She hands me the Roxy Music tape from the street.

Soft brown hair and piercing blue eyes dance in a face laced with gentle kindness. What appeared from a distance to be a white robe on further inspection reveals itself to be brushed white cotton dress that clings to her fit female body. Her hair sits nobly under a spring hat, accentuating her long neck. She is exquisite. A thin turquoise necklace hangs just above her clavicle bone, encasing a purple crystal.

"Young man, I'm glad to see you understand the discipline of the body."

Although I am completely baffled by this conversation, I have learned from past experiences to listen attentively.

"I was ill years ago and began a new ritual that changed my life. I'm watchful about what I put in my body. Thank you for noting that." I see a yellow aura circling her head, and then it vanishes.

"Many young people move to this city for one purpose and forget the values that were instilled in them during their former years. Physicality becomes their addiction, and ego becomes their demise. Eventually, this addiction has a poisonous effect on their inner spirit."

"Well, I've seen my share of perfect bodies in Hollywood, whether they are natural or induced by silicone." I chuckle, knowing that this city is the plastic-surgery capital of the world. The blue-eyed lady has my complete attention.

"Soon, very soon, not only will young actors and actresses move to the land of Hollywood with their perfect looks, but without knowing it, they will send a message to others not related to this industry, that narcissism is the key to success."

I gaze at this woman and wonder where she has been and with whom she has spoken. "This is Hollywood, lady," I say with an apology. I expect a nasty comeback, but instead she reaches inside her pocket and hands me the white rose.

"This flower is beautiful. Artificial stimulants don't make it any more beautiful. If you are truly beautiful, you don't need to wear a sign that says, 'I am beautiful.' We can see that."

I look at her, wonder how many conversations she has had today. "What is your name?"

"My name is Sulivia." She removes her hat.

"I know you? We met before? Remember?" I wonder if she forgot who I am.

"Have you ever been to Bath?" She opens her mouth in a splendid smile.

I look around and point towards Sunset Boulevard near Hamburger Hamlet. "Up there?" I ask.

"Not yet, but soon." She removes the white flower from my hand and places it back in her pocket. "Surround yourself with good people, Ethan."

"You remember me? Where is…"

"Ethan!" A loud voice from a convertible BMW yells out. It's time to go. Stop trying to pick up old ladies on the street," Carl yells out.

"Get in the car now. We need to get to Laguna." Carl catches the eye of Sulivia "Hey there."

Complete embarrassment takes over. "I apologize for this. He really isn't this obnoxious usually."

Sulivia ignores the apology. "This trip is not about Laguna, though it seems that is where you are going." She bids farewell, grabs her dog's leash, and walks up the steep hill, losing a slipper.

"Oh, let me get that." A silver toe ring sits modestly on her left foot as I hand back the tiny shoe. She smiles. "Thank you, Ethan."

"Get in the car, Ethan, now!" Carl begins pounding the horn. Chris, already quite impatient with my chivalry, yells. "Get in the car, Ethan."

***

Pacific Coast Highway is packed with cars and motorbikes. Surfers hotfoot across the oncoming traffic, avoiding speeding cars and balancing their surfboards on sun-bleached heads. Car radios spit out the latest Southern California hits, to cars full of stressed out parents and their teenagers, who have just arrived, before the serious party people show up. I hear tourists say, "Honey, why do pedestrians have the right of way in California," and "Baby, I never knew there was more than one kind of palm tree" while they look for a perfect spot for their beach towels. I also hear, "Honey, how come all those muscular men are sitting so close to each other. I don't see any women over there." It's official. Easter in Laguna has begun, and before dawn on early Sunday morning, the most beautiful men will be on display here, while the White Party takes place in Palm Springs.

Fragrant suntan lotions compete with the smell of cologne on the beach. Laguna's golden sand must have been designed and airbrushed by

Calvin Klein. Hundreds of half-naked men bask in tight swimsuits with oiled skin that has been lovingly exfoliated thanks to the Robinson's-May pre-Easter cosmetic sale.

"Ethan, would you climb down these steps a little faster? Where's my bottled water?" Carl whines, as we descend down 1,000 winding wooden steps enclosed by abundant scrubby foliage that lead us to the coast. Finally, we arrive and enter a scene of men who look as if they all dance at Chippendales. Beach towels in pastels and rainbow hues lie in rows, and if I didn't know better I would swear that someone has dyed the ocean the color of Revlon's sapphire eye shadow.

Chris locates an empty spot for our party of three and suddenly transforms into a gentleman. "Excuse me, guys. You don't mind if we sit here, do you?"

"Make yourself at home, honey. Hey girl, what's your name?"

"Ethan, he's talking to you." Chris nudges me forward. "He can be a little shy."

"Well, let me un-shy you, doll." The blonde man looks me up and down.

"Never mind, Blondie, he's a weirdo." Abruptly interrupting, Carl tosses his beach towel on the sand. "He's not shy—he's socially retarded." Placing his boogie board next to the blonde man, Carl marks his territory. "Can you move over so I can have a better view?"

"Well, aren't you rude?" The blonde man gets cross with Carl.

Uninterested in engaging in this soon-to-be brawl, I look for my Walkman and find a tape. "You don't mind if I sit next to you on this side?" I speak quietly to the blonde's friends, ignoring the two men I have come with.

"I am not rude, so pipe down." Carl demands.

Chris begins to snicker, aggravating the situation. Carl continues watching the beach crowd, pushing our friendly blonde neighbor's cooler with his foot.

"I know you didn't tell me to pipe down? Did you?" The blonde's red face, which, I might add, is most likely not from the sun, is about to unleash a tongue that has been fine-tuned on the front lines of bitchiness. His buddies, familiar with his ill temper, gather their belongings and quietly excuse themselves to another part of the beach. I make my way to the opposite side of his beach towel in order to watch the scene as it unfolds. Carl steps over his opponent's towel, prepared to defend the most precious thing he cherishes. His massive ego! The blonde is primed to defend his lightweight title. I am awestruck by something more dramatic. Twenty-four men dressed in drag—wearing red-orange drill team skirts, blouses stuffed to a full C cup, Eva Gabor wigs styled in beehives in all colors—bounce frantically with matching pom-poms. Donna Summer's disco single "Carry On," blasts throughout the shore as gay men in Speedos share beer around a makeshift dance floor.

Ignoring Carl's massive tongue-lashing, the blonde turns to me. "Be a doll, and hand me that silver pole. Would you mind, sweetie? When this is over, I am buying you a drink."

I reach for a silver flagpole that proudly screams in rainbow colors, "Cher, we love you!" and hand it to my new hero. "Here you go."

Carl glares at me, concentrating on his enemy, and shouts, "I'm going to shove that Cher flag up your ass, you freak."

Still calm, the blonde begins to wave the rainbow flag in circular motions.

"What the fuck are you doing with that flag?" Carl spits with anger.

Off in the distance I can see gay men moving about quickly. I feel a thump beneath my towel. Another round of gay men moves about at a much faster rate. Thump! Thump! I look around and see gay men diving into sand, like chorus girls in an Esther William's black-and-white movie. The thump is louder. Musclemen move aside. Something wicked this way comes. Mothers gather children and hand them off to their dads. Vendors, their faces weary with frustration, pack their containers and move to the north end of the beach. The blonde man continues to loudly egg Carl on. I can hear the soundtrack to *Jaws* in my head, knowing that what we can't see is coming. Thump! Thump! Louder and louder, I hear something approaching our beach towels. The Stranger-Ett'e Drill Team leader has her cheerleaders form a chorus line, cheering and shouting, "Go, George. Go, George!" The blonde holds the flagpole skyward leans in toward Carl, lashes out obscenities, as parents speedily cover their kids' ears. 'Give me that flagpole now!" Carl screams, drowning out Donna Summers.

Out of the blue, I recall that a sudden calmness usually occurs before the storm. But this doesn't seem to happen. The blonde man waves the flagpole, teasing Carl, igniting a verbal blaze that is out of control. "Fuck you and your silicone implants," the blonde shouts.

And they're off. Face-to-face screams introduce our first round. A right jab to the blonde's six-pack stomach is hurtful. A kick to Carl's groin is surely foul but needed. Sand in face is stupid but adds drama. A left uppercut surprises the blonde, but his agility scores him bonus points as the swing hits the biggest black man's chest I have ever seen. Standing tall and dark, a man named George faces front and center to the blonde's challenger. My expression must be priceless. How much can he weigh when he's easily 6-feet-4? A second thought comes through loud and clear. "Carl, what have you done?!"

"George, these men over here have been rude to all my friends." The blonde man points to Carl and Chris.

George grabs the rainbow flagpole, comes in for a closer look at Carl, and grunts, "Is that so?"

I look at this drama being played out, and wonder if TJ could see me now, would he be so eager to arrange my Fourth of July weekend? I quietly slip to a remote corner, lay my towel down, and ease into my new tape, *Enigma*. I lather my body with Hawaiian Tropic lotion, dig my feet into the cool sand, and slide into a space that feels peaceful. The sun caresses my toned body and the smell of saltwater reminds me of my recent trip to Hawaii. I doze. Minutes later I am awakened from a deep slumber.

"Sir, Sir." A young boy tugs at my arm. "That man over there asked me to come get you."

"What? Who are you talking about?" I open my eyes, wondering who would ask for me. "Where is he?"

"Over there." The little boy points to a white-haired young man who could easily be a Billy Idol look-alike. "Over there." He points again.

"Okay, well thank you." I remain on the sand for a few more seconds, still heavy with sleep. The little boy disappears into a crowd of new arrivals right after he collects his reward from the stranger. The white-haired man waves as though he knows me and smiles. "Over here."

Standing up, I try to find Carl and Chris. Perhaps I should scan the ocean. I wouldn't be surprised to find them bound and gagged to a floating buoy. Nope, they are not there. "Just a minute." I gather my beach gear and make my way to the white-haired young man.

"Good day to you." His thick Scottish contrasts sharply with his Nordic looks.

"Do we know each other?"

"Perhaps we do. Does it really matter?" He looks around at the multitudes of gay men with a smirk. "We eventually come to know each other sooner or later."

"I see?" His intense blue eyes have small strands of gold in them. It's hard not to stare.

"It would be a pleasure if you would take a seat and join me." Handing me bottled water first, he then clears a space. "The view here is remarkable," he says, pointing toward the cove.

"Well, maybe. I can join you for a little bit. But I need to find my ride."

"What a beautiful toe ring. Where did you get that? Oh, by the way my name is?"

"My name is Ethan. I got it in St. Thomas. Thanks. It means a lot to me." I smile, reveling in my secret.

"I love St. Thomas. I spent one of my most remarkable times in my life on that island." His eyes twinkle.

Oh, my god. Me too! That trip changed my life forever."

"I couldn't agree more. The energy on that Easter weekend was one of the most eye-opening moments. Today is my ten-year anniversary." He looks up to greet an oncoming admirer. "Yes?"

A tan, dark-haired man greets us. "My name is Gustavo. Would you men like a drink?" He looks at me, never acknowledging my guest.

"Why don't you bring us both two waters? I prefer Evian. What about you?" I point to my new acquaintance.

"Make it easy on yourself. You bring back whatever, and I will be grateful."

Gustavo leans down and comes closer to my face. "Why don't you help me?"

Not quite clear on how Nora uses charm to swim away in troubled water, I blunder with my next line. "Huh?"

"Ethan, I am absolutely capable of entertaining myself why you go for water. Go! Enjoy."

"Gustavo, I'll wait for you here," I stare at my watch, which has stopped again.

Gustavo runs an Olympic marathon down the beach to find a vender. "Where were we? Today is my ten-year anniversary too!" I notice my watch is now ticking again. "I don't understand why this new watch is so messed up?" I tap it gently, while anxious to hear my new buddy's story. "I can't believe that you were there for Easter?"

"Yes. Me too! Did you learn about the secrets of energy grids and how they function on the planet? How to anchor the ancient waves to your solar plexus? And don't forget about the triple codes. And how did you feel about the nightly reprogramming of souls to the collective-consciousness grid? Reprogramming soul alignment nightly between 3:33 a.m. to 4:44 a.m. is my favorite. But the most amazing is the awakening of the female consciousness." He speaks so quickly I can't keep up.

Obviously, my new friend learned a lot more in St Thomas than I did. Maybe I was a slow learner? Maybe Brussels didn't know any of this? "Oh, there is so much to talk about. I'm still a little jet-lagged. I'll let you go first." I say, politely.

He leans in, lowers his voice, looks around, and whispers. "I'll share something with you that I know you did not learn in St. Thomas."

"Please do." If my eyes were any bigger I could see Black's Beach from this vantage point. "What is it?"

"I am."

"What? I am? What does that mean?"

"I am. The golden grid! The most sacred site on the planet, Sri Lanka! Kataragama! Sanat Kumara!

"This is the third time I've heard the words 'Sanat Kumara.' What is it?"

"You spoke of thought energy I suppose? The power within you and the power within me can change all consciousness?"

"Yes. I'm still confused though." I feel like an idiot. "I'm becoming aware of my thoughts." It must be obvious that I am not up on this information. "Break it down for me as if I was a child." If he only knew how close to the truth that last statement is.

"The female collective consciousness will be awakened this decade. Women of power will create the beginning stages of one of the strongest shifts on the planet in our history. Unfortunately, those who hold the financial purse will see to it that this shift does not take place."

"How will they do it?"

"By creating a collapse of what you Americans know as democracy. The United States is spiritually adrift. Profit will become the new compulsion of the '90s, putting chains on the very thing that validates the flow of energy. Loss will be introduced, leading America into a *State of Terror* by the year 2001. New laws will be introduced; church leaders will fall and rise with selfish agendas, and industrialized thinking will continue. Profit will become loss. Loss will become fear. Fear will produce control. Man will become a slave to fear because he feels he has no choice. Unfortunately, man thinks he hasn't a choice because he has been told there is nothing available—unless what he wants comes at a higher asking price! The most valuable endowment we have is our values and beliefs. Once mankind realizes that the very institutions they have given their power to, such as churches, corporations, and branches of government, the sooner they can cause an effect on the collective consciousness throughout the world. This is why the rise of female energy on this planet will be the saving consideration. One simple mantra can lead mankind back to the road of true prosperity. 'I am.'"

I stare at this man, gifted with information I can only attempt to appreciate. Khaki pants and a beige linen shirt seem so inappropriate on this beach setting. His message makes me think of Brussels but on a level that is far more progressive. I'm riveted by his eyes, and his thoughts provoke my interest. These philosophies continue to astonish me. "Sri Lanka? Kataragama?" I ask, under my breath, embarrassed that I have never heard of this part of the world.

Without wavering, his answer pulls me in.

"The center of the world begins with 0 latitude and 0 longitude. The center of zero! Zero inside of zero! Many spiritualists call it the Isle of Lemuria. But we have come to refer to it as the Isle of Consciousness. *'As above, so below.'* He pauses to let me digest this matter. "The ancients believe that a great nation will lead man to a never ending war. Sanat Kumara has come forth to warn mankind. It is his mission to gather advanced souls from previous lifetimes and create a new paradigm of old-thought consciousness aligned with new thought consciousness. I am!"

All around me are families relaxing to the sounds of the ocean's waves. Radios blast and sunbathers bask in the beating sun. Gay men are everywhere, adding beauty to what would normally be just another typical vacation spot. Children run to the water's edge, thrilled and fearful of the surf. Behind sunglasses, women check out the chiseled bodies surrounding them. All in all, this is a beautiful day at the beach. So why does this information make me uneasy?

"Please help me to understand the 'I am.'"

I hesitate because I am scared to know more than I do. His eyes are kind, making this transition a little easier for me. I would later realize that this moment in time was one of the most powerful life-altering moments of my life.

Dare I cross this threshold of comfort, leaving behind the knowledge I have existed with for so many years? Brussels' words are no longer just sentences that I can trot out when the mood strikes me and ignore the rest of the time. Rather, he started me on a path to truth, one that says our planet is headed in a bad direction thanks to wrong choices made because of a few wrong curveballs thrown at mankind because of misplaced egos—it's hard to take in. I need to know what this young man knows and understand it as he does. "What do you want me to do to truly understand this? I am ready."

"We have already begun. You gave me permission by saying, 'I am ready.'" He closes his eyes and sits in lotus position. "Please listen carefully. We will begin by sitting in a divine space so that the body can receive." His arms are extended outward, pointing east to west.

"We will begin with *the breath of life*. Starting with seven separate deep breaths, you will inhale and count to seven with every breath. Then exhale. Understand?"

I nod my head.

"Once you arrive at the seventh breath, visualize the color purple in a circle with the number seven inside that circle. Let's begin."

I arrive at the final breath and can see the number seven surrounded by purple. Nothing happens. I can hear the waves hitting the shore, the sounds of laughter, people's voices drift in and out as if a radio is being tuned and catching snippets of various stations. The sun beats down on my face, and the squawk of seagulls seems louder than normal.

A hand touches my solar plexus. All of a sudden I can see myself. Gold light starts at the center of my forehead, travels to my left palm, then to my right palm and goes back up to my forehead, and out of my body. How I can see this? I don't know. My eyes are closed. I can feel the breath of my instructor. Gold light filters down from the sun and joins the purple circle. Am I doing this right? A voice answers: I am. Red-purple hues loop the purple sphere and spin, surrounded by a gold-green light. I feel fearful, inept, like I will do something wrong. A voice answers: *I am your fear.* What? I think. *I am your hopelessness.* I don't feel hopeless now. *I am your triumph.* Okay? *I am your failures and your gains. I am the sun. I am the universe. I am you. I am the divine space that holds you near when you worry. I am what you think. I am you when you do drugs. I am you when you hurt others. I am you when you cry. I am you always. I am your life. I am you when you die. I am with you always. I am your past lives. I am your future. I am your now. I am in this space you sit upon. I am always and will be forever.*

Colors surround my physical being, whirling around me like the same funnel cloud that hoisted me in the hospital. Numbers flash across a giant screen—first in diagonal corners at the bottom of the screen, then at the upper corner—in split-second glimpses.

The heaviness of this vision is instantly relieved by an image only a person having lived in Los Angeles can truly appreciate. I open my eyes. To my right I find my young white-haired guru. His eyes are open, greeting me with a lovely smile. To his right, sits George, the black man, the protector of the beach, sitting in full lotus, eyes closed. To his right, I find the blonde devil-tongued man in the same position. And to his right, a father and child sit side by side, eyes closed in deep thought. A young Asian man chants in his native language quietly, completely immersed in prayer. Gustavo has joined the group with a friend. To his right, Mr. Beautiful, the man soon to be voted the most gorgeous man to walk on this beach this Easter weekend or for that matter any holiday. He sits with an entourage of admirers, gawking at his perfect body and captivated by his extraordinary charisma. Not to be outdone, an older overly tan woman, who should have retired her bikinis years ago, sits in meditation. To her immediate right are three boys and a little girl in complete harmony with this event. And, of course, my Easter in Laguna would not be complete without the loudest voice of all. I look up and feel my first ah-ha moment of reality.

"What the fuck are you doing? What did you give them, Ecstasy?" Carl stands with his fists on his hips, unaware that he has awakened George from his slumber. I remember my third-grade teacher speaking about bears during winter hibernation and how dangerous it was to disturb their peaceful rest. I never believed her until now. "Run, Forest, run."

The little boy who brought me to this sandy spot faces me and stares with his big brown eyes. "Come with me. Hurry, now!"

"Why? Are you okay?" I look at him and can see eagerness all over his face. George has Carl under control, and the group is awakening from their peaceful interlude.

The boy grabs my hand. "Come on! Come on!" His excitement is infectious. He leads us all to the shore. "Look." He points to the water. "Big fishy! He's talking."

Immediate joy surrounds everyone. This multicultural gathering—a black man, Asian man, old lady, father and his children, gay and straight, and mothers—all discovering Easter with one another, gaze at the sea and take in a glorious sight. Twelve dolphins swim the waves. Two of the dolphins have come within touching distance for some swimmers and begin chattering in our direction. At this very moment, I look at this peculiar group and come to recognize some universal acts have occurred. Collective prayer! Unconditional love!

A swarm of kids descends upon the beach, cheering. The two dolphins swim away with their school. A young gay man brings his ghetto blaster to our circle and adds the final ingredient to this moment: Seal's, "Crazy." If I were God looking down at this scene, at the people beginning to dance in a giant circle on the beach, I would smile. But I'm not God. The white-haired young man gathers his belongings, waves for me to follow him. "I can't stay long."

"Oh, okay. Hey listen, man. What an incredible day this has been." My voice rings with excitement. "What an amazing Easter anniversary. And to share this with someone who was on the same island with me at the same time. Wow!"

He reaches for his towel, grabs his sandals, and shakes the sand from his feet, exposing a silver toe ring.

I grin. "Look at mine." I place my foot on his knee.

"That's quite a *tinker* you wear. Wouldn't you say, Ethan?"

"What did you say?" I feel chills.

"We call it a tinker. The key to your destiny," he says, nonchalantly.

"What? What? We need to talk about this." I feel like my lesson is just starting, as we are finishing.

"Hey, Ethan, it's time to go back to L.A. The 405 will be crawling with idiots." Carl and his perfect manners always seem to interrupt the perfect moment.

"Can you hold off for a while longer?" I lose my patience.

"Ethan, I must go. However, there is no place I would have rather been than with you here today. I wish you well. Be patient with him."

"What's your name? Sorry. I can't remember." He turns away into the crowd and smiles back at me. "I can't remember his name." I yell at Carl.

"Who is that real tall man with white hair?"

I look behind quickly. I scream at Carl. "Where is he?"

"Over there by the fence. He's wearing khaki pants and a beige shirt." Carl turns around. "Come on, or you can stay here. I want to go back to L.A."

I race down the beach yelling. "Brussels!"

To be continued....

Printed in the United States
By Bookmasters